# UNIVERSAL HUMAN

## ALSO BY GARY ZUKAV

*The Dancing Wu Li Masters*

*The Seat of the Soul*

*Thoughts from the Seat of the Soul*

*Soul Stories*

*Soul to Soul*

*Soul to Soul Mediations*

*Spiritual Partnership*

## WITH LINDA FRANCIS

*The Heart of the Soul*

*Thoughts from the Heart of the Soul*

*The Mind of the Soul*

*Self-Empowerment Journal*

# UNIVERSAL HUMAN

## Creating Authentic Power and the New Consciousness

# GARY ZUKAV

**ATRIA** PAPERBACK

NEW YORK  LONDON  TORONTO  SYDNEY  NEW DELHI

An Imprint of Simon & Schuster, Inc.
1230 Avenue of the Americas
New York, NY 10020

First Atria Paperback edition June 2022

**ATRIA** PAPERBACK and colophon are trademarks of Simon & Schuster, Inc.

For information about special discounts for bulk purchases,
please contact Simon & Schuster Special Sales at
1-866-506-1949 or business@simonandschuster.com.

The Simon & Schuster Speakers Bureau can bring authors to your live event. For
more information or to book an event, contact the Simon & Schuster Speakers Bureau
at 1-866-248-3049 or visit our website at www.simonspeakers.com.

*Interior design by Kyoko Watanabe*

1 3 5 7 9 10 8 6 4 2

Library of Congress Cataloging-in-Publication Data
Names: Zukav, Gary, author.
Title: Universal human : creating authentic power
and the new consciousness / Gary Zukav.
Description: First Edition. | New York : Atria Books, 2021. |
Includes bibliographical references and index.
Identifiers: LCCN 2021005274 (print) | LCCN 2021005275 (ebook) |
ISBN 9781982169879 (hardcover) | ISBN 9781982169893 (ebook)
Subjects: LCSH: Consciousness. | Self-actualization (Psychology) | Creative ability. |
Choice (Psychology) | Control (Psychology) | Social change. | Love.
Classification: LCC BF311 .Z855 2021 (print) | LCC BF311 (ebook) |
DDC 158.1—dc23
LC record available at https://lccn.loc.gov/2021005274
LC ebook record available at https://lccn.loc.gov/2021005275

ISBN 978-1-9821-6987-9
ISBN 978-1-9821-6988-6 (pbk)
ISBN 978-1-9821-6989-3 (ebook)

*This book is dedicated to*
*Emerging Universal Humans*

# Gratitude

"Gratitude" is too small a word for the love and gifts these fellow students in the Earth school have given me: Linda Francis, my co–life explorer, spiritual partner, cocreator, coauthor, and cofounder of the Seat of the Soul Institute and the Foundation for the Universal Human, for her great heart, brilliant mind, boundless courage, and joyful laughter; Phil Lane Jr. (www.fwii.net) and Phil Lane Sr. for adopting me into Lakota culture and their wondrous gifts; Oprah Winfrey, the Great Pioneer, for introducing spirituality into commercial television, sowing seeds of authentic power, and her continuing contributions to our world; Maya Angelou for the love and many blessings she gave to Linda and me; Masami Saionji for her total commitment to peace and "May Peace Prevail On Earth" poles around the world (www.byakko.org); Nipun Mehta and the Service Space community for nurturing kindness and generosity worldwide (www.servicespace.org); Elizabeth Rauscher, founder of the "Fundamental Fysics Group" at the Lawrence Berkeley Laboratory, for inviting me into the company of renowned theoretical physicists who became the godparents (my name) of my first book, *The Dancing Wu Li Masters: An Overview of the New Physics*; Ronnie Earle, district attorney of Travis County, Texas, for his thirty-two years of unwavering commitment to justice in place of convictions and his passion for community involvement instead of the criminal justice system; Brigadier General Michael Harbottle, British Army, cofounder of Retired Generals for Peace and Disarmament during the terrifying depths of the Cold War, who encouraged me as a young man to explore the deeper potential of the military; the many participants in our programs and activities; and the countless people who have graced and inspired me.

When Zukav's ideas stop
challenging you, you will laugh
with the wonderful laughter of the
discoverer who has found
a new continent.

—MAYA ANGELOU

# Contents

## OUR NEW SOCIAL STRUCTURES

## UNIVERSAL HUMANS

## THE NEXT STEP

# UNIVERSAL HUMAN

# GREETINGS

GREETINGS

# Welcome

Welcome to this book. I am so happy you are joining me in it.

This book will bring your attention to the transformation of human consciousness that is happening, so that you can understand it and use it to create a life of more joy and less pain. It will give you opportunities to experiment with a road toward meaning and fulfillment and purpose and joy, but you must use these opportunities in order to benefit from them. This road is challenging like none before and rewarding like none before. This road is the path you are walking. It is your life, and a new consciousness is now illuminating in new and different ways the opportunities and challenges it brings you.

That new consciousness is THE new consciousness. The old human consciousness evolved over hundreds of millennia. The new human consciousness is emerging within a few generations. This book shows you how to apply the new human consciousness to your life.

It's one thing to recognize that becoming loving adds love to the world. That is graspable. But how do you love, and especially, how do you love when you're angry, when you're vengeful, when you're jealous, when you want to kill someone, when you want to kill yourself, when you can't stop judging, when you can't stop looking for food, sex, or money? How do you do that? How do you become loving? This book shows you how to become loving all the time in every circumstance. That is creating authentic power. Creating authentic power is easy to understand, but it's not so easy to change your life from the ground up.

People become interested in spiritual growth when a new consciousness touches their own, expanding it, enriching it, and revealing new ways of understanding, perceiving, and loving. This is happening now to many people. People also become interested in spiritual growth because they are in a great deal of emotional pain, and they don't know

3

what to do about it. This is happening to everyone everywhere, and it always has.

What are you experiencing in your day-to-day life? What emotional pain are you in? What's keeping you up at night? What is it you are not satisfied with? This book shows you how to address that and move beyond the control of it. The thing that keeps most people up at night, the thing that they're not satisfied with, the thing that's not what it should be for them, is their life. They ask, "Is this all there is? Where's the joy? Where's the meaning? Where's the purpose? There has got to be more joy in getting money, recognition, success, sex, or fame. There's got to be more joy in getting shoes, cars, and houses. There's got to be more fulfillment in getting what I wanted. There's got to be more." In other words, fear of the world not meeting your expectations is the cause of your emotional pain.

By fear I mean experiences of jealousy, anger, resentment, superiority, inferiority, need to please, entitlement, every compulsion, obsession, and addiction, and more. Every form of fear is painful. Love is blissful. By love I mean gratitude, appreciation, caring, patience, contentment, awe of the universe, and more. Every form of love feels good. This book shows you how to recognize and cultivate love in you and how to recognize and move beyond the control of fear in you. It does this in ways that are easy to understand and explains how to experiment with them.

There are many how-to books—how to become happy, how to become wealthy, how to become satisfied, how to become attractive, how to address virtually anything that any part of any personality is concerned about. There are fewer how-to books that address meaning and purpose, fulfillment, and the joy of giving the gifts that you were born to give. This book addresses precisely that.

Meaning, purpose, fulfillment, and the joy of giving the gifts you were born to give require recognizing in yourself all the things that keep you from bliss, which means that keep you from loving. These are parts of your personality that originate in fear. Each creates painful consequences for you when you act on it. Painful physical sensations in your body and judgmental, unforgiving thoughts tell you when one of these parts, or more, are active in you. To move beyond its control you need to challenge its demands—and it is very demanding—by acting from a loving part of your personality *while you are experiencing the frightened part*—while you are experiencing its painful physical sensations and judgmental thoughts. Each time you do this, you create authentic power. When you do not do this, you do not change.

For example, anger was a big part of my life in my thirties when I lived in San Francisco, and before that and after that also. I was also addicted to sex at the same time. These were closely related. My life had so much fear in it and so much emotional pain in it (they are the same), and sex was the only thing that gave me a respite from the pain for a moment, just a moment. Then I needed more because the pain was unrelenting, and the relief was temporary. I did not change then because I did not understand these things or what to do with them.

This book does not proclaim, "I have a solution for your jealousy, and a solution for your anger, and solutions for your overwhelm, need for alcohol, need to gamble or shop, craving for sex, and each of your problems," because the solution for all of your problems is the same—become emotionally aware and practice acting from a loving part of your personality when a fear-based part of your personality is active. As you begin to see your problems from the perspective of the new consciousness, you will begin to see that they are not really problems at all, but opportunities for you to grow spiritually.

People experience emotional pain when they cannot have something they feel they need or cannot live without or they have lost something that they feel they need or cannot live without. They believe that changing the world is the only way to relieve their pain, for example, getting a boyfriend back, getting a new girlfriend, revenging a wrong, defending a right, and on and on. When they are successful, they become happy temporarily, as I did when I had sex. Their emotional pain causes them to try to change the world, and trying to change the world causes more emotional pain. These are experiences of power as the ability to manipulate and control, and the pursuit of it, the pursuit of external power.

Think of this book as a glass of cool, clear water in a time of drought. The time of drought is coming to an end. The time of drought is confinement to the old consciousness and the experience of power as external.

Arriving at the end of the drought is not merely more weather. Arriving is the new consciousness, and the drought will end as you begin to use your life and the new consciousness to create authentic power.

From the perspective of the old consciousness, you need to change the world if you don't like the way it is. From the perspective of the new consciousness, that doesn't work anymore. Change in the macro occurs in the micro. The world is the macro. You are the micro. If you want to change the world, you need to change *yourself*. Creating authentic power changes more than you. It changes every collective in which you participate from the smallest to the largest—from the individual to the group to the community to your society and far beyond. It changes your family, city, country, and your world. It is the most constructive and fulfilling contribution you can make with your life. You were born to make it.

You contribute to the emergence of the Universal Human when you create authentic power. There is no other way that you can. Universal Humans emerge from authentically powerful humans. In other words, creating authentic power is not merely a faster route to the Universal Human. It is a requirement.

The new consciousness requires a higher order of logic and understanding to comprehend and communicate it. The new consciousness conflicts with the old consciousness in every way, including the rigorous demands of its intellect. The old consciousness is not able to apprehend the largeness of what is happening to the human species, and so it attempts to shoehorn, so to speak, experiences of the new consciousness into the shoe of the old consciousness. That shoe no longer fits. The new consciousness and the old consciousness coexist in you. They overlap temporarily in this brief period of time, and this brief period of time is the one in which you are living.

As you read this book, stop each time something resonates with you and ask yourself, "What does this have to do with me? How can I use this in my life?" Then listen. An answer will come at an appropriate time, and it may surprise you.

Everything about the new consciousness is new, and this newness is something that cannot be encapsulated in a few words. Be open. We have many new things to allow ourselves to look at. Do not be hesitant about looking at them. This book brings your attention to the magnitude and the scope of what is changing, and that is the consciousness itself of the human species, and with that come open doors that did not exist before, even in a closed position. Within that comes new potential not imaginable before. With that comes recognition of the role that you are now playing in the unfolding of the Universe, and it is surprisingly intimate.

And welcoming.

# A PRELUDE

# The Great Change

A Great Change is upon us. Our social structures are disintegrating. Wars are ceaseless. Nuclear destruction nears. Global climate catastrophe is here. Individuals with little vision hold the old kind of power.

These events are NOT the Great Change. They are effects of the Great Change. Until you understand the Great Change, you will not understand these events. An obsolete world is disintegrating. Pieces of it are tumbling down, and a new world with a new kind of power is being born. We are on the ground floor of this new world. We *are* the ground floor. Human history and consciousness are changing quickly and dramatically. A new human species looks to the sky and sees beyond it. Human evolution now requires spiritual development. The dying world dismisses this, but the dying world is dying. Human evolution is becoming conscious. This is the Great Change.

New perceptions and insights fill us. The five senses no longer limit our experiences. We are learning to distinguish love from fear within ourselves and to choose love no matter what happens inside us or what happens outside. This is authentic power. We are seeing for the first time that the love and fear in the world are the love and fear in us. Therefore, only by changing ourselves can we change the world. All this is only the beginning.

Look inside yourself for these experiences. They are emerging in you. They are appearing like the sunrise of a new and different Dawn. You are more than experiencing this Dawn, more even than participating in it. You *are* the new Dawn. You *are* the Great Change. What you do with your awareness of the great change is for you to decide. A new potential has been born. *Your* new potential.

I began working on *Universal Human* thirty-three years ago. Said

11

another way, and an equally accurate way, it began working on me that long ago. It is still not finished, and neither am I. Our entire species is now beginning to participate consciously in an expansion of freedom and awareness that has no end. This expansion is not new, but our emerging ability to experience it consciously as individuals and as a species awakening—and our ability to contribute to it consciously as individuals and as a species awakening—are new and without precedent. I am happy to be a part of this awakening with you.

I offer this book as a window through which I have come to see life. I offer it to you, but I do not say it is necessary that you accept it. There are so many ways to wisdom and to the heart. This is our greatest richness, and the one that gives me the most joy.

We have much to do together.

Let us do it in wisdom and love and joy.

Let us make this the human experience.

—GARY ZUKAV

# OUR NEW CREATION STORY

# Beyond the Seasons

The sun is highest in the sky at the summer solstice. The day is longest, and the night is shortest. All has bloomed or is blooming. This is the time of maximal exuberance, but at this time all that has fully expanded begins to contract. This contraction is invisible in wheat fields in June. Glorious growth abounds. Workers wipe sweat from their brows and calves and colts graze with their mothers. Yet the crops that are growing are growing toward their harvest. Within the green of the grass the withering of the grass has begun. Fall and winter are approaching. They cannot be seen, but they are overtaking the summer.

Day by day the sun sinks imperceptibly in the sky. Days become shorter. Nights grow longer. Temperatures drop, and snow arrives. The sun is lowest in the sky at the winter solstice. Light is least, and darkness is greatest. Animals and seeds rest in deep sleep. On this shortest day, this darkest day, all is compressed into one seed of potential, and a cycle completes itself. This cannot be seen in snow-covered forests. All is silent, yet within the silence life stirs. The frozen quiet is moving toward its thaw. Spring and summer are overtaking the winter.

The season of contraction is moving toward the season of expansion, the joy of growth and expression, the abundance of life, the summer solstice. This cyclical dynamic—from potential to expression to harvest, from contraction to expansion and return, from breathing in to breathing out—governs the physical world. It governs the seasons of our lives. It is the rhythm of species, star systems, and galaxies.

A flower sprouts in the spring, but is it a new flower? Its seed carries all that a previous flower was. That seed is invisible to a child in its yard.

The sprout appears to the child as though by magic. New life appears to us the same way. The sprout amazes the child, and the neonate amazes us. The child's explanation of the flower and our explanation of the neonate both reflect limitations of experience.

The child believes that its parents produced the sprout, because only that kind of explanation is meaningful to it. We believe that a union of sperm and egg produced the infant, because only that kind of explanation is meaningful to us. The seed from which the flower sprouts is hidden from the child, and the seed from which the infant emerges is hidden from the five senses. The seed of the infant is its soul.

The soul of the infant does not age or die. It cannot be measured or weighed, yet it is real. It determines everything about the infant. It exists before the infant is born, it exists as the infant moves through the seasons of its life, and it exists as the aged adult withers and passes away like the flowers of spring and summer. Within the soul lie the wisdom and compassion that brought parents and children together and that shaped the patterns of their DNA.

All our great teachers—the Christ, Mohammed, Krishna, the Buddha, and others—spoke of dynamics that are invisible to the five senses. They called them "the Hand of God," "creative impulses of Mind," "Angels," and "devils," and more. They described consequences that are created in the domain of the five senses but that appear in nonphysical realms, such as "heaven," "hell," and "bardo states."

All our great teachers shared the same message: There is more to this life that you live than you can see. You are connected to events, experiences, and others in the realm of the five senses and in other realms that you do not perceive, in ways that you do not understand. What you choose and what you do has significance beyond the apparent. You are a part of a larger whole, a larger dynamic that impacts upon you and upon which you impact. When you choose your thoughts, your words, and your actions, choose wisely and compassionately. You are part of one Family, one Mind, one Heart, one Life, one Universe. Give all that you can to it, and you will receive more in return than you can imagine.

Now that larger dynamic is becoming visible. We are beginning to experience directly what once required faith to believe. The Earth is

Life. The galaxies are Life. The vastness of space is Life. All is Life. The Universe is a spiritual enterprise, not a material one.

Your soul is an immortal, purposeful force at the center of your being. It is your essence. You are a powerful and creative, compassionate and loving spirit that has chosen to participate in the evolution of the human species. Your origin is not merely biological. Your experiences are not only physical. Your gifts are far more than they appear.

Our species is becoming aware of the larger circumstance of which it is a part and to which it is responsible.

This is our new creation story.[1]

---

1  To learn more, read Gary Zukav, *The Seat of the Soul*, twenty-fifth anniversary edition (New York: Simon & Schuster, 2014).

# Our New Creation Story Part 1

The Lakota creation story tells of two braves who meet a young woman on a path. One brave says with awe, "Brother, she is holy!" The other says with lust, "She is *mine!*" As he approaches her, smoke envelopes him. When it clears, his bones lie on the ground. Rattlesnakes glide through them.

Then the young woman rolls in the dust! As she rolls, she becomes a white buffalo calf! The White Buffalo Calf Woman gives the Lakota people their sacred pipe and rituals. When an anthropologist asked a Lakota elder if the White Buffalo Calf Woman story is true, the elder replied, "I don't know if it actually happened that way, but you can see for yourself that it's true."

Creation stories represent the birth of human consciousness. Until now the consciousness they represent has been limited to the perceptions of the five senses. Now something amazing is happening. *Human consciousness is changing.* This change is not happening *in* human consciousness. It is happening *to* human consciousness.

Imagine a bowl with chopped carrots, lettuce, and cucumber slices. All it needs is dressing to be served. The bowl is not the salad. The salad is *in* the bowl. Now imagine the same bowl with yarn, needles, thread, and pieces of cloth in it. The bowl is not these things, either. These things are also *in* the bowl. Whatever you can imagine in the bowl, the bowl is not those things. They are content in the bowl. Now imagine that the *bowl* is changing!

This is happening now to human consciousness. Perceptions beyond the five senses are emerging in millions of humans. The appearance of these new perceptions in our awareness is the great transformation of human consciousness that is now redefining our species. These perceptions are not new content in the old bowl. Our new creation story is about a great and unprecedented change *to* our consciousness, not in our consciousness.

Your consciousness is a bowl. Your experiences are content in the bowl. They change moment to moment. You become angry, depressed, happy, vengeful, satisfied, or jealous. You succeed, fail, grow healthy, become ill, and acquire new strengths, skills, and partners. Perceptions beyond the five senses are not new content in the old bowl. *They are the new bowl.* They are more than changes in what you experience. They are changes in what you *can* experience.

Previously human consciousness was bound to the evolution of physical matter. It plodded slowly through millennia. Now it is evolving explosively. The scope, scale, and velocity of this evolution are startling. From the perspective of our previous evolution it is occurring faster than a heartbeat, faster than an eyeblink.

Hundreds of millions of humans are encountering new realms of experience and potential. Within a few generations, all humans will enter these realms. The transformation that is upon us is so profound and new that few could have imagined it or what we must now become in order to evolve.

In other words, all previous creation stories represent the birth of a five-sensory human species. They belong to the dying consciousness. Our new creation story is about the birth of a new human species that is not limited to the perceptions of the five senses. It belongs to us.

Our new creation story is unfolding inside us and outside us. *We are living our new creation story.* We stand in two worlds—the new consciousness and the old consciousness. The new consciousness and the old consciousness overlap temporarily in this time of transition. No humans have experienced this before. The dying consciousness is familiar to the five senses. It is imposing and rigid. The new consciousness is evident to our expanded perception. It is liberating and nurturing.

Fences limit the experiences of childhood. A child in a fenced yard cries when sand from its sandbox falls into the grass, even if beyond the fence lies a broad beach. Eventually the child encounters the world beyond the fence. It interacts with others whose awarenesses are in advance of its own. It encounters its impact upon the world beyond the fence and the impact of this larger world upon it.

The five senses have been our fence. They confined us to experiences that were appropriate to our level of development. We explored all that we could see, hear, touch, taste, and smell, but we could not recognize these experiences as a fence or know their purpose while they confined us.

Now we are going outside the fence.

# Outside the Fence

Outside the fence lies new awareness, deeper understanding, and greater freedom. All that troubled, confused, depressed, and enraged us; all that left us grieving, frightened, or lonely appears differently. We are lighter, see farther, appreciate more, and are grateful for everything. The world has a new meaning, a new theme, a purpose greater than we could have imagined.

Juan Ramón Jiménez, the Spanish Nobel Laureate, wrote:

> *I have a feeling that my boat*
> *has struck, down there in the depth,*
> *against a great thing.*
> *And nothing Happens! Nothing... Silence... Waves...*
> *Nothing happens? Or has everything happened,*
> *and we are standing now, quietly, in the new life?*[2]

We experience ourselves differently outside the fence. We are more than minds and bodies, more than male or female; more than black, white, red, yellow, or brown; more than intellectual or artistic, Christian or Hindu; farmer or professor. Birth is the incarnation of a soul into space, time, matter, and duality. Death is the return of a soul to nonphysical reality. Inside the fence souls do not exist, birth is random, and death

---

2 Juan Ramón Jiménez, "Oceans," translated by Robert Bly, in *News of the Universe* (San Francisco: Sierra Club Books, 1980).

is final. We are personalities. Outside the fence, we are personalities AND souls. We have a dual identity.

Said another way, inside the fence, your awareness is limited to a little you, so to speak. This is your personality—the you that was born on a certain day, bears your name, and will die on a certain day. It is mortal. Outside the fence you discover a Big You, so to speak—the You that existed before you were born, and that will exist after you die. This is your soul—the You that is immortal. Outside the fence, you become aware of your Big You at the same time that you are aware of your little you.

Juan Ramón Jiménez put it this way:

> I am not I.
> I am this one
> walking beside me whom I do not see,
> whom at times I manage to visit,
> and whom at other times I forget;
> who remains calm and silent while I talk,
> and forgives, gently, when I hate,
> who walks where I am not,
> who will remain standing when I die.[3]

We experience others differently outside the fence. Inside the fence we interact personality-to-personality. Skin colors, cultures, and languages attract or repel us. Outside the fence we connect soul-to-soul. Personalities are temporary clothing that souls choose before incarnating—they are Earth suits. Earth suits disappear when souls return home—personalities die. My Earth suit is male, white, grandfather, and American, among others. What is yours?

We experience the world differently outside the fence. Circumstances, people, and events teach us about *us*. No wall separates the inner world from the outer world. When we choose compassion, we see compassion.

---

3  Juan Ramón Jiménez, " 'I Am Not I,' " from *Lorca and Jiménez: Selected Poems*. Translation copyright © 1973 by Robert Bly. Reprinted with the permission of Beacon Press.

When we choose anger, we see anger. "Which way is the world, really?" is replaced by "Which way am I, really?" The people in your life show you. Do they care about others as much as themselves? So do you. Just a bit? So do you. Not at all? So do you. Do they care about others more than they care about themselves? (Jesus recommended this.) So do you.

Inside the fence is a limited learning environment. Circumstances, people, and events teach us about *them*. Mountains are high. Emotions are unimportant. Experiences serve the maturation of personalities. Power is the ability to manipulate and control. (This is external power.) Evolution requires survival. The universe is mechanical and lifeless. These are *five-sensory* perceptions. The five senses reveal what can be seen, heard, touched, tasted, or smelled. They are parts of a single sensory system whose object of detection is physical reality. They show us the view inside the fence. This is five-sensory perception.

Outside the fence is a boundless learning environment. It is an ocean without shores. It is everywhere around us and within us. We are not separate from the Universe, and the Universe is not separate from anything. Circumstances, people, and events teach us about *us*. Emotions are important. Experiences serve the evolution of souls. Power is the alignment of the personality with the soul. (This is authentic power.) Evolution requires spiritual growth. The Universe is alive, intimate, compassionate, and wise. These are *multisensory* perceptions. They are not limited to the five senses. They show us the view outside the fence.

The difference between the view outside the fence and the view inside the fence is epic. Multisensory perceptions are now emerging in hundreds of millions of individuals. Within a few generations all humans will be outside the fence. This is the unprecedented transformation of human consciousness that is in motion. It is changing everything.

We are becoming *multisensory*.

This is our new creation story.

# 4

# The Mothership

I magine a great sailing ship, larger than any you have ever imagined. Its masts are higher than redwoods. Its sails fill the sky. This is the Mothership. It sails always where it needs to go. Nothing can stop it.

Countless tiny vessels surround the Mothership. They and the Mothership are in the same fleet. Each small vessel has a captain and a crew. On each, the captain sets a course. The captains cannot always see the other small vessels. Sometimes they cannot see the Mothership, but they sense its huge presence.

When the course a captain sails is different from the course the Mothership sails, the voyage of the tiny vessel becomes difficult. Seas rise, waves pound, and wind howls. When the course is opposite the course that the Mothership sails, the voyage becomes terrifying. Angry oceans throw the vessel about. The captain searches for a safe harbor, but there are none. When the vessel sails in the same direction that the Mothership sails, seas protect it, waves guide it, and trade winds move it onward. (These are experiences of authentic power.)

Some crew members on each vessel are supportive. They love the sea, love the voyage, and care for one another. Some crew members are disruptive. They care only for themselves. They always want to be elsewhere. There is nowhere else to go, but they fantasize that there is, and they continually try to get there. When the captain sets a course, supportive crew members are there to help. Disruptive crew members object and obstruct.

Your personality is your vessel. You are the captain. The different parts of your personality are your crew. The Mothership is your soul. It is also the Mothership of the countless tiny vessels around it. In other words, you are one of many, many personalities of your soul.

Strange as it sounds, some captains do not even know their crew! Their vessels sail chaotically as supportive crew members assist and disruptive crew members obstruct. Your supportive crew members are the parts of your personality that originate in love—they are the love-based parts of your personality. These parts are grateful, appreciative, patient, content, and in awe of the Universe. They enjoy themselves. Your disruptive crew members are the parts of your personality that originate in fear—they are the fear-based parts of your personality. They are angry, jealous, resentful, and feel superior or inferior. They do not enjoy themselves.

Until you know your crew, you will experience setting one course and then discovering that you are sailing on a different course! This happens when a disruptive crew member (fear-based part of your personality) mutinies—takes the tiller without your permission. For example, you intend to be patient, but instead you become angry and shout, or you intend to give a homeless person money and instead you tell him or her to get a job. Your personality is splintered. Regaining control of your vessel (your personality) or getting control of it for the first time requires emotional awareness.

The great Hindu poem, the Mahabharata, tell us "Destruction does not come weapon in hand. It comes on tiptoe making bad appear good and good appear bad." Disruptive members of your crew present themselves as good. They make supportive members of your crew appear as bad. Only emotional awareness can show you which of your crew members are supportive and which are disruptive, but you must develop it.

Emotional awareness requires becoming aware of physical sensations in specific areas of your body. These are your energy processing centers. In the East, they are called "chakras." The love-based parts of your personality (gratitude, contentment, caring, etc.) feel good in these areas. Their *physical sensations* are pleasing. The fear-based parts of your personality (anger, jealousy, impatience, etc.) hurt in these areas. Their *physical sensations* are painful. For example, they ache, throb, sting, stab, churn, or burn. You will feel painful physical sensations in one of more of your energy processing centers—your chest, throat, solar plexus, crown of your head, center of your forehead, genital area, or the base of your torso when you are angry or jealous or impatient, etc.

Good-feeling physical sensations in any of these areas call your attention to a love-based part of your personality (supportive crew member) you can count on to steer your vessel into welcoming waters. Painful physical sensations in any of these areas call your attention to a fear-based part of your personality (disruptive crew member) you can count on to steer your vessel into dangerous oceans.

You are the captain of your vessel whether or not you control it. When you choose a supportive member of your crew to steer your vessel, especially *while a disruptive member of your crew demands to steer it,* you take control of your vessel.

This is very important to understand, because each time that you do that, you create authentic power.

# 5

# Authentic Power

All your duties are included in this:
Do nothing to others that would pain you if it were done to you.
**—MAHABHARATA (BRAHMANISM)**

Do not offend others
As you would not wish to be offended.
**—UDĀNAVARGA (BUDDHISM)**

Is there a maxim that one ought to follow all his Life?
Surely the maxim of peaceful goodness:
What we don't want done to us
We should not do to others.
**—ANALECTS (CONFUCIANISM)**

Hold as your own the gains of your neighbor
And as yours his losses.
**—T'AI SHANG KAN-YING P'IEN (TAOISM)**

What you don't wish for yourself
Do not wish for your neighbor.
This is all the law, the rest is only commentary.
**—TALMUD SHABBAT (JUDAISM)**

Do unto others all that you would have them do unto you
Because this is the sum
of the law and of the prophets.
—ST. MATTHEW (CHRISTIANITY)

Not one of you will be a true believer
Who does not wish for his brother
The same that he wishes for himself.
—SUNNAT (ISLAM)

Yes, Yes, and Yes. A thousand times Yes. But *how*? How can we respond with love when we are angry, when we are jealous, when we have been wronged, when we want to kill?

Authentic power is different. How to create it is different. How it works is different. What it does is different.

Knowing how to create authentic power is like owning a treasure map. Authentic power is the treasure. Everyone can reach it. No matter how many people reach it, more can reach it. No matter how many people use the treasure, it never diminishes. In fact, it grows. No one can use the treasure to create advantage. No one who has reached the treasure wants to. Once you have the treasure, no one can take it from you. On the contrary, you want to tell everyone about the treasure and how to reach it.

Authentic power is completely different from the power to make people do what you want. It is the opposite of the ability to manipulate and control. It could not be more different from trying to have more, know more, or do more.

Viktor Frankl was a Jew in a Nazi death camp. He discovered something amazing one frigid dark morning while guards beat him and his fellow prisoners with rifle butts as they stumbled over ruts in frozen muddy roads. Nazis had taken everyone and everything from him—his family, home, and the life that he knew—but they could not take his ability to love! Viktor's discovery—*no one can take my ability to love from me*—still thrills me. How many of your heroes have made this discovery? Jesus made it. Gandhi made it. Martin Luther King Jr. made it. Mother Teresa and Nelson Mandela made it. Outside the fence we must all make it.

The transformation from a five-sensory species into a multisensory species is analogous to the transformation of water-dwelling, water-breathing forms of Life into land-dwelling, air-breathing forms of Life. If we imagine the new air-breathers as being able to communicate with the older water-breathers, they would not be able to explain *anything* about air-breathing to them because water-breathers have no experiences that relate to breathing air. For the same reason, multisensory humans cannot explain *anything* about multisensory experiences to five-sensory humans because five-sensory humans do not have any multisensory experiences to relate to.

Air-breathers cannot return to the ocean because breathing water would prevent them from evolving (obviously). Multisensory humans cannot return to the limitations of the five senses because pursuing external power produces only violence and destruction (it prevents them from evolving). Metaphorically speaking, the water-breathers lived inside the fence, and external power was their water. The air-breathers traveled outside the fence, and authentic power became their air.

This is where we are now—outside the fence—and we are making a discovery that is as amazing to us as Viktor Frankl's discovery was to him. *Pursuing external power—the ability to manipulate and control—now threatens our survival!* What used to be our good medicine has become our poison. Human evolution now requires creating authentic power.

You may have experienced moments of authentic power. Everything was appropriate, like a saxophone singing the soul of a musician, drums playing a rhythm never heard, or dancers moving as none before have moved. Shared intention, movement, moment, and form fuse into a single experience. The optimal occurs. The goal is in! The shot is blocked! The impossible happens. You hit the ball farther, better, faster. Athletes call this the "zone." Musicians call it the "groove." Your personality becomes your instrument. Your life becomes your music. It flows in perfect harmony and perfect time. These are experiences of authentic power.

Creating authentic power requires changing yourself. It is an inward journey. Pursuing external power requires changing the world. It is an outward journey. Inward or outward? We stand with one foot on either side of a line. Authentic power lies on the side of uncharted land, untraversed terrain, and unclimbed mountains. The "New Spring" of Aboriginal prophecy—"the day that will not be followed by night"—lies on that side. It lies outside the fence. External power lies on the side of brutality, exploitation, and suffering. It lies inside the fence. The desolate land we are leaving lies on that side.

When we face the rising sun, we see light. When we turn our backs to it, we see shadows. These are our choices.

This is the time of our ending and the time of our beginning. Ending is the illusion of destiny and the illusion of chance. Ending is ceaseless suffering without cause. Ending is perception through the lens of the five senses. Ending is agony of isolation from other, from the world, from anything. Beginning is a new perception of health and wholeness. Beginning is a new calling toward a new place. Beginning is a new understanding of power. Beginning is the potential of the Universal Human.

Gone is the ideal of the solitary, tormented genius. Born is the perception of genius and inner health as one. Gone is the idea of an alien world. Born is the perception of the world as a reflection facing always toward us. Gone is changing the world by changing others. Born is changing the world by changing ourselves. The world no longer intimidates us. It stimulates us, enriches us, and teaches us about love.

Will you turn toward the light (authentic power) or toward the shadows (external power)? Which side of the line will you choose, moment by moment? That is THE question of our new creation story.

Only you can answer it.

# The Tools of Creating Authentic Power—Emotional Awareness

Creating authentic power is the alignment of your personality with your soul. When your personality is aligned with your soul, you are authentically powerful. Creating authentic power requires emotional awareness and responsible choice of the intention of love. These are the tools of creating authentic power. You cannot find, step into, or stumble upon authentic power. You must create it.

## EMOTIONAL AWARENESS

Your emotions show you the road you must travel to develop spiritually. If you are not aware of your emotions, you won't go far. Your emotions bring your attention to your next step in creating authentic power. They are your spiritual GPS.

Most people think of emotions, especially painful emotions, as obstacles to spiritual development. Nothing could be less true. How can you develop spiritually when you are enraged, seething with jealousy, looking down on your fellow students in the Earth school from the prison tower of your superiority or looking up at them from the dungeon of your inferiority?

Your emotions are your avenues to spiritual growth. They reveal your road map to fulfillment, joy, and love moment by moment. This is important to understand and remember because some emotions are so powerful and painful it is difficult to see how they relate to anything

31

good or wholesome. These emotions show you what is preventing your experiences of anything good or wholesome. If you do not pay attention to them, the life you long for will remain out of reach. You will remain a victim of the people or circumstances you think cause your painful emotions.

The origins of your emotions are *inside* you, not outside. Until you see your emotions this way, your attention will remain fixated on people, circumstances, and events. Your creativity and effort will focus on changing the world in order to avoid painful emotions and experience pleasing emotions. (This is the pursuit of external power.) You will ride a roller coaster—up into happiness and exhilaration when you change the world as frightened parts of your personality demand (for example, you get the boyfriend or the girlfriend) and then down into depression and pain (he or she leaves). Creating authentic power requires using that ride to explore your internal dynamics.

As we have discussed, your emotions show you when you are experiencing love—such as gratitude, appreciation, patience, caring, contentment, and awe of the Universe. With every experience of love come wonderful-feeling physical sensations. The kind you want more of. Most people are unaware that *loving parts of their personalities* create the pleasing physical sensations in their bodies.

As we have also discussed, your emotions show you when you are experiencing fear—such as anger, jealousy, resentment, superiority, and inferiority. Fear is as physically painful as hitting your finger with a hammer. With every difficult emotion, compulsive activity, and addictive behavior comes physical pain in one or more of your energy processing centers. Most people experience these sensations without knowing that *frightened parts of their personalities* are causing them (not other people).

You may need to look for these sensations in your body at first, but once you find them you will see that they are more a part of your life than you might have imagined. Without your knowledge, the frightened and loving parts of your personality have been shaping your words and deeds and creating your experiences.

If you think this cannot be happening to you, consider the possibility that it is happening to you and you are not aware of it. Dismissing this possibility is called "ignorance."

Dismissing any possibility is ignorance. Your vision narrows. You cannot create multitudes of constructive futures. You deny miracles, and so you cannot see yourself, others, and the world as miracles. You live as one who has never seen the sun. You cannot imagine anything but darkness. Plato wrote his famous Allegory of the Cave (375 BC) about such individuals. Perpetually dwelling in a cave, they remain perpetually ignorant of the world outside it. Five-sensory humans live in Plato's cave, allegorically speaking. When they become multisensory, they leave the cave. This is happening now.

Opening to the possibility that you can change your life for the better by paying attention to your inner experiences—such as your emotions—puts you on the spiritual path. The more aware you become of your emotions, the more able you become to shift your experiences from victim to creator.[4]

---

4  Read Gary Zukav and Linda Francis, *The Heart of the Soul: Emotional Awareness* (New York: Simon & Schuster, 2001) to learn more about emotional awareness. To become emotionally aware, do the exercises in it.

# 7

# The Tools of Creating Authentic Power—Responsible Choice

A responsible choice is a choice that creates consequences for which you are willing to assume responsibility.

Most people do not think much about their choices, except those they consider important. They think about which job to take, which apartment to rent, and which city appeals to them. They think a lot about which person they want to be with. They think even more about things like getting married and having children and which career they will pursue. They consult counselors, therapists, and the internet. They compare housing prices, tuitions, and consumer reports. They ask friends, relatives, and colleagues.

These choices are not always life-changing. They are circumstance-changing. Life-changing choices change *you*. You change when you expand your awareness to include the well-being of others. You change when you direct your attention inside with the intention to change yourself for the better, instead of outside with the intention to change others. These are choices of love. Choices of love are life-changing. The more of them you make, the more loving you become.

The opposite of love is not hate. It is fear. Love is a way of being. It is openness to Life, appreciation of Life, and gratitude for Life. Love is relaxing into the present moment. Love is giving without strings attached. Love is moving through the world with an empowered heart without attachment to the outcome. Love is caring for others without second agendas. Love is awe of the Universe. Love is soul-to-soul connection.

Fear is lack of trust in the Universe, lack of appreciation for yourself, lack of care for others. Fear is impatience, anger, jealousy, resentment, and vengefulness. It is obsessive thoughts, compulsive activities, and addictive behaviors. Fear is being controlled by the world around you, always needing to change it in order to feel safe and valuable. Fear is distance from others. Fear is judgment and need. Fear is self-loathing.

Choices of love and choices of fear are both big decisions. Choices of love change you for the better, and choices of fear prevent you from changing. How many big decisions do you make each year? How many do you make each month? Each week? Most people think, "Not many." They are incorrect. When you choose to remain tender in a moment of tenderness, you make a big choice. When you choose to disconnect from others and life in a moment of anger, you make a big choice. You make big decisions moment by moment, and the effects of them are far-reaching.

A person who considers him- or herself powerless and invisible creates very different consequences than a person who sees him- or herself as a powerful creator, visible to all, visible to the Universe, and responsible for what he or she creates. This is the difference between a person who lives in spiritual poverty—emptiness, emotional pain, isolation, and meaninglessness—and a person who lives in spiritual wealth—meaning, purpose, fulfillment, joy, and love. Changing your circumstances will not change your life from poverty to riches, no matter how many shoes, homes, or businesses you acquire.

You were born to create spiritual wealth. You live in spiritual poverty each time you become angry, jealous, or feel invisible, inferior, or superior. Every day gives you a tour of your life—but you need to look inside to take it. You cannot learn about yourself or change yourself by looking outside yourself. You will look outside until you *consciously* choose to look inside, until you recognize your responsibility for the intentions (love or fear) that you choose. Until then people and circumstances will distract you from the transformative power of looking inside. Then you will begin to change from an individual who manipulates and controls into one who loves.

This is the creation of authentic power.[5]

_____

5   Read Gary Zukav and Linda Francis, *The Mind of the Soul: Responsible Choice* (New York: Simon & Schuster, 2003) to learn more about responsible choices. To make them, do the exercises in it.

# The Experiences of Creating Authentic Power

**8**

INTENTION is an experience of creating authentic power. It is the most important thing in creating authentic power. It is the most important thing in everything that you do and say. Without conscious intentions of love, you cannot create authentic power.

An intention is the motivation, the reason, the purpose for acting or speaking and for not acting or not speaking. It is why you act or speak and why you do not act or speak. *An intention is a quality of consciousness that infuses your deeds and words.* It creates the consequences you will encounter.

Choosing an intention is like choosing a doorway. There are only two doorways in the Earth school. One opens to love and the consequences of acting with love. The other opens to fear and the consequences of acting with fear. Creating authentic power requires you to open the door to love and explore what lies beyond it. Your choice determines whether you will learn wisdom through love and trust (these are wonder-full experiences) or through fear and doubt (these are pain-full experiences). The Earth school is the domain of your experiences between your birth day and your death day. Until recently, it was defined by the perceptions of the five senses. Its purpose is to support you in growing spiritually.

The intention to create authentic power puts you on the spiritual path. The spiritual path may call you, beckon to you, present itself to you, but it will remain a calling, beckoning, and possibility until you choose it, until you set the intention to step onto it, or at least experiment with it. The Earth school offers you opportunities continually to learn this and more.

EMOTIONS are experiences of creating authentic power. Without experiencing your emotions, you cannot know whether loving parts of your personality or frightened parts of your personality are active. You might think that everyone is aware of his or her emotions, but this is not always the case. Most individuals go to great lengths to avoid awareness of their emotions. They drink, shop, have sex, work long hours, watch television, gamble, drug themselves into stupors and manias, and much more. They try to please others or dominate them. They strive for accomplishments, status, recognition, education, wealth—the list is endless because every activity done with the intention of fear is an effort to avoid awareness of emotions.

If you cannot distinguish between love and fear in you, you cannot create authentic power, because creating authentic power requires choosing love instead of fear. Only one of the doorways leads to love. If you are not willing to learn which one it is, you cannot go through it.

Your emotions are so very important. Take the time to locate them, as we have discussed, in terms of physical sensations in your body—in your neck, chest, solar plexus, crown of your head, forehead, genital area, and bottom of your torso. Do not dismiss any of your emotions as unimportant, even if they are painful. If you do not consider your emotions worth putting your time and energy into—focusing your attention on— you may learn about emotional awareness, and you may become able to speak about emotional awareness, but you will not be emotionally aware. Experiencing all of your emotions and creating authentic power are inseparable.

FREE WILL is a fundamental, permanent, unchangeable part of every human. To be human is to have free will. The two are inseparable. Creating authentic power requires using your free will to choose love instead of fear. You cannot make a responsible choice without using your free will. No one will insist that you choose responsibly. No one will even ask you to choose responsibly. Eventually the emotional pain that you feel will become more intense, more frequent, and more than you want to experience. Then the idea of making responsible choices, or at least experimenting with them, will occur to you. You do not need to wait that long, but most five-sensory humans do.

Using your emotions to distinguish between love and fear within you, using your free will to act with love instead of fear, *is* the creation of authentic power. When you do not create authentic power, you continue to experience your painful emotions as externally caused. They are not. They are caused by frightened parts of your personality that are activated by external circumstances.

The painful experiences of frightened parts of your personality are not inconveniences that sooner or later you will discover how to eliminate. They are avenues to your spiritual development. Until you recognize them as such—until you stop disregarding them or seeing them as nuisances or understanding them as punishments—their control over you will become stronger.

The loving parts of your personality are already aligned with your soul. When you cultivate them, you align your personality with your soul. Acting on the frightened parts of your personality prevents you from aligning your personality with your soul.

In other words, your emotional experiences serve a purpose. That purpose is clear to multisensory humans, but it is invisible to five-sensory humans. Experiences of frightened parts of your personality show you what your soul incarnated for you to experience and move beyond the control of. You do that by experiencing their painful physical sensations fully and observing their judgmental thoughts, and then using your free will to make a responsible choice to put your attention on the experiences of a loving part of your personality.

The experiences of loving parts of your personality show you what alignment of your personality with your soul (authentic power) feels like so that you can cultivate them. You do that by consciously experiencing their pleasing physical sensations and appreciative, grateful thoughts, setting the intention to remember them, and returning to them when frightened parts of your personality become active. When you put your attention on the experiences of a loving part of your personality, you direct your attention to that part. This is where your attention would be—on a loving part of your personality—without the frightened parts of your personality. Where your attention goes, you go.

Then act from the most loving part of your personality you are able to access *while you are experiencing the painful sensations and judgmental thoughts of a frightened part of your personality.* This is the experience of creating authentic power, the moment of manifestation, the moment your life moves beyond fear and into love—the experience of choosing to respond to the circumstances of your life instead of react to them, the experience of choosing to act consciously with love instead of unconsciously with fear. The more often you create authentic power, the more the frightened parts of your personality lose their control over you.

～

Creating authentic power is a PROCESS, not an event. These experiences are part of the process. They are the experiences that you must bring into being again and again in yourself in order to create authentic power. Patience, focus, and practice are all involved. Commitment, courage, compassion, and conscious communications and actions are all involved. *You* are involved totally, and the thing you are totally involved in is your life.

Each experience of your life, when made conscious and consciously utilized—when seen, accepted, and used as the gift that it is—is an opportunity to cultivate love and challenge fear in you, to move toward wholeness, to create authentic power. Remind yourself as each of your experiences come to you that it is not only for yourself that you are cultivating loving parts of your personality and challenging frightened parts. It is for the world that you desire, because your contributions to the world change as you cultivate love and you challenge fear.

When you see from this perspective, even your most painful emotions show themselves as blessings. It is as though you ask Divine Intelligence, "Please show me what I need to know to live a life of joy and meaning no matter what I am experiencing. I am so exhausted from emotional pain and anxiety and stress and lack of trust. *Please* help me." Then look at the emotions you are feeling and the experiences you are encountering and realize that your request has been granted.

Now what will you do?

# The Process of Creating

# Authentic Power

For any reason or anywhere you are, you can experience joy because of the perception in which you hold what is happening. You can experience joy at any time or any place. Appreciation of the perfection that is the process of your life and awareness of the opportunities that process brings you to create authentic power are always yours to experience.

When you reach for a part of your personality that is appreciative, grateful, caring, or patient, you move yourself in that direction. You move toward appreciation, gratitude, caring, or patience. You do not move yourself in the direction of a frightened part of your personality.

While you are jealous, for example, you can begin to challenge your jealousy. One challenge is to recognize that you are in a frightened part of your personality. Another is to begin to recognize that the person of whom you are jealous is a soul like you, or if you cannot do that, to recognize that he or she is a personality like you with loving and frightened parts, and that the path of his or her life is as difficult and complex as yours. These are examples of moving yourself in a direction of understanding and away from judgment. In other words, you begin to open yourself to compassion for the other person, and that will affect your words and your deeds.

When you are fully compassionate with the other person, that is an experience of authentic power. Compassion is the experience of authentic power. Patience, care, gratitude, appreciation, contentment, and awe of the Universe are also experiences of authentic power.

Many individuals think that the tools of creating authentic power—emotional awareness and responsible choice—are steps that they must go through, or that it is natural for them to go through, and yet that is not the case. They confuse the order in which these tools have been presented with an imaginary order in which they think their experiences must present themselves.

There are different experiences in the process of creating authentic power, but creating authentic power is not linear. For example, it is possible for you to be angry or in the midst of resentment or jealousy and suddenly see through the eyes of love, and that begins with recognizing where you are and where you would like to be and then finding yourself there.

Frightened parts of some personalities have a tendency to take comfort in step-by-step instructions. First this, then that, and then the third, and then the fourth in order, and then at last the destination. There is no need to impose this structure or imagined rigor upon yourself or others.

When you are creating authentic power, you are unraveling yourself, so to speak, in terms of experiences that you can encounter, but these experiences are not steps in the creation of authentic power. They are possible experiences in the process of creating authentic power. Some individuals, especially those with intellectual tendencies, burden themselves with what they feel ought to be and how that should be done and how it is going to be done. They focus on what should be rather than simply involving themselves in the experience of fear and challenging it with the intention to move into an experience of love, for example, an experience of patience or acceptance or gratitude. That is the important thing to remember. That is the process of creating authentic power.

There are many different experiences that you can encounter while creating authentic power. If you get stuck in one of them, recognize that it is one experience among many in the process of creating power. It does not itself lead to the experience of authentic power. It leads to more of the same because there is stuck-ness. There is a refusal on the part of a frightened part of your personality to move beyond it.

That is why some individuals who are creating authentic power feel that emotional awareness—especially experiencing the painful physical sensations of frightened parts of their personalities—is a swamp, a morass from which they cannot extricate themselves. They do not yet understand that any of their experiences in the process of creating authentic power are only *parts* of that process, a process that frees them through awareness and choice.

There is value in experiencing the pain of a frightened part of your personality repeatedly because eventually you will realize that it will not change until you change it. That could take lifetimes. Therefore, do not judge yourself or others who are involved in the process of becoming aware in their lives. You can leap from any position of fear into love at any moment. Do not judge yourself or them for not leaping from fear to love in a single bound. That can happen, but be gentle with yourself if your path at the moment is different.

There is an example in the New Testament of a man controlled by frightened parts of his personality named Saul who suddenly, in the midst of a long foot-journey, found himself in Love, and that change was so strong and powerful for him that he renamed himself Paul. The importance of this story, for me, lies in its illustration of the power of human consciousness to move beyond fear and into love instantly.

When you feel that you cannot extract yourself from the painful physical sensations of frightened parts of your personality, remind yourself that you are in a particular part of this process, in this case, feeling pain continually. Remind yourself that this is not the end point of your journey, that your continual experience of pain through the practice of emotional awareness is a choice that you are making to avoid moving beyond that pain.

Creating authentic power requires not simply following steps or instructions. It requires your will, your intention, your openness to experimenting with moving beyond all that you thought was appropriate and effective. Yet remaining closed to this experimentation is the path that you have chosen until that moment. It is not for you to judge that path, but to see where you are on it without attachment to the outcome and with compassion, because the emotional pain you feel, and the emotional pain that others feel, is real and deep.

Your experiences are each part of a process that is taking you beyond your fears and the goals and aspirations of the frightened parts of your personality. They are each part of a process that is leading you to where you incarnated to go.

# 10

## Choices That Matter

When you turn left instead of right, it is because you intend to turn left. You may or may not be aware of your intention, but without it, you would not turn left. You would continue straight, or veer to the right, or climb up some stairs. Behind everything you do lies an intention. You are always in motion, and the direction, intensity, duration, and everything about the motion is determined by your intention.

Most people are unaware of their intentions most of the time. Their lives are robotically repetitive. They shower, eat, go to work, return from work, and daily do countless things without awareness of their intentions for doing them. They bounce from experience to experience, not knowing what brought their experiences into their lives. They blame others for their pain and credit them for their pleasure. These are experiences of five-sensory humans.

Until you become aware of your intentions and choose them consciously, your life appears to unfold out of your control. Actually, it is unfolding as you intend, but you do not know what you intend. If you are surprised by your experiences, it is because you are unaware of the intentions that created them—your intentions. This is a realization of multisensory humans.

The first step in uncovering your unconscious intentions is to examine your belief system. A belief system that causes you to contract—for example, that tells you the universe is dead, random, frightening, or merciless—generates a background of fear in your life. Every belief system that includes fear—such as fear of abandonment, rejection, or punishment—does the same. Your guard is constantly up, and everything becomes a tense experience, even starting your car, going outside, or answering the phone.

A belief system that causes you to expand does the opposite. For example, a belief that the Universe is alive, compassionate, and wise opens you. When you adopt a belief system like this, the love in it infuses your actions and words the way that fear permeates them when your belief system includes fear. Love fills your awareness, and you become freer to create with intentions of love.

Most individuals adopt the belief system of their parents or peers without examining it. For example, they adopt a belief that only their "Savior" can keep them from unbearable never-ending pain, without asking themselves, "If Divine Intelligence exists, could it be so mean and small-minded to condemn even individuals who do not know about this belief system and its 'Savior'?" Or they adopt a belief that white people are superior to people of color, without asking themselves, "Could all white people be more wise, brave, kind, and compassionate than Jesus from Nazareth, Mohandas Gandhi, Martin Luther King Jr., and Nelson Mandela?" Obviously not.

If you find any fear in your belief system, experiment with belief systems that do not contain fear. Then look for the one among those that most calls to your heart.

For example, the belief system that the Universe is wise and compassionate; you are a compassionate and loving, powerful and creative spirit; authentic power is the alignment of your personality with your soul; and every experience in the Earth school supports you in creating it is a belief system that contains no fear. Belief systems that demand you adhere to a dogma (unchangeable and unchallengeable rules); accept historical accounts without question; disdain, pity, condemn, or intend to change others with different belief systems; declare themselves the best, most effective, or only belief system that can lead you to the goodness in yourself that you long for; and belief systems that offer rewards or/and threaten punishments all contain fear. In fact, they are *built on* fear. Fear is fundamental to them and inseparable from them.

Experimenting with the belief system that most calls to you (as opposed to the belief system that calls to your parents or peers) will help you understand that you are responsible for choosing the most healthy belief system for yourself. Whichever belief system you experiment with, approach it with skepticism—for example, "Can this be true? Does it really work?"—not with cynicism—for example, "This belief system is shallow, rigid, authoritarian, etc." See what it produces in your life. Does it lead to goodness, acceptance (of all), and love (for all)? If not, experiment with another belief system. You alone are responsible for the consequences of your choices. This is good news.

Five-sensory individuals see intentions as goals. Their "intentions" are really "out-tentions," for example, the out-tention to make money, get married, change jobs, visit Europe, save the rain forests, or learn to weld. They believe that actions create consequences.

Multisensory humans see an intention as a *quality of consciousness*. They see that the consciousness behind an action or word—NOT the action or the word—creates consequences. For example, five-sensory humans think the Golden Rule is about actions. ("DO to your neighbor what you want your neighbor to DO to you.") Multisensory humans see that the Golden Rule is about consciousness. ("INTEND for your neighbor what you want your neighbor to INTEND for you.") What consciousness do you hold toward your neighbor when you speak or act? Is it anger, jealousy, or resentment? Is that the consciousness you want your neighbor to hold toward you? Is it gratitude, appreciation, or caring? Is that the consciousness you want your neighbor to hold toward you?

Intentions of love, as we have seen, create constructive and joyful consequences. Intentions of fear create destructive and painful consequences. Actions and words are irrelevant. For example, you can donate money to a charity to publicize your personal goodness (fear), create a tax deduction (fear), or project a positive image (fear). The intention of fear always creates destructive and painful consequences. You can also give to a charity to support others, with no strings attached (love). The intention of love always creates constructive and joyful consequences. If you are not aware of your intention when you speak or act, you will be when its consequences appear in your life. If they are not what you expect, your intention was not what you thought.

Your choices of intention create the road upon which you walk moment by moment. All roads lead to awareness and love, although some are more direct and joyful, and some are longer and more difficult. The choice of love fuses the consciousness of love with matter, and the choice of fear fuses the consciousness of fear with matter. The point of choice is the hourglass point between energy and matter. It is the seat of your soul. It is the point where energy becomes matter.

You are always at this point.

You *are* this point.

You are always choosing.

# 11

# The New Use of Courage

I was a member of a Special Forces (Green Beret) "A Detachment" in Vietnam. An "A-team" was a highly trained twelve-man unit. Each A-team had two officers and ten enlisted men. I was one of the officers on my team (the executive officer—second in command). A-teams, in my opinion, were the heart of the Special Forces. The mission of the Special Forces was to infiltrate enemy lines by air, land, or sea, and support local people in resisting their dictatorial government.

Things were different in Vietnam. First, there were no "lines." The enemy—the North Vietnamese Army and the Viet Cong—were everywhere, and so were we. Second, many of the local people we were supposed to be supporting were fighting *us*. Third, many Vietnamese saw us as occupying their country.

Everything else was war as usual. American planes bombed Vietnamese villages. American soldiers waded through mud and rain forests to attack Vietnamese soldiers, and Vietnamese soldiers did the same to ambush American soldiers. All were doing their best to kill one another. (The commerce of this conflict was also war as usual—American factories sold bullets to the Americans to shoot Vietnamese soldiers, and factories around the world sold bullets to the North Vietnamese to shoot American soldiers.)

Still our job was special. Everything about us was Top Secret. We were inserted clandestinely, usually by helicopter, into Laos or Cambodia to do Top Secret things. Coming into a landing zone—a clearing in a rain forest—was one of the scariest parts. Our helicopters were completely vulnerable as they settled down. I think even the gunships, which stayed higher, were vulnerable. If the Viet Cong had learned about our arrival, we would probably have died.

How could the Viet Cong have learned about our arrival? From one of the many mercenaries we trained and took with us on our missions. These were usually local tribesmen trying to feed their families. No one knew their loyalties. We kept them in our compound, always ready to go without notice (so they would not know in advance of a mission), and isolated them as much as possible to prevent them from sharing our plans. We met them at the helicopters in the dark of morning to launch our missions. They knew only to fight as we had trained them to fight.

One mission was to conceal a motion-sensing device on the side of a dirt road that was part of a large network known as the Ho Chi Minh Trail. It would transmit a signal when a truck passed it, and attack aircraft standing by for the signal would be airborne in minutes, on their way to bomb the device (and the trucks that had activated it). The mission took about a day and a half from insertion to extraction.

I became fatigued, but I could not rest. The ground was hard, and my fear was intense. My eyes would close now and then in the night, but my body would not sleep. It seemed to know the danger it was in. Laos missions (our missions) were code-named "Prairie Fire." We had been told that calling a Prairie Fire Emergency—"We have been discovered!"—would immediately divert all attack aircraft in the air toward us and launch standby aircraft to our defense. I believed this. I had seen our own pilots spiriting toward their helicopters in response to a Prairie Fire Emergency. No effort would be spared to extract a Prairie Fire team from an emergency.

If that were unsuccessful, we would get no further help, and we expected none. Our uniforms had no insignias. We wore no identification. Serial numbers were ground from our weapons. Many of them were foreign-made. President Johnson regularly denied the presence of American troops in Laos and Cambodia. We did not officially exist. If we were captured, we would be dismissed as mercenaries.

Enlisting in the US Army, volunteering for the Special Forces, requesting Vietnam duty, and planting the motion sensor were examples of my old use of courage. Parachuting at night with equipment at Fort Bragg and from helicopters into the ocean off Okinawa were more examples. I had plenty of courage, but I never thought about how I was using it. I felt compelled to do these frightening and dangerous things, and then to do more of them, but I had only a dim understanding of why, which I could not allow myself to even consider.

I did them to be admired. In retrospect, I did them to be loved. I did not realize how strong my needs to be admired, recognized, and valued were. Those needs lifted me out of Harvard, enlisted me in the army, and put me down by the side of a dirt road in Laos, all without my awareness of them. I was too frightened to realize that I was frightened. The street name for this is "macho."

I still have courage, and now I think a lot about how I use it. The same courage that once enabled me to "stand up, hook up, shuffle to the door" of a C-130 aircraft in flight and jump into the emptiness between me and a drop zone far below now enables me to look at myself in ways that I never suspected were possible.

Now I use my courage *every* day, but I use it in a new way. I use it when anger or rage erupts in me and demands action and I choose instead to act from the most loving part of my personality I can access. I use it when jealousy closes my heart and I choose instead to act from the most loving part of my personality I can access. I use it when I want to kill someone or kill myself and I choose instead to act from the most loving part of my personality I can access. I use my courage when I feel the painful physical sensations of these emotions and I choose to act from the most loving part of my personality that I can access *while I am feeling them*. These are examples of the new use of courage.

I never imagined how much courage entering my life consciously would require. As I began to look into myself, all I found at first was fear—fear of failing, fear of not living up to the expectations of my parents, fear of not living up to my expectations of myself, fear of rejection, fear of abandonment, and more. Slowly I realized that looking with integrity at my own fears required more courage than any danger the army provided.

I never dreamed how much courage acting with compassion requires when the people around me are enraged and vengeful, or parts of my personality that originate in fear are enraged and vengeful. The day after the World Trade Center buildings collapsed into rock and blood, a movie star in New York City suggested that we respond with compassion. His huge audience booed him and shouted him down. I admired him. I had heard about a Tibetan monk just released from a Chinese prison where he had been tortured. He told the Dalai Lama, "I was in danger." The Dalai Lama quickly asked, "What danger?" The monk replied, "I was in danger of losing my compassion for the Chinese." I asked myself, "How much courage did this monk require to remain compassionate to his tormentors?" I still do.

The greatest pain is needing to belong and not belonging, needing to be loved and feeling unlovable, wanting to love and feeling unable to love, not wanting anyone to see you inside the way you see yourself lest they detest you, feeling inherently flawed and intrinsically defective. This is the pain of powerlessness. Every human—five-sensory and multisensory—has the pain of powerlessness deep inside. Five-sensory humans mask it by trying to change the world. This is the pursuit of external power. Multisensory humans look inside themselves to change their internal sources of it permanently. This is the creation of authentic power.

Creating authentic power requires the new use of courage.

# 12

# Intentions of the Soul—Harmony

The intentions of the soul are significant.

The intentions of the soul cannot be recognized without multisensory perception. In the same way, the intentions of the soul cannot be understood without multisensory perception. Yet with multisensory perception they open a new vista onto human experience.

Harmony is a reflection of the material world even though five-sensory perception cannot perceive that harmony. Five-sensory humans speak of ecosystems, balance, and sustainability, but the harmony that is the natural world on our planet—natural meaning realms other than human—goes far beyond what they can see. It is an exquisite and delicate balance in which all aspects of Life have their place. The aspects of Life are beyond countable. Not even insects upon our planet can be numbered, much less microbes, yet each of them has its place.

These are not larger places and smaller places, as we might think in physical terms. All the aspects of Life are precious and equal. Each is necessary for the compassionate unfolding of the Universe. This perception is quite different from the five-sensory perception in which bigger is better, bigger is more. Even though five-sensory humans are not physically bigger or more than other forms of Life, they see themselves that way.

Multisensory humans see themselves as part of Life. They see animals, plants, and minerals as part of Life. They see the smallest and the largest forms of Life as equally important. Five-sensory humans cannot grasp this except as a grand idea. The experience of it eludes them. Multisensory perception begins the process of opening them to that experience. Creating authentic power brings them into it.

Authentic power is the alignment of the personality with the soul, which means the alignment of the multisensory personality with the intentions of its soul. As we begin to understand harmony as an intention of the soul, we see that harmony is simply a reflection of that which is. Little in the Earth school appears harmonious to five-sensory perception because it is the domain in which personalities come to learn the difference between love and fear so that they can choose love instead of fear. The entire Universe is harmonious, or balanced, but in ways that are beyond the human experience.

The best way to approach harmony is experientially, that is, in terms of your emotions. As you interact with other students in the Earth school, those interactions activate parts of your personality, and each of those parts is a way of perceiving a realm of emotion. The realm of fear has multiple sub realms, and all of them express fear, for example, jealousy, rage, resentment, superiority, inferiority, and more. These experiences are well known to multisensory individuals who are creating authentic power, and they are painful. The realm of love, if love could be called a realm, also has multiple sub realms, such as gratitude, appreciation, caring, contentment, and awe of the Universe, and experiences of them are blissful. These experiences are also well-known to multisensory individuals who are creating authentic power. It is in experiencing both of these realms that the creation of authentic power becomes possible, for it is only through the use of your will, your free will, that you can choose which realm your awareness will illuminate for you—love or fear. As you become aware of your experiences of love, of your constructive intentions and the consequences they create, you begin to experience the harmony of the Universe.

Nothing in the Universe exists that is not harmonious from the perspective of the Universe. This harmony is not negotiated. The Universe does not negotiate with aspects of itself. Neither do aspects of the Universe negotiate with one another. Experiences such as the death of one animal feeding the life of another animal, or the transformation of energy from one type into another, obviously cannot be obtained by negotiation, for who is there to negotiate with?

Five-sensory humans negotiate circumstances of minimal conflict.

A circumstance of minimal conflict is very different in every way from a circumstance of love flowing through every aspect of the Universe, combining, reordering, dissolving, restructuring, rebirthing—Love reconfiguring Love, or said another way, birth reconfiguring five-sensory forms of Life within the Earth school.

As multisensory humans cultivate love and challenge fear in themselves while they interact with one another—while they are creating authentic power in themselves—they can reach a common resonance of a high frequency in the process. That is what, in the Earth school, we would call harmony. That frequency is not only a little bit higher, it is inexpressibly higher, than the frequency of a negotiation to create a circumstance of minimal conflict. It is an interaction in which the needs of all involved are considered and honored, the needs of love are given priority over all, and the desires of fear are given no priority except as they serve the purpose of illuminating the distinction between love and fear within individuals who are creating authentic power.

In our part of the physical universe, which is a very small part, harmony is evident everywhere. As each new morning arrives on our planet, so does a new perception of the sun, whose warmth and light allow Life as we know it on our planet—food to grow and species for us to grow with. This harmony is invisible to five-sensory humans. They see ways to benefit themselves, to exploit animals, one another, and the Earth. Multisensory humans look at the same situation as an exquisite dynamic portrait of harmony. They experience that harmony within the spheres of their own lives in the Earth school when they resonate with others—not with the needs or desires of others, but with the essence of others.

In human emotional terms, this would be when we care for one another, we are interested in one another, we seek the well-being of one another, and we experience that in one another. That is the nectar of the Earth school. That is harmony. That is the new potential awaiting us, a potential that is beyond contentment, beyond even joy. It is the beauty, the fulfillment, the richness of Life itself. It is the experience of ourselves as part of Life, and others as part of Life, and others as part of ourselves, and ourselves as part of others and all else.

Your soul intends to create with harmony in the Earth school. When

you align yourself with that intention, you move yourself into new domains. These domains are beyond five-sensory experience. They are not
beyond multisensory experience. They are calling multisensory humans
to the experience of the Universal Human.

Universal Humans live in these domains.

# Intentions of the Soul—Cooperation

# 13

Cooperation is the natural course when competition no longer dominates consciousness. This is the same as saying that love is the natural course when fear no longer dominates consciousness. Cooperation requires reaching out to others. It requires listening to them and appreciating their intelligence and their wisdom. Competition requires creating a barrier to others, disregarding what they want, what they offer, and substituting for that at the center of your consciousness what you want and what you need from them and then how to get it.

Competition assumes that only one party can win, so to speak, that only one party can come out on top. Cooperation assumes that there are no winners or losers, there are only cooperators, individuals who have set the intention to merge their creativity, their intelligence, and their wisdom toward a common goal.

Five-sensory individuals can cooperate in the pursuit of external power. Indeed, that is what they do when they are competing. For example, competing entities, such as corporations, encourage, and in fact require, cooperation among their employees. Employees in groups—one within one corporation and one within another—cooperate among themselves, but the bottom line is to ensure the successful competition of the entity that employs them.

Multisensory humans cooperate, but their cooperation is a special type of cooperation. It is cocreation. Cocreation is cooperation soul-to-soul. It is cooperation in the service of love. There are no competing individuals or entities. There are only students and collectives of students in the Earth school. When the benefit of all of them is the primary objective of multisensory humans who are merging their creativity and intelligence with compassion, that is cocreation.

Cocreation is satisfying in ways that cooperation cannot be. Cooperation allows individuals to touch one another in creative ways. Yet the objective of that cooperation may be counter to the benefit of all involved. It may be, for example, the development of a nuclear weapon, or an advertising campaign that captures more market share.

Multisensory humans do not see in these terms. They see one another as souls, and they strive to utilize their creativity in ways that benefit Life. The rewards of this in terms of fulfillment, meaning, purpose, and joy are immense. Not immense in a sense of bigness that is overwhelming or impressive, but immense in the sense of satisfaction and gratitude and appreciation that goes deep, that comes from the heart and reaches the heart.

Cocreation is the joining of multisensory individuals in ways that they were meant to join just as cooperation is the joining of five-sensory individuals in ways that they were meant to join, which is in the pursuit of external power, for the pursuit of external power enabled their survival, and survival was the only requirement of their evolution. Multisensory humans require spiritual development to evolve. Spiritual development requires moving beyond the needs of fear, the perceptions and desires of fear, the goals of fear, in other words, the objectives of frightened parts of the personality.

Multisensory evolution requires creating with the intentions of the soul—harmony, cooperation, sharing, and reverence for Life. As one individual cocreates with another individual, they bring into being one or more of these intentions. They cocreate to experience harmony. They cocreate to share. They cocreate with reverence for Life.

The experience of cocreation for the benefit of Life has a by-product, you might say, that is itself remarkable. That is the experience of harmony. We have explored harmony in the previous chapter. The experience of harmony is without bounds because love is without bounds, and cocreation is a route toward the experience of love. Multisensory humans were born to cocreate. They cocreate naturally. The only obstruction to their cocreations are the frightened parts of their personalities. In identifying, experiencing, and challenging the frightened parts of their personalities they are able to move beyond them. In other words, creating authentic power leads to cocreation. It enables cocreation, and cocreation becomes the desired objective itself.

Cooperators cooperate in order to achieve a physical goal. Cocreators cocreate in order to experience a merging of their creativity, intelligence, wisdom, and joy. The process of cocreation is more important to them than an objective. The objective is the vehicle that brings multisensory individuals together. Cocreation allows them to move toward that objective. Yet as they do, they move toward it in a way that is open, wide open. They are not confined to that objective, although eventually, if they choose, they will reach it. The journey is as significant and meaningful and fulfilling to them as the objective itself. Cocreators cocreate for the fulfillment of cocreation, for the joy of cocreating.

, As multisensory individuals create authentic power, the experience of cocreation becomes a delicious by-product, something that they long for and strive for and consciously bring into being. As they become authentically powerful, cocreation becomes as natural to them as breathing. It becomes as natural as smiling when their hearts respond with love to the energy of another. Their cooperation turns into cocreation, and the two-dimensional black-and-white sense of satisfaction that comes from achieving a five-sensory goal is replaced by the multidimensional, full-color fulfillment that comes with cocreating. Cocreating brings into the Earth school not only the energy of the soul, but the energy of the Universe itself.

Cocreators desire more of the experience of cocreation. It is not a craving. It is not a need of the personality. It is more like the natural way in which flowers turn toward the sun. When cooperators cooperate they cooperate within a limited sphere of openness, for they do not wish to share that which might benefit one of their cooperators in the future. Just as cooperators cooperate within the context of competing entities, alliances within those entities and between those entities come into being and disappear, and therefore, a cooperator will not share that which may put him or her at a disadvantage in the future, for example, an idea that might be patented by another cooperator.

Cocreators are not bound in that way. Love has no secrets. It is transparent. Cocreation is not possible without an open heart, and when the open heart is there, it leads to satisfaction and fulfillment without end. Cocreation requires caring for the other. It requires considering the benefit to others and the collective. Put it this way: cocreation has no favorites. It is a natural flow of love between the cocreators. They may or may not think of it that way, but that will be their experience as they discover the joy of cocreating.

# 14

# Intentions of the Soul—Sharing

S haring is at the heart of authentic power. Sharing is a natural expression of love. When love is not present, sharing is not possible. The appearance of sharing is possible, but that is an activity generated by fear, for example, when the sharing will ultimately benefit the one who shares.

Sharing feels healthy and wholesome and good. Sharing comes from trust in the Universe. It comes from trust that the experiences in the Earth school are what they need to be for the individuals involved, given the wisdom of the choices they have made.

What is shared from the perspective of the soul? In the Earth school it is love. There is nothing else that can be shared that is worth the effort. All else is pursuit of external power. There are many ways that a gift can be given or something can be shared with a second agenda of self-benefit. Sometimes even a gift as significant as an education can be given with a second agenda of self-benefit. Parents often participate in this dynamic, but without awareness. They desire the education of their children to reflect positively upon themselves. Donating to a cause for the purposes of self-promotion or to create an image as a philanthropist or a generous person is also part of this self-benefiting dynamic.

None of this is sharing. Sharing is spontaneous. Sometimes the implementation of a sharing needs to be thought out, such as planning for the future of a child or the future of a worthy endeavor, but the decision to share comes from the heart, and it is recognized more than made. Sharing is an intention of the soul. The soul knows only sharing. Souls do not withhold. Souls support their personalities with their availability. They support their personalities with their impersonal perspective. These must be asked for, and they are always there.

Reverence is relating through your soul. Reverence connects your personality with souls in advance of your own. It is engaging in a form and depth of contact with Life that is beyond the shell of form and into essence. It is contact with the essence of every person, bird, plant, animal, and thing, with the essence of the Earth and all upon and in it. It is contact with the interior of its beingness. Reverence is accepting the principle of the sacredness of Life, any way that you define sacred. Reverence is the experience that all Life is, in and of itself, of value and that everything is Life.

All this is sharing. It is sharing not as an action but as an environment, an atmosphere, so to speak, just as the air that we breathe is not shared. It is. We need not ask for it. We need not receive it. It is a gift. It is as our world is. Sharing is as souls are.

When you share, you bring the energy of your soul directly into the Earth school. That is why the choice to share without second agendas creates authentic power. It aligns your personality with your soul. The Earth school continually offers opportunities for each of its students to discover the frightened parts of his or her personality that require challenging and the loving parts that require cultivating. Spiritual partnerships accelerate this process. In all these ways sharing is fundamental. Without sharing you go nowhere on the spiritual path, and yet you must embark upon the spiritual path in order to share.

As you embark upon the spiritual path, you develop a new understanding of sharing. The five-sensory understanding of sharing is more akin to the concept of lending. It is not really giving. It is sharing, but there is usually an agenda beneath the sharing or the giving. It may be the satisfaction of giving or, as we discussed, the creation of a self-image that is philanthropic. This type of sharing does not create constructive consequences.

Multisensory humans perceive sharing very differently than five-sensory humans. Five-sensory humans consider sharing to be giving of their wealth, for example, to a charity or public event or building. That is not the criterion of multisensory humans for sharing. Their only criterion is the intention of love.

Sharing is the same as giving, and giving is the same as sharing when there is no hidden agenda. When love is the inspiration, love is the giver. Love is also the receiver. One of the greatest gifts you can give to others is to receive their love. This does not mean to exploit their love. It means to open yourself to the love they have to give. They do not open themselves to give this love to you. They open themselves to fulfill themselves, to live with meaning and purpose and joy, yet they cannot do that when they have a second agenda. Nonetheless, they themselves grow spiritually as they develop the ability to receive the love that you have to share as well as the ability to share the love that they have for you.

All of nature is based on sharing. Every ecosystem demonstrates sharing. As you breathe, you inhale oxygen which is created for you by the plant kingdom, and as you exhale you give the plant kingdom carbon dioxide which it uses to create oxygen, and so it goes. The sharing is endless. That which appears to be sharing is giving, and that which appears to be giving is sharing because the two cannot exist apart.

As you develop the ability to share without second agendas, your sharing becomes like light from the sun or warmth from the sun. The sun has no hidden agendas. It has no requirements. It gives and gives and gives. Its sharing is complete. Eventually the energy in the sun will exhaust itself, yet that is another activity, so to speak, in the endless giving and sharing that occurs in the Universe.

Even when you create with fear, and painful consequences come into being for yourself that affect others, that is sharing. Others experience an individual who is creating with fear and learn from that individual how to create with love in themselves. This is the impersonal perspective of the soul. From the perspective of the personality it is enough to know whether or not there is an agenda beneath your sharing or your giving. In other words, do not think to yourself that you have license to behave insensitively or cruelly because others will learn from the insensitivity or cruelty of frightened parts of your personality that you do not challenge.

Your intention is not hidden from the Universe—only sometimes from yourself and others. As you incarnate and reincarnate into the Earth school, the Universal Law of Cause and Effect, or karma, will help you to recognize your intentions until you recognize them all. That is a long path to walk. Creating authentic power shortens it considerably. As you discover multisensory perception in yourself, you enter the potential of this accelerated spiritual development. Thus you have the ability to evolve far more quickly than five-sensory humans.

We have referred to creating authentic power and knowing how to do that as possessing a treasure map, but this treasure map is of no use to you if you do not share it with others. The more you use the treasure you find by following the map, the more you want to share the treasure with others. The more you share it with others, the more they desire or learn to share with you. As they share with you, the more they desire to share. This is a microcosmic glimpse into the nature of the Universe, where give and take, good and bad, merge into one beneficent dynamic that has no beginning and has no end.

There are some gifts that you have to share that might surprise you. One of them is your joy, is simply enjoying your life. That is a priceless gift, and you cannot give it to yourself without giving it to others. Support in creating authentic power is a gift that you give to others. In other words, as you create spiritual partnerships, you commit to your spiritual development above all else, and the partnerships you form are with others who are committed to their spiritual development above all else, you find that your role is one of support because you cannot create authentic power for them, but your support is precious to them, for it is through your support that they can identify parts of their personalities that they need to challenge to move beyond the control of fear that they might not have observed.

You and your soul are inseparable. Your soul and sharing are inseparable. Creating authentic power helps you to experience these things.

Then you can share.

# 15

# Intentions of the Soul— Reverence for Life

When you speak of reverence, you speak of the Universe. When you speak of the Universe, you speak of reverence. You might imagine, in five-sensory terms, the Universe in front of a mirror and being reflected in the mirror, but in such a way that it is difficult to distinguish the reflection from the reflected, the reflected from the reflection. The difference is that the reflected does not require the reflection to exist. The reflection does.

Reverence is the reflection. The Universe is the reflected. In other words, the Universe does not depend upon our experience, in this case, upon your experience of reverence or not. The Universe is. To the extent that humans can reflect the Universe, they revere the world. They revere the Universe of which the world is a part. They revere one another. They revere themselves, that is, they honor themselves. They see themselves, one another, the world, and the Universe as holy, as beyond value as a mountain is beyond admiration. That is reverence.

You experience reverence when, for a moment, you drop your judgments and angers and resentment. In other words, when you drop your fear. Fear is not so easily dropped, yet the experience of fear dropping away is one that many humans have encountered. It is the experience of grace, the experience of ease, of effortlessness in your life, of a lack of fear entirely. Thoughts of judgment are not present. Thoughts of right and wrong are not present, for they do not exist.

You were born to create a permanent state of grace, so to speak. The tool for doing that is the creation of authentic power. As you create authentic power, as love becomes more and more a part of your awareness and then becomes your awareness, your life fills with grace. You fill with grace. With that grace you perceive your experiences, your life, and the Universe. That perception, that experience, is reverence.

Reverence is one of the intentions of your soul, reverence for Life, for all reverence is reverence for Life. You cannot revere one person without revering all people. You cannot revere one flower without revering all flowers. You cannot revere one worm without revering all worms. You cannot revere any aspect of Life without revering all of Life, for your reverence is the reflection. The Universe, Consciousness, Love, Life are the reflected.

Without reverence your experience becomes hollow, shallow, without substance. Without reverence your goals are determined by fear, and your aspirations are motivated by fear. Without reverence, the world is cruel and brutal. Without reverence you are cruel and brutal. Without the ability to revere all forms of Life, all actions, all thoughts, you become that which you judge. In other words, if you cannot revere those who are brutal and those who are cruel, you become as they.

To revere Life is to revere all of Life, for Life is all that is. The experiences of brutality and cruelty and ignorance, in other words, the experiences of fear, that you encounter in yourself you encounter in the world. As you revere the world, as you revere yourself, nothing stands beyond your reverence, for nothing stands beyond the Universe. Therefore, when you judge cruelty or brutality in another, the experience of reverence ceases in you. The holiness of the Universe, the beneficence of the Universe, the miraculous unfolding of the Universe does not cease. Only the reflection of it in you ceases when you judge. That is the pursuit of external power.

To value something is to judge it. The more value you give it, the more positive the judgment and the reverse. To revere something is not to revere it equally. "Revere equally" are meaningless words. They are products of five-sensory perception. From the multisensory perspective everything is precious—not equally precious, not less precious, not more precious. All is precious.

When you discern an activity, you are not judging it. When you judge it, you lose power. When you judge it, you have no reverence. When you judge, you give yourself permission to experience pain. You open yourself to the pain of powerlessness. When you discern, you are able to revere what you discern clearly, for every experience in the Universe, and therefore in the Earth school, has value, has a purpose. In the Earth school that purpose is your spiritual development.

Creating authentic power aligns your personality with your soul. As you create authentic power, your personality becomes an accurate reflection of the Universe. You become lighter and lighter. You become more aware. Love replaces fear. Lightness replaces darkness, and you become able to fly rather than to crawl. Yet both flying and crawling are part of the Universe, and they are to be revered.

That is not the same as being valued. To revere anything in the Earth school is to revere everything that exists, for nothing stands apart from the Universe. As you create authentic power you challenge fear, and as you challenge fear you cultivate love, and as you cultivate love you begin to reflect the Universe.

Love and reverence cannot be distinguished. Soul-to-soul connections and reverence cannot be distinguished. The path to authentic power is the path to awareness, to love, to reverence, in other words, to the direct experience of the Universe. Yet there is no single perception of the Universe that can encompass the Universe. That which is perceived reveals the structure of the perceiver, and the perceivers are without number. Said more accurately, the points of possible perception are without number.

Your soul reveres them all.

# 16

# The Illusion

When you act from a frightened part of your personality, you are caught in an illusion. It seems real, and you believe its thoughts and suffer its pain. In other words, the illusion becomes apparent to you through your painful emotions.

For example, imagine a child lying unconscious on a sidewalk. That is not an illusion. It is a circumstance. From a larger perspective, the impersonal perspective of the soul, it could be called an illusion, but from the perspective of the Earth school, it is something that actually happens. However, the fear, anxiety, and other difficult emotions that the parents of the child experience do not have to do with this circumstance. This circumstance activated *internal dynamics* within the parents, and these dynamics—*not the circumstance*—created their painful emotions.

The entire domain of painful emotions is an illusion. When an individual appears to cause painful emotions in you, your experiences do not have anything to do with that individual. That individual activates an internal dynamic in you, and that internal dynamic creates painful emotions in you. That internal dynamic is a frightened part of your personality. Your emotions are freestanding energies in you, so to speak.

When you experience the painful physical sensations and troubling thoughts of a frightened part of your personality, you enter the illusion. When you act on them (react), you move further into the illusion. You think that your pain will disappear if the individual that appears to cause it changes, in other words, if you can change the world. Within the illusion, that sometimes is the case. For example, if you are able to change the behavior of the individual or the circumstance (with anger, tears, rea-

68

soning, threats, bluster, etc.) to satisfy a frightened part of your personality, its painful physical sensations and judgmental thoughts disappear, but only temporarily. The internal dynamic that caused them remains intact within you to be activated again in the future.

When you create authentic power, you function on the reality of internal dynamics in you that create pleasing physical sensations (loving parts of your personality) and internal dynamics in you that create painful physical sensations (frightened parts of your personality). How can you use knowledge of this reality? First, you can recognize your experiences for what they are—products of dynamics *inside you*. Changing the external world does not affect these dynamics. Changing yourself does.

Second, you can choose not to act on the physical sensations and thoughts of these internal dynamics. That means not to act in relationship to the individual who activated them. That is a reaction. You can choose instead to respond from loving parts of your personality that create pleasing physical sensations and joyful thoughts in you. That is a response. When you respond instead of react, you create authentic power.

For example, imagine that a friend becomes angry because you refuse to do something she asks. She is caught in the illusion. A frightened part of her personality is in pain because it is not getting what it wants, but she believes that *you* are causing her pain. Actually, the pain she feels does not have to do with you. She is responsible for continuing to experience her emotional pain by trying to change you instead of addressing the interior dynamic in her that is creating it. She is pursuing external power.

Your decisions do not and cannot not create painful emotions in others. Others create painful emotional experiences and disturbing thoughts in themselves by acting on the illusion—in other words, trying to escape their pain by changing the world. Frightened parts of personalities are rigid and strong. If you refuse a friend's request because your integrity requires you to refuse it, a frightened part of her personality will demand that *you* step out of your integrity to relieve *her* pain! That part of her personality is caught in the illusion, and she believes the illusion. The only emotions that are possible in the illusion are painful emotions, such as anger, resentment, disappointment, humiliation, and frustration.

*The illusion is the realm in which painful emotions occur and are blamed upon the external world.* Fear distorts your experiences and relationships while you remain in the illusion, and you are unable to distinguish between the reality of loving parts of your personality and the illusion of frightened parts.

Creating authentic power takes you beyond the illusion.

# 17

# Beyond the Illusion I

An individual without authentic power is controlled by frightened parts of his or her personality. That is, most of her experiences of emotions are experiences of emotions of fear, and often experiences that she thinks of as loving have a needful component, in other words, a fearful component. An authentically powerful personality is the opposite in every way. It is a personality without fear. It has no constraints of fear. It has no memory of fear. It moves through the Earth school with an open heart, without attachment to the outcome.

The four characteristics of an authentically powerful personality are humbleness, clarity, forgiveness, and love.

HUMBLENESS is a comfortable, in fact a delightful, experience. It is one that cannot be shaken. Humbleness is the experience of one who sees that everyone in the Earth school is on a path that is as difficult as his or her own. A humble person walks in a friendly world. All individuals in it belong in it from this perception. All are fellow students in the Earth school, each with frightened and loving parts of his or her personality.

Individuals in pursuit of external power focus on personalities, and their interactions are personality-to-personality. They look at what their personalities need and want and do their best to obtain that, and they look at what the personalities they encounter need and want and do their best to obtain. In other words, they see the pursuits of external power in others.

Multisensory humans create authentic power. They see souls in the

71

Earth school. It is here that comfort, pleasure, delight, and a joyfulness come into the picture, for all souls enter the Earth school voluntarily. They all seek the experience of physicalness in order to grow spiritually. They all know prior to incarnation the nature of the Earth school—that of time, space, matter, and duality. Duality requires choices, which means for every "this" there is a "that," and each choice brings either the "this" or the "that "into being. If the choice is unconscious, one or the other comes into being unconsciously. The consequences of unconscious choices are always surprising. When you encounter one, you think, "Why did this happen to me?" or "What did I do to deserve this?" or "I did not intend to create this." In fact, you did, but you were unaware of your intention when you chose the "this" or the "that." That is the life of an unempowered individual, an individual without awareness, one who is in the control of frightened parts of his or her personality.

A humble person sees these things clearly, sees the difficulty of continually choosing consciously, which requires emotional awareness. Therefore she or he is a natural friend to others and views others as natural friends to her- or himself. A humble personality cannot go where there are strangers, for there are no strangers to it. It responds with love to all that it encounters. Its life is joyful.

A humble personality cares not for appearance. It may appear erratic or irrational or foolish to others. This is of no concern to the personality that embodies humbleness, for its concern is not to pursue external power. It does not care to capitalize on experiences or individuals, but to support individuals and to support them with joy.

Humbleness is not an intellectual process, although you can think of it as a natural joy that has no end, that has no boundaries, a natural curiosity about all that exists, and an openness to it.

CLARITY is multisensory perception, but multisensory perception that is recognized and utilized. Many individuals have an occasional multisensory experience or a glimpse of multisensory perception, but they do not recognize it for what it is. They make no attempt to use it. That is not clarity. For example, I remember as a teenager my grandmother standing beside me at her funeral holding my hand in hers. When I laughed at something that amused me, she jerked my hand downward as she often did when she was impatient with me. She wanted to enjoy her funeral! At the time I did not recognize this experience as unusual, although I did not share it with my parents until later. I knew they would think I was hallucinating. This experience was a multisensory perception, unrecognized by me and unused by me. It was not clarity.

Many individuals have glimpses into the lives of others. For example, they know things about an individual that their five senses did not reveal to them. They see these things clearly, and they recognize their experience as a multisensory perception. This is clarity. It is different, for example, from projecting onto another individual aspects of yourself that are too painful or shameful for you to acknowledge in yourself, such as resentment, jealousy, or anger. Clarity is not projection. Clarity is simply perception.

Clarity goes hand in hand with humbleness, because clarity is the multisensory perception of personalities as Earth suits and an interest in the souls that are wearing them. Clarity is seeing beyond the shell or form of appearance and into essence. It allows essence-to-essence experiences, soul-to-soul experiences. It enables Life-to-Life experiences, for example, the life of a tree, of a forest, of a cliff, of a stream, of a bird, or of the sky and your relationship to it. Experiences of this kind are meaningless to individuals without clarity, that is, to five-sensory personalities. Clarity brings reverence, and reverence is clarity.

An individual with clarity lives in awareness of essence—his or her essence and the essence of all that he or she encounters, a world of essence, a Universe of essence, and that essence is Life itself.

# 18

# Beyond the Illusion II

ORGIVENESS is moving beyond the confines of fear. It is the ability to leave judgment behind and to encounter Life as it is with clarity. An individual with clarity has no understanding of or need for forgiveness. What is to be forgiven for the air we breathe? What is to be forgiven for the ground beneath our feet? What is to be forgiven for the breeze that softly touches us? These are experiences that are. There is no need or meaning in "forgiving" any of them or where they come from, for they come from the Universe. They come from the Earth school, a part of the Universe.

When experiences are seen in this way, when the Earth school is seen in this way, when personalities are seen in this way, they are as they are. They require choices—to react or to respond. For example, a car approaches a stop sign, but the driver does not appear to see it. A natural choice would be to stay out of the intersection. That is a choice, yet there is no forgiveness necessary.

Frightened parts of a personality feel otherwise. They judge the driver or the sign or the intersection. They become offended, angry, frightened, and disturbed. It is for these experiences that the term "forgiveness" has meaning, for these experiences create distance. They prevent the experience of humbleness. They are experiences of lack of clarity, and it is only in that context that something called "forgiveness" is possible.

Forgiveness is challenging a frightened part of your personality and choosing to respond with love to the experiences that part has created in you. The experiences of that part of your personality are an illusion. Forgiveness has nothing to do with another individual. Forgiveness is an energy dynamic in *you*. It affects *you*. When you forgive, you challenge a frightened part of your personality that has judged another individual. You choose not to continue in the illusion—not to continue to judge, not to indulge bitterness, vengeance, righteousness, or anger. The freedom that comes from moving beyond the control of a frightened part of your personality is the experience that comes from what we call forgiveness.

Forgiveness, in other words, is an experience of love.

LOVE is the Big One. Forgiveness is the decision to love. It is a direct challenge to frightened parts of your personality. The decision to forgive is the creation of authentic power. Therefore, forgiveness is a part of an authentically powerful personality. Forgiveness is, you might say, a re-equilibrium. If there is a lapse in the experience of humbleness, if there is a lapse in clarity, then forgiveness eliminates that lapse. It removes the gap in humbleness. It removes the gap in clarity. It reestablishes both. It puts you back in the harmonious, wholesome, fulfilling, and creative experience of Love.

Love is the natural state of an individual in the Earth school that is aligned with the Universe. The Universe is alive, wise, and conscious. It is loving. Nothing that occurs is without conscious benefit. Whose consciousness? The consciousness of the Universe. The consciousness that is the Universe. There is no distinction between the Universe, Consciousness, Life, and Love. Love is entering into that alignment.

It is not alignment in the sense of driving a vehicle on a road that requires paying attention to the road so that the vehicle remains on it. Love is an ocean. A traveler on the ocean need not worry about running off the ocean as the driver of a car is concerned about running off the road. Wet is the nature of the ocean. Wherever the ocean is, it is wet. Now imagine that the ocean is the Universe, and wet is Love. The Universe and Love cannot be separated. Therefore, Love is a characteristic of an authentically powerful personality.

Love is the end point and the beginning of authentic power. It is the creation of authentic power and the experience of authentic power. Love is the birth of the personality and the return of the soul to nonphysical reality. Love is the brutality of an executioner, and Love is the terror of the executed. Love is the greed that cannot be satisfied, that drives individuals to endless competition and exploitation. All of that is Love. Nothing is not Love.

Your awareness is Love. You can direct your awareness. Your ability to direct your awareness is Love. There is no end to Love. There is no beginning to Love. There is no exit from Love. There is no entrance into Love. To say that Love is a characteristic of an authentically powerful individual is to say that the authentically powerful individual is aware that there is no distinction between itself and Love, yet at this point language fails, for there is no "itself." There is.

That is Love.

# 19

# Temptation

The choice between love and fear is called temptation.

Five-sensory humans misunderstand temptation. They think it is an offering from an external, negative, and evil source. By evil they mean purely destructive and malevolent. Multisensory humans have a different understanding based upon a different perception of themselves, the world, and the Universe. A multisensory individual understands temptation as an opportunity to view the plans of a frightened part of his or her personality before that part implements those plans.

Those plans will always be ways of pursuing external power. There are no other intentions that are important to a frightened part of a personality. This dramatic difference in understanding leads to an equally dramatic difference in what to do when a temptation presents itself. A five-sensory human interprets that experience as being attracted to or manipulated by a malevolent external presence. A multisensory human interprets it as an opportunity to explore in detail a frightened part of his or her personality so that it can be challenged and changed.

The origin of this thing called temptation, when seen from a five-sensory perspective, places responsibility for it on something outside the individual, something that wishes the individual harm. When seen from a multisensory perspective, the origin of this thing called temptation places responsibility for it on a frightened part of one's own personality, which means that the responsibility for doing something about it does not involve doing something to change the world or defend oneself against the world, but exploring the frightened part of the personality that is producing these experiences.

Creating authentic power is becoming the authority in your own life. A multisensory individual must choose to react to a temptation—which is to contract in fear, to defend him- or herself against an external enemy—or to respond in love and trust—which is to explore the temptation, the plan, the intended implementation of a frightened part of his or her personality—and to see what consequences it will most probably produce.

In other words, temptation from a five-sensory perspective is a negative thing. Temptation from a multisensory perspective is a positive thing. From the five-sensory perspective, temptation is a danger. From the multisensory perspective, temptation is a gift and an opportunity to grow in compassion and clarity, which is to grow spiritually, to create authentic power.

You can look at a temptation as a dress rehearsal for a negative karmic event. A dress rehearsal is the last step in the preparation of a production before the production is shown to the public. This situation is identical in the case of temptation. A temptation is the counterpart of a dress rehearsal. It is the last stage before the plan of a frightened part of the personality is implemented. It is an opportunity to review the production that has been produced to that point. At that point the production has been seen only by those who need to see it. In this case, that is you. Once the production goes public, so to speak, the doors to the theater are opened, the audience flows in, and the production moves into the world. It moves beyond the sphere of your own experiences and energy and into the spheres of the experiences and energy of others. That is the moment when karma is created.

Therefore, by paying attention to the dress rehearsal, appreciating it in its detail, you are able to avoid the painful consequences that will follow from it, which means you are able to shape your life with a decision based in love rather than a decision based in fear. The temptation is not merely attractive to a frightened part of your personality. It is a masterpiece of that part, so to speak.

Suppose, for example, that a frightened part of a personality desires to have a sexual interaction with another individual. To make this situation more graphic, assume that the other individual is married or is in a spiritual partnership with another individual with whom there is an agreement that sexual interactions with others are not appropriate for their partnership. The frightened part of the personality will provide images of what that interaction might be like, or what it might feel like, or how attractive it is, or how attractive the other individual is, along with illusions, or fantasies, that these interactions represent more than they do, that they represent genuine connections, or that they represent no connection at all other than the satisfaction of an addictive craving.

Whatever it is that a frightened part of your personality is planning to do, it will present that plan to you in the temptation, and the temptation will be attractive. It will be a whole, preplanned story with reasons for why it should happen, with justifications for every action large and small.

Take, for another example, the desire to steal from an employer. To make it more specific, assume that the employee is an accountant who has access to bank accounts. In that case, the frightened part of the personality will provide a video, so to speak, except that it is much more than sounds and words. It is feeling. It is tactile. It will show how the money will be stolen, what the manipulation will be, what the cover-up will be, what the profit will be for the one who steals—who embezzles—what the embezzled funds will provide for the one who embezzles, the satisfaction and pleasure of that. Perhaps it is to escape a debt that the one who embezzles has created. Perhaps it will be to purchase something that the one who embezzles feels it is important to purchase in his or her own pursuit of external power.

All of this will appear in the temptation. A temptation is not the work of an evil entity existing outside you.

It is the creation of a frightened part of your personality.

# 20

# The Gifts of Temptation

There are multisensory individuals who have yet to understand the magnitude and the enormity of being able for the first time to recognize themselves as souls as well as personalities. They do not recognize the intentions of the soul—harmony, cooperation, sharing, and reverence for Life—and the intentions of frightened parts of the personality that produce the opposites, and therefore their responsibility to choose between love and fear, between constructive parts of the personality and destructive parts.

As multisensory perception emerges in five-sensory individuals, they begin to make the connection between the pursuit of external power and all that is empty, meaningless, and painful in their lives. Eventually they will make that connection as their emotional pain becomes more intense and difficult to bear. That is why it is supportive for multisensory humans to have a way of exploring what they are beginning to experience internally—the soul as a reality, themselves as an immortal being as well as a personality that is mortal, and power as alignment of the mortal aspect of themselves with the immortal aspect of themselves.

Temptation assists in this process. Most individuals think of temptation in terms of significant moral violations such as stealing, adultery, or murder. Multisensory humans see that temptation occurs each time a frightened part of a personality becomes activated, in other words, each time emotions that are violent, that are disconnected, and thoughts that are judgmental and comparative, enter into the awareness of the personality. As multisensory perception emerges in them, so also does awareness of different aspects of their personalities.

Every experience of a frightened part of a personality is identical to a temptation in its energy. It originates in fear, for example, the desire to be right, the need to dominate, the need to please, feelings of superiority and entitlement, feelings of inferiority, and more. When you are angry with an individual, your anger is more than a simple matter of thinking of what you dislike about that individual. It is an energy dynamic, and a painful one, that you can experience by placing your attention in your energy processing centers. This is emotional awareness. When you place your awareness in your energy processing centers, you feel physical sensations that are either painful or pleasing. These are more than thoughts.

Once you realize that every experience of a frightened part of your personality is a temptation, you will recognize how essential the dynamic of temptation is to spiritual growth. It is a magnet that draws negative energy from your consciousness and puts it on the screen of your awareness so that you can see it clearly.

An apparent contradiction that exists in the New Testament confuses many individuals, and not only Christians. On the one hand, it presents evil as external and malevolent, and it presents temptation as an instrument of that evil. Therefore, the most well-known prayer in the Christian realm (the Lord's prayer) implores the Christian deity to protect Christian adherents from temptation, which specifically means to protect them from evil, and more specifically, not allow them to be tempted. On the other hand, the New Testament directs individuals not to resist evil. These cannot be reconciled by five-sensory humans or comprehended as other than contradiction by the intellect.

From the multisensory perspective, there is no contradiction. Evil is an absence of Light. It is the absence of Love. "Resisting evil" is an orientation that places evil outside oneself. Not resisting evil is an invitation to explore this absence, not to act on it. In other words, this guidance does not invite an individual to act on a temptation, but to explore it as a frightened part of his or her personality.

It is an invitation not to resist experiencing the painful physical sensations that frightened parts of your personality create in your energy processing centers—what you feel in your body. It is an invitation not to resist the thoughts of frightened parts of your personality, but to become aware of them. It is an invitation to observe all these things in yourself clearly so that you can challenge frightened parts of your personality and understand what it is you are challenging. Once it is clear that temptation is a product of a frightened part of the personality—and that becomes clear quickly as an individual develops emotional awareness and practices responsible choice—the way forward is clear. It is one of challenging fear and cultivating love.

You are not at war with the external world. The external world is part of the Earth school, and the Earth school exists for your spiritual development. You are not at war with evil, for there is no such thing as evil. There is only your own ignorance, your own lack of awareness of your own internal dynamics. Temptation moves you toward that awareness strongly. Then it becomes a question of how you will use that awareness. This is where responsible choice enters the picture, as we have seen.

Temptations are part of learning in the Earth school. The Earth school is a domain of duality, and duality requires choices. The fundamental choice in the Earth school is the choice between love and fear, and that choice becomes obvious in the case of a temptation. There is no punishment for deciding to act on a temptation. That creates consequences, and those consequences are destructive and painful to experience. There is no reward for choosing not to act on a temptation, for acting from a loving part of the personality instead also creates consequences. Those consequences are constructive and blissful to experience. It is only a view of experience that includes punishment and reward that sees from the perspective of punishment and reward, and that perspective is the perspective of fear.

The Universe does not punish, and it does not reward. The Universe supports your spiritual development. Your spiritual development is the purpose of your incarnation into the Earth school. As you make choices that align your personality with your soul, you move into health, into consciousness, into Life more fully, and into Love completely. These are the gifts of temptation.

They are for you.

# 21

# Nonphysical Dynamics

onphysical dynamics support you in growing spiritually (creating authentic power). In other words, they support you in choosing love. They support you even if you do not know about them, and if you know about them, they support you even if you forget about them. You can always depend on them.

## THE UNIVERSAL LAW OF ATTRACTION

The Universal Law of Attraction brings individuals into your life who have the same energy as you.

I spent hours in my favorite coffee shop in North Beach, a part of San Francisco near Telegraph Hill. I met friends there daily for coffee and conversation. The sweet aroma of espresso and cappuccino filled me with warmth, and I loved it. Mostly we discussed physics, philosophy, other people, and ourselves. I was intellectual, arrogant (frightened), and I felt superior (frightened) to the people we talked about, usually in derogatory ways. We laughed together and enjoyed ourselves. If I had known how to step back from my experiences enough to see them clearly, I would have noticed that all my friends were also intellectual, arrogant, and felt superior. They laughed freely at other people, other people's theories, and other people's ways. We held court daily in the coffee shop, and we were the royalty—but only to ourselves.

Around us other people laughed or had serious discussions about serious things or read while sipping coffee. I know now that many of these people were loving and caring. They were virtually invisible to me then. The people in my group cared about ourselves, and we connected only to ourselves and others like us. I was experiencing the Law of Attraction without the least awareness of it.

The Universal Law of Attraction does not ask you what kind of energy you want to experience. It shows you the energy that you *are experiencing*.

A young couple visited a small town in Vermont. They asked an old man rocking on his porch, "What are people here like?" "What are they like where you live?" he asked them. "They don't care for others," the couple answered. "People here are like that also," the old man told them. The following week another visiting couple asked the old man the same question. "What are people here like?" "What are people like where you come from?" he asked them. "They are kind and friendly," the couple answered. "People here are much like that also," the old man said. He understood the Universal Law of Attraction.

The world always validates your belief—reflects your energy. If you believe the world is loving, a loving world will surround you. If you believe the world is cruel, a cruel world will surround you. Five-sensory humans think, "I will believe it when I see it." Multisensory humans know, "I will see it when I believe it."

## THE UNIVERSAL LAW OF CAUSE AND EFFECT

The Universal Law of Cause and Effect is a message delivery system. It delivers messages from you. Your messages always arrive at the right place and time. Even if the recipient moves, they arrive at the right place and time. They arrive at the right place and time even if the recipient dies! You send a message each time you act with an intention. Since you are always acting, and since each of your actions has an intention, you are always sending messages. All of your messages are addressed "RETURN TO SENDER."

Said another way, when an action that you take activates an experience in another individual, the Universal Law of Cause and Effect sends

YOU that same experience. For example, if you betray your fiancé or fiancée, the Universal Law of Cause and Effect will send you his or her experience. You will experience the same surprise, confusion, and pain. A fiancé or fiancée in another time and place might betray you, but not necessarily. A platoon leader might abandon you in combat, or a friend might embezzle from you. You may not recognize the wrapping around your message when it arrives, but you will recognize the message immediately when you open it. You have been betrayed.

You may have sent your message yesterday, ten years ago, or four centuries ago. If you sent it with love, it will feel wonderful when it arrives. If you sent it with fear, it will hurt when it arrives. Count on it. The Universal Law of Cause and Effect operates flawlessly. Think of each message you send as a personal communication from you to you that arrives via laser-guided boomerang, so to speak.

In other words, *all your experiences are karmic necessities.* When you see this, you will start paying attention to the messages you send and stop blaming or thanking others when you receive them. The Universal Law of Cause and Effect is the Universal impersonal teacher of responsibility.

The Universal Law of Cause and Effect does not judge your messages. It does not read your messages. It does not discuss your messages.

It delivers them.

# 22

# How Does the Universal Law of Cause and Effect Work?

The experience of a karmic consequence is the experience of an emotion that an intention and action of yours activated in another individual. That experience may come to you as a mirrorlike reflection. In other words, the roles you play may be identical but reversed. You may have been an employer, for example, and you have treated an employee the same way that your employer is now treating you. The same souls are involved. This is not often the case. What is significant and central is that an experience which an action, and the intention behind it, activated in another individual is now coming to you so that you can experience that same energy exchange from another point of view, the opposite point of view.

As you create authentic power, you become able to recognize painful experiences in yourself in terms of emotional awareness. Those are the experiences that frightened parts of your personality create when they are active. These may appear clothed differently, so to speak, from the action and intention that you or another personality of your soul took toward another individual, which activated similar or the same frightened parts in him or her.

In other words, the frightened parts of your personality that are reacting are reacting to that which they themselves, or another personality of your soul, have experienced toward another individual. For example, you are betrayed by a friend. You thought that he was caring for you, and he was not. You thought that he was attempting to support you, and he was planning to exploit you. Now that comes into clear focus. As you experience that and challenge the frightened parts of your personality that react to it, you begin to move beyond the control of those parts. As you move beyond the control of those parts, you move into love. As you move into love, you change your karma. You change the consequences that you are creating with your intentions and your actions.

It is not a matter of identifying exactly what energy exchange caused that which you are experiencing between you and your friend. It is the energy *itself* that requires attention, and that energy is fear. As you continue to interact with others with an intention of fear, for example, to exploit them, to prove yourself right, to dominate them, to gain from them—you continue to create painful consequences for yourself. When you challenge frightened parts of your personality as they become active, and replace their intention with the intention of a loving part of your personality, a part that is aligned with your soul—which means you choose to act from a loving part of your personality while a frightened part of your personality is active—you change the energy exchange in that moment. In that moment of choosing an intention of love and acting with it to the best of your ability, instead of reacting with fear, you move yourself beyond the control of the parts of your personality that are reacting. Those are the parts that create painful consequences for you when you encounter them.

The point is the energy that is created when you choose an intention to infuse an action or a word, and when the intention that you choose is fear, can activate frightened parts in another individual. It can create reactions in him or her. The reactions that it creates in the other individual are the experiences that *you*, having initiated the karmic exchange, will experience in *your* life or in the life of another personality of your soul. As you change the energy with which you interact with individuals, you change that entire dynamic, or rather the entire dynamic remains precisely as it is and always has been, but what it creates in you in terms of experience changes radically as your intentions change from fear to love.

When you choose to respond from the healthiest part of your personality that you can access instead of react from a frightened part of your personality, you create different karma for yourself. In other words, each emotionally painful experience in you is a consequence of an intention of fear that you held while you, or another personality of your soul, interacted with another individual in the past. Responding with love to that experience instead of reacting to it with fear creates emotionally pleasing experiences in you and prevents you from creating more painful consequences.

As you create authentic power and align your personality with your soul, you enter a new phase of experience in the Earth school. The phase toward which you are traveling, and toward which all individuals in the Earth school are traveling or will travel, is learning to move through the Earth school with an empowered heart, without attachment to the outcome. This means you bring the clarity of your heart to all that you do, without attachment. When attachment enters the picture, pain enters the picture, which is the same as saying that fear enters the picture. It is redundant to say, "an empowered heart without attachment to the outcome," because an empowered heart has no attachments. Yet it is helpful to use these words because they illuminate the components that are essential for you to recognize and understand: the energy of the heart, which is love, and what prevents the energy of the heart, which is fear.

From an empowered heart you can say, "This is not appropriate," "Let us cease immediately," "Let us proceed," or "Let us experiment," all of which and more are options that can be taken without attachment to the outcome when the choice is made with love. The choice of love is not made for another individual or individuals, although love knows no distinctions. It is made in order to challenge a frightened part of your personality.

What another personality does or does not do does not enter that picture. It is an internal dynamic that you are discovering or again recognizing in yourself, which you are challenging with the intention to move completely beyond it. The other individual is performing a service for you, so to speak. Everyone in the Earth school performs that service for you when you interact with him or her. They activate frightened and loving parts of your personality so that you can distinguish between them and create authentic power.

The response from love is always "Thank you."

*23*

# Nonphysical Teachers

Understanding about nonphysical Teachers comes easily to some multisensory individuals because their first experiences with them are unambiguous. They know what is happening, and they feel the value of it. Not all individuals who are becoming multisensory have those experiences or that introduction to nonphysical Teachers. Whatever your experiences are or will be, your nonphysical Teachers will assist you appropriately.

The transformation of human consciousness from five-sensory to multisensory includes awareness of, access to, and receiving the support of nonphysical Teachers.

A nonphysical Teacher is an impersonal energy dynamic. Sometimes we attempt to personalize them by giving them names, such as Michael or Gideon (I made this up), but they are not that. They are in the Earth school but not of it, just as a parent is in the experience of its child, but not of it. The parents' perspective is different than that of the child. They see more, and they know more. Their consciousness and experiences cannot be grasped by the child. Your nonphysical Teacher(s) is always with you, knows everything about you, and supports you in your spiritual growth.

There are ways that you can experiment with the existence of nonphysical Teachers. The first step is to understand that they exist, and that they have always existed. Five-sensory humans had nonphysical Teachers, but they were unaware of them because of the limitations of their experiences. Now that humanity is becoming multisensory, all humans are becoming aware of nonphysical Teachers. Like all multisensory perceptions, these experiences are new. You invite deeper understanding of your nonphysical Teachers each time you remind yourself that they are real. That means reminding yourself of our new creation story, and that you are participating in it.

The easiest way to engage a nonphysical Teacher is to ask yourself the question "What is my intention?" before you speak or act, especially when you are not certain what your intention is. You will not be alone in your answer. The answer may come immediately, days later, or in whatever time is necessary. Be patient. Understand that the moment you ask for nonphysical guidance, the answer is pouring in. You may need to relax yourself in order to receive it. You may need to walk in nature or do an errand, so long as you are not distracting yourself. The answer may come to you as an insight or an idea that is new to you. It may come with a feeling of excitement. You may hear words. A memory may emerge in your awareness or a song or an event. Let the meaning of that song or memory or event or those words appear to you.

This is also the process of getting in touch with intuition, for intuition is the voice of the nonphysical world, and the nonphysical world is the home, metaphorically speaking, of nonphysical Teachers. As you become aware of the reality of the existence of your nonphysical Teachers, you will begin to ask your nonphysical Teachers more and more questions, especially when you are confused, which means that frightened parts of your personality are active. As you calm yourself, as you challenge frightened parts of your personality, you will find it easier to access intuition, to access your nonphysical Teachers.

As we discussed, nonphysical Teachers are in your life to support your spiritual development. They will answer your questions, but you must ask them. Be aware of the questions you ask. Are they important questions to you? How will you use your time with a nonphysical Teacher? Your nonphysical Teachers will answer all your questions. They will not run out of patience, so to speak.

When you have an insight or you feel that a thought or memory or song is activating understanding in you, assume that the understanding is coming from a nonphysical Teacher and allow yourself to deepen the connection. A nonphysical Teacher will not tell you what to do, but will offer you insights, or show you possibilities that you might not have considered. You must decide whether or not to accept or experiment with an insight that you feel a nonphysical Teacher is sharing with you. If you feel that you are being given instructions or told to do this or to do that, know that you are *not* in communication with a nonphysical Teacher, but with a frightened part of your personality. This is where emotional awareness and responsible choice enter the picture. As you involve yourself in this process, you will become more comfortable with it, and, in fact, quite confident in it.

Do not be concerned that you will become dependent upon a nonphysical Teacher. Enjoy the dependency. Delight in the dependency, for it is dependency upon the Universe. What is wrong with depending upon the Universe? Experiment with your nonphysical Teachers. They are sources of great joy for you, for they will help you move beyond fear and cultivate love.

Individuals who cocreate with nonphysical Teachers have always walked among us. Each great religion claims one or more of them as its own. Five-sensory individuals are not aware of nonphysical Teachers. Multisensory individuals are becoming aware of them. In other words, interaction with nonphysical Teachers is now becoming a species-wide phenomenon.

This is inseparable from our new creation story.

# 24

# As Within, So Without

As Without, So Within appears to be the natural order of the world for five-sensory humans. They experience the world as primary and consciousness as secondary. That is, they believe that the world determines their consciousness. Therefore, they strive to change the world in order to change their consciousness. They pursue external power. The opposite of this, As Within, So Without, is the natural order of the world for multisensory humans. They experience consciousness as primary and the world as secondary. That is, they believe that consciousness determines their experiences of the world. Therefore, they change their consciousness in order to change the world. They create authentic power.

In other words, five-sensory experiences of the world teach five-sensory humans about the *world*, for example, mountains are high, rain is wet, the speed of light in a vacuum is 186,282 miles per second. Multisensory experiences of the world teach multisensory humans about *themselves*, and herein lies the relationship between our awareness and the world.

This dramatic change in perception has dramatically changed the way that humans understand their relationship with the world. Five-sensory humans think changing themselves and changing the world are entirely different. Multisensory humans see that they are the same.

Changing your consciousness does not change the Earth. The Earth is a living entity that exists with or without us. Yet when we are not aware of the relationship that we have with the world, we cannot learn about ourselves from the world. When we become aware of this relationship, the world shows us parts of our personalities that we have not yet seen.

For example, it shows us parts of our personalities that we do not want to see, parts that are too shameful or painful for us to acknowledge. Until we become aware of those parts in ourselves, we see them in others! This is called projection.

Imagine that you encounter an individual who is out of integrity or who is predatory. If you are aware of the parts of yourself that are out of integrity or are predatory, and you are challenging them, you will be able to see that individual more accurately as one who is in the control of parts of his or her personality that are out of integrity or predatory. If you are not aware of these frightened parts in yourself, or you have not challenged them, or you feel that you cannot challenge them adequately or at all, then you will attempt to challenge them *outside* of yourself, in the individual that displays the same frightened parts.

The power of emotional awareness is the power to identify frightened parts of your personality and to recognize them when they are active. That which activates them is a projection. In other words, that which needs to be healed is within you. That which appears to need correcting or challenging when a projection is in process appears outside of you. This is the intimate and powerful relationship between within and without. It is fundamental. It is what allows emotional awareness to help you grow spiritually.

Emotional awareness is the ability to distinguish between frightened and loving parts of your personality. The frightened parts of your personality are those that impose themselves because they are painful and compulsive or addictive. When there is a reaction (projection), there will always be the attempt to stop the emotional pain or reduce the emotional pain by acting upon the external world, which is fruitless.

Take, for example, an addiction to a drug or to alcohol or to food. When emotional pain comes (a frightened part of the personality is activated), rather than looking inwardly, attention goes outward searching for ways to stop the pain, whether it is a fix, a drink, sex, another meal, or another dessert. That which is being sought from without is an illusory healing, for it is that within which requires healing, which means challenging and moving beyond the control of it.

Learning through projection and reaction also occurs in large collectives, such as national and international collectives. For example, when individuals see a lack of integrity or awareness in a president or a prime minister of an externally powerful nation, acting in ways that could create far-reaching harm, such as accelerating climate change or igniting a nuclear war, they strive to prevent those actions in the world without realizing what they represent—frightened parts of their own personalities that are out of integrity and at war continually or threatening destruction continually.

When they recognize that, they become able to challenge the activities and policies of the individuals responsible for them without making those individuals villains, which means without disempowering themselves, as Gandhi was able to do with the British and Martin Luther King Jr. was able to do with white supremacists. Then they can become effective activists. Then they no longer seek refuge in mocking, disdaining, and disparaging others or venting the disgust of frightened parts of their personalities at them, all of which is useless.

Instead they can look within themselves at what they disdain, reject, and find disgusting, and challenge experiences of disdain, disgust, and rejection within themselves. As they move beyond the control of the parts of their personalities that are activated by what they see in the world, they are able to set their intentions to change the world not in order to feel better themselves, and not to make others villains, but to contribute to the world with an empowered heart, without attachment to the outcome.

This dynamic of projection and reaction continues in us until we find in ourselves all that we are reacting to, until we realize that we are pushing away parts of *ourselves*. Then our hearts melt toward those who have repulsed us because we can recognize in them the parts of ourselves that we did not previously see, and we become thankful to them for showing those parts to us.

The world teaches us about ourselves each time we see connections between it and choices that we have made. For example, we see hurricanes more violent, droughts dryer, fire seasons longer, and fires uncontrollable. We see arctic ice disappearing, glaciers melting, islands sinking into the sea, and coastal cities beginning to flood. We see fracking poison aquafers, and pesticides, rodenticides, and fungicides make us ill. We see microplastics in the oceans, crops shrivel, hunger spread, and fellow students in the Earth school starve and die—and we realize that we have created all of this. None of it would have happened, could have happened, without choices that we made. This is collective learning.

We see, when we look, the Universal Law of Cause and Effect bringing into our lives experiences that our choices have brought into the lives of others, and we see that our experiences will not change until we change our choices. This is individual learning. Seeing the same at the level of collectives is collective learning.

As more missiles are prepared for flight, more bombs drop, more corpses rot beneath rubble, and more water from more faucets bursts into flames, millions of multisensory humans are declaring to themselves, "I will no longer contribute to the cruelty that has characterized the human experience."

The world reflects us everywhere so that we can cultivate love in ourselves, challenge fear in ourselves, and give the gifts that we were born to give. How could we not have seen this relationship that we have with the world before? How can we not see it now? Where is the line between the world and you?

Where is the line between you and the world?

# 25

# As Below, So Above

"As Without, So Within" is as obsolete as the understanding of power as ability to manipulate and control. They go together, and they are both part of the old consciousness, the consciousness that is dying. "As Above, So Below" is in the same category of misunderstanding. It was accurate when humanity was five-sensory and the unspoken, unreasoned, and unrecognized assumption was that the external world determines the consciousness of the individual. Now that also is as obsolete as the old consciousness.

From the perspective of the new consciousness, the perspective of multisensory perception, the opposite is the reality in which you are now operating. That reality is As Below, So Above. What does that mean? It means that you as an individual in the Earth school are a micro. The macro is the collective experience of humankind. Yet it is the micro that determines the macro. This is something that five-sensory perception cannot discern and the intellect cannot grasp.

You are the micro with fear and love. The macro is also a container, so to speak, with fear and love. From the perception of the five senses, the micro and the macro are forever separated by a wall. The barrier is the difference between "in here" and "out there." That is the barrier that is now dissolving, for the fear and love in the world that you desire to change are the same fear and love in you. Now you have the ability, the power, to change the fear and the love in you. That is authentic power.

The ability to distinguish between love and fear in yourself, to challenge fear by choosing to act from a loving part of your personality, instead of react from a frightened part of your personality, and to cultivate love when you recognize it by realizing that it comes from a loving part of your personality, is real. Fear is not real. All of that is the creation of authentic power. Therefore it is no longer accurate to say that the micro changes the macro, for there is no distinction between micro and macro. This is what the intellect cannot grasp. Lakota wisdom declares that the center of the Universe is everywhere. That is correct. The center of the Universe is in you. It is in me.

Changing the Universe from the center of the Universe, from the old perception, might be thought of as changing the Universe from the inside out, if such a thing could exist. It does not exist, just as no such a thing as changing the Universe from the outside in can exist or could exist, for you and the Universe are not separate. You are a part of it. It is a part of you.

The scope of your comprehension as you move into multisensory perception becomes far greater. From that perspective, although you cannot experience the identity of the Universe and you, you can feel it at times. Those are the feelings that come when you disappear, and all that remains is what you are seeing. Yet what you are seeing is inside you as well as outside you. For example, while you watch a mountain light with alpenglow as the sun sets, and it turns from Earth tones and snow and ice tones into pink and then begins to glow and then turns violet and then turns shades of purple as darkness envelops it, and you stand fascinated. You stand absorbing the beauty, in the beauty, and the beauty is in you. That is what generates the feeling of awe, of appreciation, of fullness, of completeness.

Inverting the old and obsolete sayings "As Above, So Below" and "As Without, So Within" to "As Below, So Above" and "As Within, So Without" reminds you that the power to change the world is the power you have to change yourself. The power that you have to change yourself is the power to remove the obstacles to love with which you were born, in other words, the frightened parts that your personality that your soul contributed to your personality when an aspect of your soul incarnated into the Earth school.

To change yourself is not a trivial matter. It is more than significant. It is the transformation that you were born to accomplish, to experience, and to utilize—not from the perception of a personality, but from the expanded perception of Love. From that expanded perception Love is Love—outside, inside, there is no distinction. As you develop the ability to contribute love, as you develop the ability to begin by distinguishing love from fear and further the ability to cultivate love, which requires challenging fear, and as your awareness begins to fill with love, eventually you become love, and you recognize, not from the deduction, not from the conclusion, not from the assumption, but from your experience, that love is all there is. These inversions are simply reminders that the work you are doing on Earth as you excavate your fears, challenge them one by one, and move beyond their control is world-changing.

Do not attempt to fill in the gaps in the linear logic of the intellect, for there is nothing that can fill them. Those gaps do not reflect gaps in the world or gaps in the higher order logic and understanding of the heart, but simply the limitations of the intellect. It is an instrument that was designed for one thing: to gather, evaluate, and recommend data from the five senses to assist the personality in pursuing external power.

Let that go. Use your intellect to learn the instruments that technology has created, for example, apply the biological learning that five-sensory research has uncovered for the good of all life. Yet the contribution you were born to make to all life is the transformation of your life from a life of fear and unconsciousness to a life of love and conscious contribution of love.

"As Below, So Above" and "As Within, So Without" are not corrections to five-sensory clichés. They are completions. For As Above, So Below is incomplete without the recognition that As Below, So also is Above, and As Without, So Within is incomplete without the recognition that As Within, So also is Without. As you create authentic power, you become more than complete. You become the completion.

The Christ transformed the collective consciousness of fear with the power of His own consciousness of love. This was His greatest gift, the gift He was born to give, and His life modeled it. Five-sensory humans think of the Christ in terms of walking on water, manifesting food and wine, healing the sick, giving sight to the blind, and resurrecting a dead body into a vibrant, living, physical vehicle. When I think of the Christ, I think of His clear and powerful statement, unambiguous, unmistakable, and shocking: You can do all that I have done *and more.*

Do you believe this? What would be your first step?

The Christ walked the Earth in the times of five-sensory humanity. We are becoming multisensory. Our understandings of ourselves, the world, the Universe, and power are different. Our capabilities are different. Our way of evolving is different. It requires changing the Below and the Above, the Within and the Without—ourselves and the world. It requires us to transform the collective consciousness of fear with the power of our own consciousness of love. It requires us to do this with each choice of love instead of fear, each action of love instead of fear, each word of love instead of fear, each thought of love instead of fear.

And more.

# Spiritual Partnership

Friends have expectations. These are often hidden (and unconscious) agendas, such as psychological agendas (validate my needs, feelings, decisions), physical agendas (help me build a business, pass my exams, care for my children), emotional agendas (make me feel lovable, safe, worthy), financial agendas (help me make money, borrow money, get a job), and others. When friends cannot accomplish their agendas—when they do not meet one another's expectations—their friendships dissolve. For example, if a friend no longer has time for you, gossips about you, or lies about you or to you, do you keep that individual as a friend?

Friends are allies. They say, "Lean on me, and I will lean on you," but closeness is not necessary. Friends often share surface interests, interactions without substance, and exchanges without depth. They chat about jobs, homes, vacations or lack of vacations, plans, other people, health, children, etc. They strive to create mutual comfort. When they are unsuccessful, their friendships dissolve.

In other words, friends pursue external power. They ask, "What's in it for me?" If the answer is "nothing," a friendship is not possible. Collectives also pursue external power. They ask, "What is in it for us?" What is in it for us workers, professionals, parents? What is in it for us Americans, Europeans, Japanese? What is in it for us white people, yellow people, black people? If the answer is "nothing," an alliance is not possible.

These dynamics are invisible to five-sensory humans. Multisensory humans see them. Five-sensory humans cannot see (and do not believe) the relationship between friendship and the pursuit of external power.

Therefore, they cannot see the relationship between friendships and climate disaster, species extinction, and threats to human survival.

The new consciousness is changing this.

We live in a time of double vision. In the old vision, the vision of the five senses, we are mortal and separate. The world is the source of our suffering and joy. We are small, victims, and seek fulfillment through others. The Universe is inert (dead). We cling to people or resent them, and death is the ultimate disaster.

In the new vision, the vision of multisensory perception, we are more than bodies and minds, the world reflects ourselves back to us, and the Universe is wise and compassionate. We are large and powerful, but not larger or more powerful than others. Our struggles are meaningful, and fulfillment is a choice. We create our experiences, and death is the completion of a journey through the Earth school and the return home of a soul.

These visions now overlap. Sometimes the new vision beckons us like a face in the clouds or music in moving water—ephemeral but there, insubstantial but present, gently shaping our experience. Sometimes it takes us boldly toward new values and aspirations. Rapidly or slowly, boldly or delicately, the new vision shows us a world that is being born—a world of new meanings, understandings, and ways of being. Its inhabitants create authentic power.

The old vision shows us an obsolete world of external power, empty successes, and unattractive goals.

These are big differences. The personal interactions of five-sensory humans are friendships. The personal connections of multisensory humans are spiritual partnerships. Spiritual partnership is a new archetype. *Spiritual partnership is partnership between equals for the purpose of spiritual growth.* The idea of relationships between equals for the purpose of spiritual growth was far too advanced for five-sensory humanity. Multisensory humans know they have souls. They know they are together for a reason, and that reason has to do with their souls. They create authentic power, and they help one another create authentic power. Spiritual partnership is part of the new consciousness.

An archetype is an energy dynamic. Marriage is an ancient archetype.

It is part of the old consciousness. It creates a natural division of labor that enhances probabilities of survival. Marriage partners are not equals, and they do not consider themselves equals. They do not share experiences of frightened parts of their personalities, for example, sexual attractions to others, jealousy, anger, superiority, and inferiority. They do not "rock the boat." The energy of "husband" (provider, overlord, owner) and the energy of "wife" (property, chattel) are parts of the old consciousness. Multisensory humans do not experience themselves these ways.

Spiritual partnerships are replacing every five-sensory form of relationship. The dynamics of spiritual partnership are entirely new. Spiritual partners stay together as long as they grow together spiritually. They choose their roles in their partnerships. They say the things they are most afraid will destroy their partnership.[6]

Spiritual partnerships are not only for couples. They are for neighbors, classmates, coworkers, family members, organizations, teams, companies, communities, and countries. The things for individuals to learn in spiritual partnerships are the same for groups, communities, and countries to learn in spiritual unions.

Spiritual partnerships are voluntary. They are possible only when there is openness to spiritual development. Spiritual partners ask one another: "If you think you see a part of my personality, and you think I do not see it, and you think it might help me to see it, will you tell me?" They say "think" deliberately because they know they may be projecting onto others unconscious parts of their own personalities that are too painful or shameful for them to acknowledge.

A tsunami is sweeping the beach of human experience clean of all that served our evolution in the past and depositing upon it all that our evolution now requires. Gone is external power. Arrived is authentic power. Gone is evolution through survival. Arrived is evolution through spiritual growth. Gone is friendship.

Arrived is spiritual partnership.

---

6   To learn more about spiritual partnership, read Gary Zukav, *Spiritual Partnership* (New York: HarperOne, 2010). To experience spiritual partnership, use the Spiritual Partnership Guidelines in your life.

# 27

# The New Perception of Community

ive-sensory communities are created by fear. The largest five-sensory communities, the smallest five-sensory communities, and all five-sensory communities in-between are created by fear. Five-sensory humans think communities are collectives of mutual support, care, and appreciation. That is one side of a coin, but every coin has two sides. As we become multisensory, we become able to see the other side of the coin we call "community."

The other side of the coin is discomfort, danger, and vulnerability. Individuals who are not in the community threaten the community. For example, a community of white individuals provides safety, comfort, and protection to white members. Individuals who are not white experience this community differently. They are threatened by it, whether or not the white individuals want their community to be threatening. The community (or communities) of nonwhite individuals provides safety, comfort, and protection to nonwhite members. Individuals who are white experience this community differently. They are threatened by it, whether or not the nonwhite members want their community to be threatening.

The pursuit of external power produces these problems endlessly. This means that fear generates communities endlessly. Commonalities that appear to bring five-sensory individuals together, such as white skin and white culture, black skin and black culture, Christian beliefs, Buddhist beliefs, American citizenship, and Chinese history, do *not* bring them together. Fear does. Any commonality that appears to be the core of a community—such as a community of intellectuals, artists, athletes, scholars, parents, etc.—is not the core of that community. The core of every community is fear of those who are different.

Even members of professional associations, who have no reasons to fear others who are not members, generally feel more comfortable with one another. Dentists feel more comfortable with dentists than with welders. Sailors, skiers, scholars, soldiers, and students generally feel more comfortable with those who share their experiences. Communities come into being and disappear, grow larger and become smaller, but wherever they exist, they exist because of fear.

Communities separate us and keep us apart. "Others" cannot exist without communities, and communities cannot exist without "others." Five-sensory humans believe communities form around similarities. Multisensory humans see they form around differences.

When you speak from (instead of about) frightened parts of your personality or allow others to speak to you from (instead of about) frightened parts of their personalities, you participate in community-creating. Frightened parts of your personality seek agreement with frightened parts of other personalities. They look for others who share their illusions (blacks are dangerous; whites are oppressive; lesbians are abnormal, etc.). They distance you from love, no matter how loving your communities appear to you or how loving you want them to appear to others.

Ask those who are not in your community (do not share your illusion), if you have the courage, whether they feel comforted by your community (illusion) or threatened by it. They will tell you, if they have the courage, that the communities (illusions) you hold most dear are those that the frightened part of their personalities most distrust, dislike, or hate.

You participate in community-creating when you identify with a collective. Fear is the glue that holds you and the community together, that holds individuals in all communities together.

Every community is a prison of fear. Some are very large prisons, such as the communities of white individuals, yellow individuals, black individuals, and brown individuals. Even the smallest communities, such as dyadic friendships, are prisons. Every experience with a community, such as a sense of safety, smugness, or superiority, is an experience of fear.

When you see both sides of the "community" coin, you can use your communities to show you your fears, if you look for them. Look carefully at the individuals who are not in your communities, and ask yourself why they are not.

# 28

# The Biggest Community

The Biggest Community has always been, and it will always be. It does not get larger, and it does not get smaller. We were in the Biggest Community when our personalities were born, and we will remain in the Biggest Community when our personalities die. It is not possible to leave the Biggest Community.

The Biggest Community includes everyone and everything. Individuals in the Biggest Community think, appear, speak, behave, and believe differently from one another—often very differently. Mother Teresa—inspiration of kindness—and Adolf Hitler, Joseph Stalin, and Mao Zedong—savage murderers of millions—are in the Biggest Community. Individuals sleeping in penthouses are in the Biggest Community, and individuals sleeping on sidewalks are in the Biggest Community. Individuals exploring the wonders of wilderness and individuals in concrete cages, tormented by harsh lights and brutal captors, and their captors, are in the Biggest Community.

Those who forgive and those who condemn; those who nourish and those who deprive; those who contribute and those who deny; those who care and those who do not; are all in the Biggest Community.

Mountains, continents, and the Earth are in the Biggest Community. Stars, planets, meteors, nebulae, and stones are also in the Biggest Community. The entire physical universe is in the Biggest Community. The Biggest Community contains much more. Countless realms of Life and Consciousness, far different from those we experience, are in the Biggest Community.

Five-sensory humans are not capable of conceiving space, galaxies, and celestial systems, including our own, in terms of community. Their understanding is limited to a context of time, space, matter, and duality. This is the only context that the intellect can comprehend. There are countless other contexts in the Universe, and they also are in the Biggest Community. There is nothing in the Universe that is not conscious. When we demand that consciousness be only as we experience it, we exclaim as blind people that there is no such thing as "color" or as deaf people that there is no such thing as "sound." The great Navajo Prayer to Beauty becomes our Ode to Ignorance.

> *Ignorance before me.*
> *Ignorance behind me.*
> *Ignorance below me.*
> *Ignorance above me.*
> *All around me ignorance.*

This is the multisensory perception of five-sensory perception. It is the Before of darkness and destruction in contrast to the After of light and unity. The light is our first glimpse of meaning and purpose, wisdom and compassion in our lives and in the Universe. The unity is the Biggest Community. Both are coming to us now, and our species is changing forever and for good. This change—the change from five-sensory perception to multisensory perception—is emerging in hundreds of millions of humans. They long for constructive lives of mutual support, and they intend to create them. They journey into joy, explore wholeness, and express the new consciousness.

The same change is coming slowly or not at all to millions of others. They grasp for external power, claim superiority or cling to inferiority, brandish accomplishments, exult in victories, and despair in defeats. Their lives are endless struggles to change the world, endless entreaties to powers beyond their own for salvation from the senselessness of their lives, from the callous cruelty in them, from the unbearable weights of poverty and oppression, and from the inescapable indifference of others. No matter how much or how little they have, they are terrified that they will lose it or that others will take it from them. They embody and express the dying consciousness.

Within a few generations all humans will be multisensory, and five-sensory perception will be a remembered experience of the most significant summit that five-sensory humans did not climb.

Five-sensory humans filled their history with warfare and brilliant technology that they turned against themselves. They created art, music, and literature that called to the noble aspirations in their hearts, but for the most part they did not themselves live toward those aspirations. Five-sensory humans gave little attention to kindness. Kindness impeded their pursuits of external power. It appears in no curriculum of their great universities. It appears nowhere in five-sensory education at all. Five-sensory humans wrote their history with their blood. Noble and bold as parts of it are, it is written in blood.

Five-sensory humanity was not negative. It was limited. Within the old consciousness glimpses of compassion flew like color-filled banners high above the onward flow of brutality that swept five-sensory history through endless fields of death and depravity and deposited it at last in a barren waste of war without end, scarcity for most, and plenty for few, where it now comes to its empty end, its vitality spent, its potential unfulfilled. Paradise on Earth was the shining potential of five-sensory humanity—water, shelter, food, safety, and comfort for all created by all. Five-sensory humans instead channeled their creativity into conflicts and conquests. The old consciousness is now dying, and its potential has turned to dust.

Electricity did not make candle-power negative. Candles served their purpose at the appropriate time, and five-sensory perception did the same. The birth of the new human consciousness does not make the dying human consciousness negative. It is simply obsolete. It prevents human evolution. Those in whom the new consciousness is emerging are not superior to those who are still limited to the old consciousness or refuse to release it. We are all students in the Earth school following preconsidered pathways of possibilities that we chose with the assistance of nonphysical Teachers prior to incarnation. Who among us is superior, and who is inferior?

The time of multisensory humans creating with the intentions of the soul—harmony, cooperation, sharing, and reverence for Life—is here. Their ourstory is filling with courageous words and deeds of love, of spiritual accomplishments in a world that does not yet recognize spirit, of contributions to the Biggest Community. They strive toward a world of immense power and immense peace.

Multisensory humans utilize experiences of discord, competition, hoarding, and exploitation in themselves and that they see in others to challenge fear within themselves and change themselves instead of trying to challenge and change others. There are no others in the Biggest Community. The Biggest Community does not exist, cannot exist, could never exist for "us" and not for "them." "We" and "they" exist only in the context of five-sensory communities. They exist *because* of five-sensory communities. Everything that ever has been and ever will be is in the Biggest Community.

That is the community of the Universal Human.

# 29

# Transition

Darkness disappears at sunrise. What was hidden becomes visible. Sunrise does not take you elsewhere or beyond. You remain where you are, but your awareness includes more. This is happening now as we transit from five-sensory perception to multisensory perception. Multisensory perceptions appear in ways small and large, but whenever they appear, they expand your awareness. You sense yourself as more than a mind and body. You glimpse purpose and potential in "chance" encounters and "random" events. Words and experiences take on new meaning. Your life becomes deeper and richer, like a black-and-white movie becoming color while you watch it.

You begin to see things about yourself and others that your five senses cannot show you. You sense that your life has a purpose, and you thirst to find it. Old goals fall away, and new interests replace them. People and circumstances become more interesting. Nonphysical beneficent Presence becomes a part of your life. You cannot see or touch it, but you are drawn to it. Against all reason the world sometimes feels completely appropriate. There is something to learn everywhere, all the time, and sometimes you remember to look for it.

These are multisensory perceptions. There are more. We become aware of ourselves as souls as well as personalities—aware of a part of ourselves that is more than physical, that sees more than we, that lives in a greater place. Cocreations with our souls, with other souls in advance of our own, and with nonphysical wisdom and compassion become possible.

New insights appear. We see that we could have pursued external power with reverence. We did not need to kill without reason, mutilate, starve, and torture one another to survive. We did not need to destroy species, collapse ecosystems, poison rivers, and pollute oceans to evolve. We see that pursuing external power now creates only violence and destruction. A realization shakes the ground beneath us: The very thing that enabled us to survive and evolve now works against us! Our good medicine has become poison. The unthinkable stands before us, undeniable and inescapable. *The pursuit of external power now prevents our evolution and threatens our survival!*

Love, awareness, compassion, and wisdom alone take us where we want to go. Creating authentic power alone creates healthy futures. There are no other paths. We must each become the authority in our own life, the decider of our own decisions, the determiner of our own future. No one can do these things for us, and we cannot do them for others.

A consciousness like none in our past is being born, calling us to health and wholeness, sanity and responsibility, meaning and joy. An old consciousness, caustic and familiar, spent and righteous, life-defying and death-promoting, is dying. They both surround us in this special moment, in this special span of a few generations—the unfamiliar and the familiar, the healthy and the toxic, the vibrant and the exhausted. One consciousness moves us forward, and the other has taken us as far as it can. One consciousness is love, and the other is fear.

All the rules have changed. What brought us to fulfillment now leads us only to emptiness and pain. What enabled our survival now endangers our survival. Awareness of emotions is essential to human evolution—not a hindrance to happiness. Intentions create consequences—not deeds or words. What is behind our eyes is now more important than what is in front of them. This is a game changer.

We are the new makers of new maps. We stand in this unanticipated moment with one foot in the world that is emerging and the other in the world that is disintegrating. We must choose at each moment between them. Multisensory perception is replacing five-sensory perception with startling velocity and breathtaking boldness.

Millions celebrate these changes. They welcome them. They are awed by them. Millions still pursue external power. They were born into the old consciousness, and they deny the birth of the new consciousness. Five-sensory perception and the pursuit of external power *are* the old consciousness. Multisensory perception and the creation of authentic power *are* the new consciousness.

We long for harmony, cooperation, sharing, and reverence for Life, and we are waking into a world of discord, competition, hoarding, and exploitation—a world in which life is a cheap commodity.

What will we do?

What *can* we do?

What can *I* do?

30

# What Can I Do?

You can create authentic power wherever you are, whenever you are, however you are. You can create authentic power when you are joyful, solemn, or suffering. You can create authentic power at home, at work, at school, and on vacation. You can create authentic power with caring people and uncaring people, sensitive people and callous people, loving people and hateful people.

You create authentic power when you consciously change yourself for the better. You pursue external power when you try to change the world in order to feel valuable and safe. Pursuing external power cannot change the world, and it cannot permanently change your experiences. The only way you can change the world is by creating authentic power, and the only place you can create authentic power is in yourself.

Our world is built on external power. Corporations hunt customers more efficiently than our ancestors hunted elk. They hunt continually. So do we. We hunt for individuals to influence with our wealth, intelligence, appearance, or sexuality. They hunt us for the same reasons. Airlines continually change prices to maximize profit. They shift seat availabilities for the same reason. We scour the internet for bargains. We purchase products produced by children, slaves, the children of slaves, and the toil of grandmothers and grandfathers suffering in servitude. Poverty is servitude, and poverty is everywhere.

Christian Crusaders, malicious progeny of malevolent European royalty, thundered on horseback through Muslim cities savagely slashing flesh with their sharp swords. Cossacks, ruthless and vicious, thundered on horseback through Jewish villages savagely slashing flesh with their

113

sharp swords. American cavalrymen, heroes of Hollywood, thundered on horseback through Native American villages savagely slashing flesh with their sharp swords. Only the ground beneath pounding hoofs varies from scene to scene. American soldiers thundered through the Middle East in their armored vehicles savagely slashing flesh with their sharp shrapnel.

Multisensory personalities see all of this as a single drama running through millennia without cessation. The same actors play different roles in different scenes in the same ongoing production. Sometimes they play wealthy characters and sometimes they play indigent characters. Sometimes their characters exploit, and sometimes they are exploited. Sometimes they kill, and sometimes they are killed. Each character is a personality. Personalities come and go—they are born and die. Each actor is a soul. Souls do not die. They enter and reenter the domain of the five senses—incarnate and reincarnate into the Earth school—again and again as they choose on their journeys to wholeness.

In other words, multisensory humans are beginning to see in themselves the naked greed of the brutal banker, the callous cunning of the financial speculator, and the brazen brutality of the Nazi executioner. They also see the kindness, caring, patience, gratitude, and awe of the Universe in themselves. The journey to authentic power requires unearthing in us everything that we create with fear and everything that we create with love. The farther we travel on this journey, the more we realize that *our* love and *our* fear are the love and fear of the world. We begin to experience the joy and suffering of others as our own joy and suffering.

This is the beginning of our awakening: We realize that the problems around us are not in "them." They are not in the "world." The problems around us are in *us*. We cannot solve these problems by changing others or the world. The world that we have inherited from five-sensory humanity is built on external power. We cannot change it by adding more external power to it. Pursuing external power changes nothing. Can love be legislated? Should we imprison those who do not love? Would that help them to love? Would it help us to love? Would it instead ignite in them the rage that we can no longer ignore in ourselves? Who is left to blame for the anguish, the suffering, and the despair of the world?

There is no way forward except into ourselves, into the darkest jungles with the most fearsome beasts, filling us with terror and hopelessness, dangerous at every turn, endlessly horrifying. That is the landscape we all flee, and it is in each of us. We flee into the pursuit of accomplishment, wealth, sex, food, belligerence, superiority, inferiority, vengeance, acquisition, and austerity. We lash out with words and weapons. We strive to control, to manipulate whatever needs to be manipulated in order to avoid the terrible pain of powerlessness, the pain of needing without end and not obtaining, the agonizing ache for love and the excruciating inability to love.

This pain drives every angry deed, word spoken in rage, withdrawal into hopeless silence, tidal wave of helplessness, and supernova of sorrow and destruction. It is the source of all exploitation, brutality, intolerance, and hatred. We create these things each time we grasp for appreciation, sex, food, alcohol, any fix to obliterate forever the unbearable pain of powerlessness. Running from it does not diminish it. Nothing can prevent it. Work, play, study, and accomplishment cannot shield us from it. It lies beneath every drugged stupor and manic excitement. It is the dragon emerging from its den breathing fire and destruction. It is our healing demanding attention.

There is no way to experience the heights of our love, altitude of our aspirations, exhilaration of our giving, fulfillment of our caring, gifts of our gratitude, or the grace of a smile without experiencing all that prevents these things. We cannot bask in the sunshine within us while we are armored against the suicidal, homicidal, genocidal darkness within us. We cannot know ourselves without knowing all of ourselves.

Which of your mountains seems unclimbable? Your anger, jealousy, resentment, need to please, or need to dominate? Your need for sex, alcohol, drugs, or food? Which of your experiences do you blame on others? Your depression, rage, superiority, inferiority? What judgments do you proclaim? Your superiority? Your inferiority? That your belief is a better belief? The best belief? The only belief? That homeless people do not feel pain? That you are a victim of anyone? Anything? The universe?

Human evolution now requires inner ascent, not outer conquest. Both victories and defeats feed the need for external power. Pursuing external power now leads nowhere. We are waking to ourselves as powerful and creative, compassionate and loving spirits that are responsible for what we create. We recognize the dynamics of our lives in the Earth school.

When we fear that the Universe will not provide for us and doubt that it will, we learn wisdom through fear and doubt. We live in pain. When we love Life and trust that the Universe will cocreate with us circumstances most appropriate for our spiritual growth, we learn wisdom through love and trust. We live in joy. We see emotions as messages sent from beyond, to use Rumi's beautiful words, each showing us a frightened part of our personality to challenge and change or a loving part to cultivate.

Our evolution now requires us to create a world of harmony, cooperation, sharing, and reverence for Life. You cannot do that without creating a life of harmony, cooperation, sharing, and reverence for Life. Authentic power is the new means and end of our evolution. It is the goal and reason for your incarnation. Nothing else suffices or satisfies. Nothing else can transform you into a Universal Human.

This is the new lay of the land. *To change the world, you must change yourself.* You must learn to distinguish between love and fear in yourself and choose love no matter what is happening inside you or what is happening outside you. Then you must do it again.

And again.

# 31

# The Limited Logic of the Intellect

The intellect is the creator of tools and orchestrator of possibilities. It organizes data from the five senses to pursue external power. It identifies advantages and disadvantages. It shows five-sensory humans how to survive.

The intellect thrills at new inventions, connections, and possibilities. It utilizes everything physical to manipulate and control everything physical. It creates both better bathtubs and hydrogen bombs with passion. It invents innovative ways to heal bodies and kill them. It delights equally in designing helpful machines and armor-piercing bullets. The intellect was more important to five-sensory humans than strength, speed, and endurance together. It enabled them to survive.

The intellect connects dots, for example, between a cold cave and heat from a burning tree ignited by lightning. Connection! Bring burning branches into the cave. It connects dots between sharp edges on a rock and animal skin too tough to tear. Connection! Cut the skin with the rock.

Five-sensory humans used the intellect to pursue external power without reverence. The intellect could have sheltered, fed, and clothed five-sensory humanity without harming Life. Instead five-sensory humans used it to create assault rifles, aircraft carriers, and nuclear weapons. It could have created peace and food and clean water for all. Five-sensory humans used it to create starvation, undrinkable water, unbreathable air, violence, and suffering. Five-sensory humanity benefited itself from agriculture, science, art, and music, but not the Earth or the other forms of Life upon it.

The pursuit of external power without reverence sent Mongolian horsemen into China, Roman soldiers into Palestine, and American armor into the Middle East. It created the "Holy" Roman Inquisition and every form of cruelty. It flooded Europe with Nazi armies, China with Japanese armies, constructed labor camps and death camps, exploited animals, plants, and minerals, demoted the Earth to a "resource," and soaked it in blood. None of this was necessary to the evolution of five-sensory humanity.

The intellect explains physical effects in terms of physical causes which, in turn, are physical effects. It disregards phenomena without a physical cause as "chance," "random," "will of God," "accident," or "abstract," which all mean the same thing: It has no explanation.

The intellect cannot answer our most important questions. "Who am I?" "Why am I?" "What is death?" "What is Life?" It translates every "Why?" into "How?" For example, it cannot explain why a drunk driver killed your mother. It calculates the momenta of their vehicles at impact, but it cannot explain why *she* died. It re-creates circumstances leading to her death, beginning at an arbitrary moment, but it cannot tell you why *she* died. It does not know. It cannot tell you how experiences of other personalities of your mother's soul affected the decisions of your mother because it has concluded that your mother's soul and other personalities of it do not exist.

Multisensory perception reveals the Earth school as a part of the Universe, and not the larger part. The intellect was created to comprehend only the smaller part, but multisensory humans reside, so to speak, in the larger part. The intellect cannot tell them anything about the larger part, much less guide them through it.

"Beginning" and "end" are artifacts of five-sensory perception. Where does the Universe begin? Where does it end? Five-sensory humans see the limits of the intellect also, but they do not acknowledge them. They use concepts such as "infinite" and "eternal" even though no human has ever detected anything physical that is infinite or eternal.

The intellect aligns perfectly with the perceptions of the five senses, but it does not align at all with multisensory experiences. This is not a matter of scope or scale. Multisensory experiences are not too large, small, grand, or complex to be comprehended by the intellect. They are *different* from the experiences that the intellect was designed to comprehend. Now we are entering territory that the intellect has never seen and will never see.

This is the territory of the heart.

# 32

# Higher Order Logic and Understanding of the Heart

The higher order of logic and understanding of the heart is a higher order of comprehension, perception, and understanding. It is a fusion of experience and understanding, yet the experience that is infusing the understanding is multisensory perception. Multisensory perception infuses understanding, and understanding enriches multisensory perception. In order for this to occur new logic and new understandings are required. These are the higher order logic and understanding of the heart. The relationship of multisensory perception to the higher order logic and understanding of the heart is as intimate as the relationship of five-sensory perception to the intellect.

The higher order logic and understanding of the heart are as different from the logic of the intellect as multisensory perception is from five-sensory perception. No attempt to understand multisensory experiences from the limited logic of the intellect can be satisfactory or effective. It will produce confusion on an intellectual level. That is not difficult to create, however, confusion does not resolve the matter. Resolving the matter, so to speak, is the function of the higher order logic and understanding of the heart, and in that resolution there is often a matter of contradiction from the perspective of the five senses and the intellect.

In other words, there are multiple truths, or multiple experiences, that are mutually exclusive from the perception of the five senses and the understanding of the intellect. Evolution without time is one of the more obvious, for souls evolve in nonphysical reality, and yet time exists only in the Earth school. The intellectual understanding of evolution and the five-sensory perception of evolution both require time. From that limited perspective evolution is change over time. Yet in nonphysical reality there exists an ever-increasing movement or motion or direction toward freedom and awareness—more freedom from fear and awareness of more.

In other words, from the multisensory perspective, evolution is an experience that is timeless, a new orientation in an evolution that cannot be oriented in terms of the five senses. Multisensory perception is its own orientation. It is there. It does not need to be explained or justified. Yet to communicate it, to fully comprehend the depth and power of multisensory perception, requires a higher order of logic and understanding, and that requires engaging the abilities of the heart.

The heart includes. The intellect compares. The heart embraces. The intellect excludes for each inclusion it creates. The heart has no limitations on its ability to include. That is impossible to five-sensory perception and incomprehensible to the intellect. The heart delights in all that is. That also is impossible from the perception of the five senses and the intellect, for there is an orientation toward survival as the ability to manipulate and control. That which is seen as worth manipulating and controlling because of its ability to enhance survival is considered superior or more worthy of attention and effort than that which is not. In other words, judgment is built in, so to speak, to five-sensory perception and the understanding of power as external.

The understanding of power from the perspective of the higher order logic and understanding of the heart is alignment of the personality with the soul, the alignment of a vehicle with that which created the vehicle, and the vehicle was created for the alignment. That appears redundant to the intellect, yet it is not. Authentic power therefore is both the means and the goal. It is the means and the end. In the realm of the five senses and the intellect, an end has means to attain it, yet the means and the end are not the same. The end cannot be attained without the means. From the higher order logic and understanding of the heart, authentic power is the means and the end of human evolution.

The journey to the soul is a journey without distance. No ground is covered. No mile markers are passed, yet we frequently speak of mile markers along a road. We often speak of a journey, and that also is true. How can that be true when the journey has no distance, no beginning, and no end? Understanding these things requires the heart. These things cannot be articulated in ways that do not produce a collision of meanings or a dissonance of words. Yet there is no dissonance in the higher order logic of the heart. There are no collisions. There is what is, and what is is perfect.

That also cannot be grasped by the intellect or perceived by the five senses, for their perfection is measured against a standard that is imaginary. Yet it cannot be imagined. Who can imagine perfect form, perfect thought, perfect movement? Yet from multisensory perception and the understandings of the heart, no movement, thought, or form is not perfect.

The transition of human consciousness from five-sensory perception and the pursuit of external power to multisensory perception and the creation of authentic power is complete. That is, there is no overlap. The insistence on retaining standards of perfection, standards of morality, standards of behavior, standards of thought, standards of goodness, and standards of brutality are all part of a limited domain of experience that humankind is now moving beyond and into new realms of experience.

When there is a difference of perception between five-sensory and multisensory, experiment with giving precedence to the multisensory perception, not because it is right and the other is wrong, but because it is less limited and the other is more limited. When there is apparent disagreement or conflict between the limited logic of the intellect and the higher order logic of the heart, experiment with holding the higher order logic of the heart as a guide or a polestar. For as you move closer to that star, you are able to experience that it includes everything within it, and all is perfect. Yet all is evolving. All is distinct and unique, and yet all is one. All is holy.

There is no "yes, but" in the realm of the higher order logic and understanding of the heart. There is only "yes, and." There is no "this" and "that." There is only that which is. There is no "more," "less," "larger," "smaller." There is only that which is, and that which is is perfect beyond all standards of perfection, without all standards of perfection, including all standards of perfection.

This has been known by humankind since its origin. It has not been understood. It has been feared. Five-sensory reverence is not only a matter of awe, but a matter of fear. Awe of the Universe, wonder at the Universe, is a part of the human experience. Yet emerging with that sense of smallness is fear. There is no smallness from the perspective of the higher order logic and understanding of the heart. There is no largeness. There is all that is, and at the same time, there is nothing. In other words, all that is includes all that is and all that is not.

This cannot be comprehended, cannot be perceived, and cannot be embraced by five-sensory humans understanding power as external. This is celebrated by the heart and celebrated by multisensory humans as they experience it and strive to understand through the higher order logic and understanding of the heart.

Think on these things, but not too much. Rather allow yourself to absorb them. Do not fear not understanding. Do not fear not not understanding. Do not fear. This is the higher order of logic and understanding of the heart. As you strive to understand, you move in a direction opposite to the one that you want to travel. Yet at the same time, you do not move. You are where you are.

Enjoy yourself.

# 33

## Trust

When we say, "I trust something," we mean that the thing (or person) we trust is what it appears to be or it will do what we trust it to do. We even say, "I don't need to see it happen. I trust that it will happen." The sun rising in the morning is an example. We trust that it will rise. Everything in our experience tells us it will. Of course we know that past performance does not guarantee future performance, but we feel comfortable moving forward without the guarantee. If we think about it, we realize that we are taking a leap of faith, but nothing about expecting the sun to rise tomorrow feels like that. It doesn't even seem worth thinking about.

Nevertheless, that leap of faith is the source of all emotional pain. When we take the leap and do not fly, when we fall to the rocks below, when we say in bewilderment, "How could this have happened?" we realize that our faith was misplaced. We were not standing on the ground as we thought. We were in the air somewhere, and our fall showed us unmistakably where the ground is.

This is the origin of all painful emotions. We attach to people or things being one way and then discover that they are another. The person we thought was our partner for eternity says, "I don't love you anymore." The doctor says, "Your child is dying." The doctor says, "*You* are dying." After going through the experiences that Elisabeth Kübler-Ross described—denial, anger, bargaining, depression—we finally reach acceptance (if we remain emotionally aware instead of fleeing into alcohol, drugs, sex, food, work, etc.). We discover where the ground is. It is where our leap has left us—in the present moment, in the present circumstance, with our present experiences. It has taken our awareness abruptly to Now.

This experience is so painful that many people use it to justify not trusting. They declare, "I will never trust again. I will not allow myself to be hurt again." They miss a big point here. They are still trusting. Before they trusted that things would be as they desired. Now they trust that things will not be as they desire. In both cases they trust in ignorance. This is a common five-sensory experience.

Ignorance to five-sensory humans is lack of awareness of facts. Ignorance to multisensory humans is lack of awareness of the origin of their experiences. There are countless more facts in the world than you can be aware of. From the multisensory perspective there are only two origins of experience—love and fear. Awareness for a multisensory human is awareness in the moment of whether his or her experience originates in love or in fear. For example, if you are grateful, your experience originates in love. If you are angry, your experience originates in fear.

Five-sensory humans trust that external circumstances, such as people, events, beliefs, and religions, when rearranged as they desire, can make them feel valuable and safe. Said another way, and the most important way, five-sensory humans "trust" these things to mask the pain of the frightened parts of their personalities that fear they will not get what they want, need, or expect. These parts fear abandonment, inability to care for themselves, losing friends, going to hell, dying, and more. They search for a solid place to stand in an always-changing world; they seek safety from the unknown, always approaching and terrifying.

Eventually they realize that the world—people, circumstances, events, beliefs, religions—cannot provide the safety that frightened parts of themselves seek. They do not know what other individuals will choose in the future. They do not know what *they* will choose in the future. Not even their nonphysical Teachers know what students in the Earth school will choose in the future. *None of these things can be known in advance.*

Therefore, in what can you trust when the darkness of depression closes around you, the fear of loss envelops you, the terror of death approaches? What can you trust when, above all, you *need* to trust, to hope, to see Light, or at least the possibility of Light? What is left to trust?

You can trust the Universe. You can trust the process of your life. You can trust your experiences to support your spiritual development. You can trust the Universe even when frightened parts of your personality do not want the experiences that they encounter. You can trust that all of your experiences, including the most difficult, are designed to bring the awareness of your soul into the consciousness of your personality.

When you trust these things, you trust the Universe. You see from the impersonal perspective of the soul. Gratitude appears, sometimes like the flame of a small candle in a large cathedral, and it grows. Sometimes it appears suddenly like a supernova. Appreciation, patience, and contentment flicker into your awareness or rise in it like suns. You relax into the present moment. You feel at home in your life, at ease in the world, and joyful in the Universe. These are experiences of authentic power.

You were born to create authentic power. You can trust that everything supports you in creating authentic power. Trust in the Universe is that which takes you toward wholeness. When you trust what parents, preachers, and peers tell you because they tell you, fear underlies your trust. When fear underlies your trust, you will fall, and your fall will offer you lessons to learn. When love underlies your trust, you will fly, and your flight will offer you lessons to learn.

When you trust the process of your life, when you trust your experiences in the Earth school, when you trust your own fullness—when you trust the Universe—you go where only love can take you.

# 34

# Multisensory Prayer

Multisensory experiences of prayer are very different than five-sensory experiences of prayer. That is because multisensory perception includes the understanding of power as alignment of the personality with the soul, and five-sensory perception includes the understanding of power as the ability to manipulate and control.

Multisensory prayer is cocreation. It is communion with the Universe. Multisensory prayer is direct two-way communication with Divine Intelligence. Multisensory humans trust the Universe. They know they have a part to play, and they do. They create authentic power—develop emotional awareness, practice responsible choice, and consult intuition. They do their best. Then comes prayer.

Five-sensory humans seek to appeal to a divinity that they feel is above and beyond them, yet somehow within them. They fear this divinity as much as they depend upon it and look to it. Their fear has nothing to do with divinity or Divine Intelligence. It is a projection of their own understanding of power in the limited domain of the five senses—the ability to manipulate and control. As five-sensory humans strive for external power, they imagine that their deity does the same. In other words, they create their image of divinity after themselves. They project onto it a need to manipulate and control all around them, including humankind, the Earth school, the Universe.

In other words, they imagine external power concentrated into one source, and they call that source whatever is their name for the divine. Therefore, they fear it. They supplicate it. They submit pleas to it, and those pleas are their prayers. Their prayers have to do with manipulating and controlling, as does their projection. When they pray for the health of others, for the well-being of others, what they are actually praying for is relief from their own experiences of the pain of powerlessness.

For example, when a five-sensory human prays for a longer life for an ill parent, it is praying for itself. The soul of its parent will return home to nonphysical reality at an appropriate time of its choosing. The five-sensory human is praying for relief from the anxiety or grief or sense of loss that it fears will accompany the departure of a soul from the Earth school and the death of the personality.

Multisensory perception and the multisensory understanding of power are the opposite of this in every way. For example, imagine that five-sensory individuals project the loving parts of their personalities onto their images of divinity—the parts of themselves that are grateful, appreciative, patient, caring, and in awe of Life—and that they naturally see these as parts of Life. Imagine five-sensory individuals projecting onto their image of divinity an unending patience and support of themselves and others in growing spiritually. Imagine they project that there is nothing they would not do to support others in healthy ways to grow spiritually. Five-sensory humans do not project these things because they do not live them. In other words, if their lives were ongoing experiences of the loving parts of their personalities, they would naturally see the Universe and their understanding of divinity in the same way.

Therefore, when they pray they would communicate, they would share their aspirations and share their fears. They would discuss with their image of divinity the frightened parts of their personalities that hinder their spiritual development and prohibit them from loving with the fullness that they desire to love and are capable of loving.

Imagine a human without the pain of powerlessness. There is no such thing at this time, yet in the course of evolution, such a human will emerge. Such a human will have a loving, appreciative, grateful, patient, and caring understanding of divinity because he or she *is* that. Human evolution is moving in that direction. Beyond the multisensory human is the Universal Human, and beyond that are other phases of other expanses of awareness and freedom.

Loving parts of a personality do not see others as separate. They see

one another as souls originating in the Universe that, like all things originating in the Universe, *are* the Universe. Multisensory humans cultivate
the loving parts of their personalities as they create authentic power.
They consciously focus their volition into intentions of love and cocreate
with their understanding of Divinity that reflects love and cocreation
back to them, not the experiences of frightened parts of their personalities. Their prayers are celebrations.

Multisensory humans pray in joy, openness, and love. Fear is absent.
Five-sensory humans pray in fear, to satisfy the frightened parts of their
personalities that live in fear. The difference between multisensory
prayer and five-sensory prayer is the difference between love and fear.
When multisensory humans pray, they enter love more deeply, more
consciously, with more awareness, and with more openness. When
five-sensory humans pray, they do the opposite. They enter more deeply
into fear, contraction, and helplessness.

The final step in creating authentic power is releasing your own
power into one that is greater. There is no greater power than love. The
Universe is love. All in the Universe is love. When multisensory humans
communicate with that, open themselves to that, and cocreate with that,
they are praying. As they ask for help in creating authentic power, their
lives become continual prayers. Eventually they seek not to dominate
or eliminate frightened parts of their personalities but to use them as
they were meant to be used—to show them what they need to change in
themselves so that they can love without limit.

This is how multisensory humans pray.

# Compassion

# 35

Begin with the assumption that all experience originates in compassion, the compassion of the Universe. When an experience in the Earth school activates fear, it activates a part of the personality that has no compassion. Yet that part of the personality itself was created with compassion. It was created by your soul in consultation with nonphysical Teachers as it formed the personality that became its incarnation into the Earth school that became you.

The parts of the personality that originate in fear are designed to bring the awareness of the personality to the parts of itself that show it clearly what it must change in order to move beyond the control of those parts. While it is in the control of those parts, it cannot experience compassion. It cannot experience tenderness. It cannot experience concern for others. It cannot open itself to the experiences of others as if they were its own experiences because it cannot see others as anything but separate from itself. In other words, it cannot see others as anything but objects.

Said another way, when individuals experience frightened parts of their personalities through painful physical sensations in their energy processing centers or critical, judgmental, unforgiving thoughts, they are experiencing parts of themselves that have no compassion. Those parts are concerned only for themselves and are driven by fear to attempt to alter the outside world. That is the pursuit of external power. There is no compassion in the pursuit of external power.

Emotional awareness is a big part of this process. As individuals use their emotional awareness to distinguish frightened parts of their personalities from loving parts so they can challenge the frightened parts and cultivate the loving parts, they move themselves toward compassion, for when a frightened part of a personality is challenged repeatedly, the control of that part lessens, and as it does, so also does the cruelty, the coldness, the lack of care, the lack of compassion that control the personality, and the personality moves more into the softer, healing energy of love. In this movement, there is compassion.

Therefore you can utilize or build upon all that you learned about authentic power to learn about compassion. You can simply begin to see the creation of authentic power from yet another healing perspective, the perspective of the development of compassion within yourself.

A frightened part of a personality cannot be challenged without awareness and volition. Without these, the frightened parts of a personality that the soul gave the personality at its incarnation remain strong and create powerfully throughout the time that the personality is in the Earth school. As the personality creates without awareness, it creates with fear. In other words, it creates painful and destructive consequences. When, in turn, it does not bring its awareness and volition to bear upon those experiences, it creates yet more of the same in ignorance, that is, unconsciously.

Were the Universe not one of compassion, none of this dynamic would be happening or possible. Buddhists call the continual creation of karmic consequences the Wheel of Samsara. It is always turning. Creating authentic power stops the Wheel from creating painful and destructive consequences.

The experience itself of temptation—which, as we have seen, is awareness of the plans of a frightened part of the personality before it acts on them—is also an experience of the compassion of the Universe. Through temptations the Universe shows the personality what it will create if it acts on those parts. It gives it a dry run, a dress rehearsal for its consideration, so that it can choose to implement those plans or challenge the frightened part of itself that intends them. In other words, temptation gives the personality the opportunity not to act on a frightened part of itself before the energy of fear spills over into the energy spheres of other students in the Earth school and creates painful karmic consequences of fear.

In short, temptation allows the creation of the conscious, constructive consequences of acting with love rather than the unconscious, destructive, painful consequences of acting with fear, of acting in ignorance. All of this has to do with compassion, and you can bring all of this into your life. *Everything you do in creating authentic power has to do with the creation of compassion, for without creating compassion for yourself, in yourself, you cannot be compassionate to others.* It is impossible.

Therefore, when you remain unaware of frightened parts of your personality or indulge them, you allow yourself to continue living a life of pain, and that life of pain manifests itself as a lack of compassion for others because the two are identical. If you have no authentic power, you are in the control of frightened parts of your personality that create painfully and destructively. Everything that you have learned about creating authentic power is a gift of compassion.

Students in the Earth school generally think that compassion has to do with others. It does not. It has to do with themselves, for as they become compassionate with themselves, which means as they learn to recognize fear in themselves and challenge it rather than indulge it, they begin to act with love. As they act with love, they become sources of compassion.

Compassion cannot be created by simply intending or desiring to become compassionate, any more than love can be created simply by intending or desiring to become loving. You must first find and eliminate all within yourself that prevents experiences of love. Creating authentic power gives you a guided tour, so to speak, of the parts of your personality that do not experience the love of the Universe, that do not experience the compassion of the Universe, even while they live it in terms of what they are creating.

Explore this perspective. As you approach compassion in this way, you need not begin at the beginning, so to speak. You have been beginning at the beginning since your first glimpse of authentic power or the idea of authentic power. You can now bring to bear all that you have learned about authentic power in a context of understanding compassion.

In other words, it is not as though you need to learn everything again, for you have already learned a great deal. You have learned about the transformation of human consciousness that is now underway. You have learned about your internal energy processing system. You have learned about intuition. You have learned about responsible choice. And you have learned about all of these things in the context of creating authentic power. Now you need merely to shift your perception so that all of this is held in a different way. Not that any of it changes, but simply that it is held in a different way, or allows a different perception.

With each challenge of a frightened part of your personality, with each responsible choice to act with love—to respond instead of react—experiences of compassion come into being, and perceptions of an emerging life of compassion. With each indulgence of a frightened part of your personality—with each choice to ignore or discard an experience of a loving part of your personality, with each unchallenged experience of a painful life with no compassion—experiences devoid of compassion, and perceptions of a painful life without compassion, come into being.

In short, there is nothing new to learn. You need only look at what you already know from a slightly different yet valid and insightful perspective. Giving the gifts that you were born to give is an act of compassion. Manipulating and controlling others or the world in order to achieve the desires of frightened parts of your personality are acts without compassion.

Eventually you will become compassionate with others. Until then you will spin your wheels, so to speak, attempting to become compassionate with others while you have no compassion for yourself. None of the frightened parts of your personality have compassion for you or others. Why spend time spinning your wheels, which means acting from frightened parts of your personality yet again and creating without compassion yet again? Creating authentic power gives you traction.

More and more individuals are discovering the tools of creating authentic power as our species becomes multisensory, but many do not value that what these tools can create for them, and that we have been calling authentic power, is the same as compassion.

If you want to be compassionate, you will fall short of the mark if that compassion does not extend to you.

36

# Heartfulness Meditation

reating authentic power is a meditation. It brings attention to
your internal dynamics—your experiences of them, the thoughts
that accompany them, and the intentions that you choose as you act on
them or challenge them. At the same time, it brings your attention to
activities in the world—the activities that stimulate your emotional experiences, that illuminate within you that which needs to be challenged
and changed and that within you which needs to be cultivated in order
to fulfill your sacred contract with the Universe.

Creating authentic power occurs in the new context of a new consciousness. Creating authentic power is not possible for five-sensory
humans because five-sensory humans understand power as the ability
to manipulate and to control. There have always been humans who were
not limited to the five senses, and who expended the effort to awaken
to and focus upon their internal dynamics and the relationship of those
dynamics to their external experiences.

As the new consciousness replaces the old human consciousness, this
becomes the case for all humans. Yet now there is a very big difference
because all humans are becoming multisensory. They are able to see with
the impersonal perspective of the soul the workings of the Earth school
to bring awareness of the soul into the consciousness of the personality.
The intellect and the pursuit of external power which accompanies it and
which it serves were the common experiences of humanity prior to the
birth of the new consciousness. Alignment of the personality with the
soul in the environment of the Earth school is now the new content of
the new consciousness and the new humanity.

The heart is at the center of creating authentic power. That is the same as saying that love is at the center of creating authentic power, and that is the same as saying that the Universe and the direct experience of the Universe are at the heart of creating authentic power. Meditation for five-sensory humans could be called mindfulness, for it fills the mind with awarenesses and understandings. Meditation for multisensory humans would more accurately be called heartfulness, for it fills awareness with the experiences of the heart. These are necessary.

Commitment to spiritual growth is a heartful commitment. This is not in the consciousness of many individuals when they begin the process of creating authentic power, for they begin it as they become aware of the extent of the emotional pain in their lives and their inability to remove that pain. That is when most humans look to a spiritual path. As they learn to create authentic power, they learn to distinguish within themselves between love and fear, between the blissful, healthy, good-feeling, constructive experiences of love and the painful, destructive, contracting experiences of fear, and to cultivate love. As this occurs, love begins to enter awareness more clearly, more frequently, and eventually begins to be a larger and larger part of awareness.

The shift from five-sensory perception and the intellect is the shift to multisensory perception and the heart. This is identical to the shift from the understanding of power as the ability to manipulate and control to the understanding of power as alignment of the personality with the soul.

*The creation of authentic power is an ongoing heartfulness meditation.* It is a meditation in which all emotional experiences are noted, are observed, and are felt in terms of physical sensations in the energy processing centers. It is a heartfulness meditation in which the energy currents of love are identified and cultivated. It is a heartfulness meditation in which the control of frightened parts of the personality dissipates, and the fulfilling, healing, energizing, invigorating, creative energy of the heart replaces it.

This does not mean that specific meditations at specific times are not helpful. They can be quite helpful provided that they are undertaken in the service of creating authentic power. Many individuals seek to escape the world through meditation. They undertake five-sensory meditations or meditations that are mindful as a way of distracting themselves from pain. In other words, they meditate to move beyond the emotional pain of the frightened parts of their personalities. They quickly learn that is not effective, and yet that remains their intention until they move beyond the control of that pain.

The creation of authentic power is quite different. It redefines the process of "moving beyond" into the explicit experience of moving into the energy of the heart. It takes you into the world through meditation, and as you enter the world fully you challenge those very parts of your personality that five-sensory individuals seek to escape, and you consciously move beyond the control of them.

Intention is primary. Intention is always primary. When a multisensory human meditates in heartfulness meditation, it is to move into the painful emotional experiences of the frightened parts of his or her personality and use them as they were meant to be used and as multisensory humans understand them to be used—to eliminate within themselves those aspects of themselves that prohibit them from giving the gifts that they were born to give, from fulfilling their potential, from living in love, from being love consciously.

There is no need for volition at a certain level of awareness. Yet to reach that level of awareness, volition is necessary. In other words, conscious choice of intention is necessary. Creating authentic power is the conscious choice of love and learning how to make that choice continually.

As we have discussed, there have been multisensory humans throughout the history of five-sensory humankind who strove for the awareness of the heart. That cannot be distinguished from awareness of the mind once awareness of the heart is understood in experiential terms. Traditional Eastern meditations guide individuals eventually toward the experiences of the heart, toward connection, toward oneness with all that is. Creating authentic power does that continually. The Universal Human is the product of this process. Universal Humanity is the phase of human evolution that lies beyond the multisensory, beyond the emergence of multisensory humanity and the understanding of power as authentic.

Creating authentic power transforms the experiences of the Earth school moment by moment into a meditation. These experiences occur

without awareness until meditation enters the picture. When that meditation is the creation of authentic power, it is heartfulness meditation.
From the impersonal perspective of the soul, heartfulness meditation
does not transform the individual. The individual transforms him- or
herself by bringing his or her awareness to the energies of the heart
through the creation of authentic power.

This process appears circular if you look at a circular journey as one
that begins at a point, continues, and eventually returns to the same
point. That is one way of looking at a circle. Another way of looking at
a circle is in terms of completeness. There is no point on the circle that
is not the beginning and the end of every other point of the circle. That
is what you are. You are complete, and yet as you experience the circle,
you become aware of the circle and its completeness and your own completeness. Five-sensory meditations call this various things, among them,
"enlightenment."

Heartfulness meditation leads you to the oneness, the fullness of Life.
It is awakening to the process of your life, and yet it is the process of your
life that is awakening you when you use it consciously.

# 37

# Heartfulness Meditation and
# Mindfulness Meditation

Heartfulness meditation and mindfulness meditation were designed for different audiences. Mindfulness meditation was designed for five-sensory humans. It is a product of the old consciousness. Heartfulness meditation is designed for multisensory humans. It is a product of the new consciousness.

Creating authentic power, as we have seen, is a meditation. Everything about creating authentic power is about the heart. It is about love and the creation of love within a human life in the Earth school. Heartfulness meditation begins and ends with the heart. It encompasses all human activity and yet in the context of the heart. The context of the heart means a context of love. Love is one of the aspects of the fundamental duality in the Earth school. The other aspect of it is fear. Creating authentic power is distinguishing between love and fear and choosing love. It is, therefore, a heartfulness meditation.

Creating authentic power requires recognizing the difference between love and fear in all ways possible, which means in terms of physical sensations in the body, in terms of emotional currents in the body, and in terms of thoughts. Five-sensory humans and five-sensory meditators have understood the difference between energy that creates constructively and energy that creates destructively. However, their emphasis has been simply on the recognition of energy.

Heartfulness meditation is on both types of energy, love and fear, and learning how to use the energy of love and to challenge the energy of fear. Mindfulness meditation allows individuals to detach from their experiences—physical, mental, and emotional. It brings their attention to the external world and their attention to their internal experiences and does this in different ways depending on the form of mindfulness meditation. Creating authentic power does all of that and in the context of love.

Heartfulness meditation does all of that and, further, in a next context—the context in which incarnation is intentional, in which the energy of the soul chooses to incarnate in accordance with its karmic obligations and with the potential that it seeks to achieve. It is more than witnessing the processes of Life in the Earth school. It is engaging them consciously. Yet this engagement is done without attachment to the outcome.

Mindfulness meditation emphasizes detachment from outcomes. Heartfulness meditation does as well, yet again in the context of love. Mindfulness meditation emphasizes allowing thoughts and experiences to flow. It allows individuals to see the dynamic of life in the Earth school and how in each individual it supports the dynamic of life in all other individuals. Again, heartfulness meditation does the same, but in the context of love and intentional choices of love.

Mindfulness meditation is analogous to enjoying a ride in a self-driving car. You need not focus on driving. You simply are aware of the ride. Heartfulness meditation is stepping into the driver's seat and directing the vehicle. It puts the meditator behind the steering wheel, distinguishes between those parts of consciousness that would drive the car in destructive ways or toward destructive destinations and those parts of the personality that would drive the car toward constructive destinations, and then puts those parts of the personality—the loving parts—in control of the driving. The end of heartfulness meditation is more than enjoying the ride, is more than experiencing the vehicle. It is a shift of emphasis from observation and detachment to observation, detachment, and then focused intention without attachment to the outcome.

All meditations are intentional to a degree. The decision to meditate is itself an intention. Meditations in Eastern cultures focus on intentionality. For example, the Buddha explained how desire is the source of all suffering, and then explained what to do about that. Yet his explanation was not in the context of love. It was in the context of five-sensory perception, and his explanations were designed for five-sensory humans who evolved by pursuing external power.

Heartfulness meditation excavates the word "desire." It explains it in clear and simple terms. It explains it as the core fear of all individuals in the Earth school. It explains it as the pain of powerlessness. In other words, heartfulness meditation goes beyond the assertion, the accurate assertion, that desire generates all suffering, and in more accurate terms explains that as fear generating all suffering. Fear generating all desire. The pursuit of external power generating all desire.

Mindfulness meditation focuses on detaching from the outcome of intentions. Heartfulness meditation also focuses on detachment from the outcome of intentions, and distinguishes intentions of love from intentions of fear. The objective of heartfulness meditation is an individual who moves through the Earth school with an empowered heart, without attachment to the outcome, beyond the control of fear, able to express love without reservation, without limit, able to receive love without limit and without reservation.

The focus of mindfulness meditation is the mind. All is assumed to begin and end in the mind. The source of all experience is said to be an original mind. From the perspective of heartfulness meditation, the source of all experience could be said to originate in an original heart, for the Universe is not a mind. It is not thought. It is consciousness. It is love.

Mindfulness meditation separates consciousness from all else, which is a way of saying that consciousness is all else. Heartfulness meditation illuminates the same, but also that Consciousness, Love, and Life are identical. Mindfulness meditation strives to include all experience in the context of mind, in an expanded understanding and experience of mind. Heartfulness meditation includes all possible human experience in the context of love, in an expanded, clarified context of love far different from that of the sentimental experience of love, which is an experience of fear.

Mindfulness meditation encompasses all intentions and detachment from the outcome of all intentions. Heartfulness meditation focuses upon the intentions of love and detachment from the outcome of intentions of love and the elimination of intentions of fear. It is purposeful. It reflects the birth of a species that understands its place in the Universe in new ways and is willing to accept its new understanding and experiment with it.

The purpose of mindfulness meditation is to detach from everything and to experience it. Mindfulness meditation is specifically not to align with currents of energy, with thoughts, with actions. The purpose of heartfulness meditation is to align the personality with the soul and with the intentions of the soul—harmony, cooperation, sharing, and reverence for Life. It is the discipline of learning how to create with those intentions without attachment to the outcome.

Heartfulness meditation illuminates the Universe as a source of love, and that love is in all aspects of the Universe and in all experiences. Mindfulness meditation would say, in effect, all that is, is. Heartfulness meditation would say, all that is, is love.

Meditation is valuable in all of its forms, for it allows individuals to detach from their experiences and their thoughts and their emotions. Heartfulness meditation is valuable for the new multisensory species because it enables that species to use this detachment consciously to create authentic power, to cultivate love and to challenge all parts of the self that prevent love.

Mindfulness meditation in its many forms is a life-long practice. The goal is awareness and detachment. Heartfulness meditation is also a lifelong practice. The goal is love and the continual natural creation of consequences with love. The purpose of mindfulness meditation is to become aware of the nature of your own life. The purpose of heartfulness meditation is to become the authority in your own life.

If you are multisensory, which you are, you are already beginning to experience the nature of your life—that it is more than physical aspects, that it is a part of a larger reality, that the larger reality influences it, and that it influences that reality. Mindfulness meditation aims at these realizations. Heartfulness meditation incorporates also intention, conscious direction, and conscious use of all that the new awareness brings in order to align the personality with the energy of the soul. It is an ongoing, lifelong meditation. Its focus is the heart. Its destination is the heart. Its means of getting there is the heart.

At its heart is the heart.

# OUR NEW SOCIAL STRUCTURES

# 38

# What Are Social Structures?

Mountains emerge from the Earth. Mountains and the Earth are inseparable. The Earth is their source. Human social structures emerge from human experience. Human social structures and human experience are inseparable. Human experience is their source.

Mountains develop dramatically. Molten lava flings itself into astonished air from fissures in the firmament or explodes from craters long considered safe summits, building upon the Earth. When lava reaches the sea, as lava from volcanos on islands often does, it builds upon the Earth in cataclysmic clashes of water and fire. Mountains grow, islands grow, land rises and stays risen. In other cases, continent-size tectonic plates collide, thrusting new mountains into unsuspecting skies. Mountains appear where none were, and they stay thrust.

Mountains shape the Earth as they emerge and as they develop. Ranges of mountains cross continents—Sierra Nevada, Cascade, Rocky, Pyrenees, Alps, Andes, Himalayas. They cannot be ignored. The Earth is their mother. When Mount Lassen in the United States erupted in 1915 (Cascade range), superheated ash exploded thirty thousand feet into the stratosphere. When Mount Saint Helens erupted in 1980 (Cascade range again), one thousand three hundred feet of mountainside disappeared in an instant!

We can build highways and hotels on mountains, drill tunnels through them, mine their tops, and cut their forests, but we cannot change them. Our activities are trivial compared to the processes that produce mountains. Only changing the Earth itself could change the processes that produce mountains.

Human social structures develop in similar ways. Endeavor by endeavor they emerge from human experience. Exploration of the physical world with primitive tools morphed through millennia into exploration with subatomic particle accelerators. Settlements morphed into metropolises.

Just as mountains shape the Earth as they emerge and develop, human social structures shape human experience as they emerge and develop. They cannot be ignored. Human experience is their mother. They shape human activity across cultures, customs, epochs, and geography. The social structure of commerce, for example, is the same in Asia, Europe, India, and Africa. It is the same in Latin, Caucasian, Buddhist, and aboriginal cultures. It is the always-current culmination of countless individuals pursuing external power. Today we call some of these pursuits businesses.

The social structure of health care is the culmination of countless attempts over hundreds of millennia to escape illness and death. We can nationalize health care or privatize health care, but we cannot change the social structure of health care. We can replace capitalism with socialism, but we cannot change the social structure of economics. We can replace dictatorships with democracies, but we cannot change the social structure of governance. We can replace fact-based curricula with faith-based curricula, but we cannot change the social structure of education. Our changes are trivial compared to the processes that produce social structures. Only changing human consciousness itself could change the processes that produce human social structures.

THAT CHANGE HAS HAPPENED! Human consciousness has transformed beyond the five-sensory ability to comprehend or imagine. This transformation changes human experience in every way. It changes the ways that we see ourselves, one another, the world, and the Universe. It changes our social structures.

The new human consciousness is epic and unprecedented. It is replacing a world built on five-sensory perception and external power with a world built on multisensory perception and authentic power. It is reshaping terrain known to our ancestors for hundreds of thousands of years and known to ancestors of our ancestors for millions of years. It is replacing our five-sensory social structures of the personality with multi-sensory social structures of the soul. This is happening NOW. This is the big moment, the big day, the big epoch, and we are on the ground floor.

Five-sensory humans cannot create new human social structures because they create with the old human consciousness. Multisensory humans bring new human social structures into being as they create with the new human consciousness, as they create authentic power.

Our disintegrating social structures are the products of five-sensory humans. Now five-sensory humans are disappearing, and so are their social structures. Our new social structures are the products of multi-sensory humans. Now multisensory humans are appearing, and so are their social structures.

This was not visible before, but it is obvious now.

# 39

# Why Our Social Structures
# Are Disintegrating

I discovered a once-beautiful dilapidated house in a coastal town in
Northern California. That town was my new home. Close to yet remote from San Francisco, it gave me a respite from my life in the City. I
loved its isolation, its sense of community, and its intimate relationship
with the ocean. I supposed these were the things that had brought people
to it for decades, and had now brought me.

The house was condemned. Yellow tape cordoned off a weed-covered
yard and a broad porch beyond it. It was a Victorian house, like many I
had seen in San Francisco. Gingerbread trim connected lathed porch pil-
lars, and a round turret with a conical top gave it an elegant distinction.
I could imagine stained glass in the windows. From the sidewalk where
I stood, the old house continued to exude the gaudy tastefulness of that
era. It was clearly the summer home of a wealthy family. It had a family
feel about it.

I liked the house immediately. I knew that the ocean view from the
back would be magnificent. I could not imagine why someone had not
renovated it long ago. In my fantasy, I imagined doing just that. I walked
down the winding road to the beach to get another view of the house. I
looked up, and I gasped.

The house, once separated from the edge of the cliff by a large yard,
extended precariously over empty space! Cantilevered on a rotting un-
derstructure, half of it hovered over a void between its exposed under
flooring and the rocky beach below. It seemed to float high above me,

as though about to journey seaward like a hot air balloon. It was, in fact, ready to plunge downward, and its doom was imminent.

Spectacularly poised at the moment of its demise, the house stood on a precipice like a trapeze artist high above a hushed crowd. This surreal apparition of majestic ignorance and impending disaster hung suspended against a vacant sky. The cordoned beach silently awaited the massive intruder. As the cliff continued to erode imperceptibly, more under flooring imperceptibly became exposed. Faded signs and yellowed tape on the rocks testified to the longevity of this slow-motion drama.

None of this was visible from the top of the cliff. Tape and cones kept passersby on the sidewalk, overgrowth concealed the ocean behind the house, and nowhere was the problem of the missing cliff apparent. Only a sad and broken facade of a once happy structure remained on the otherwise pleasant street. The sea had taken the ground on which the house had stood. Soon it would take the house. Once solid and strong, it had become unstable and weak, and its own weight would soon bring it down. Nothing could prevent it.

Five-sensory perception is like the view from the sidewalk. We see from a limited perspective, and therefore, we see less. We look around us, and we see our social structures in dysfunction. We look for reasons, but we cannot see the deeper causes beneath the dysfunctions, just as we cannot see from the sidewalk the reason that the house is condemned. The reason exists nonetheless. Analyses, calculations, or new plans cannot remove it. Without recognizing that reason we have no way of knowing that an unstoppable collapse is in motion. No reengineering, renovation, or remodeling can salvage the house. It is doomed.

The same is true of our social structures. From the sidewalk, so to speak, their increasing dysfunctions appear to be understandable and fixable. From the beach, hope of saving them disappears. Reality obliterates wishful thinking. Creativity refocuses toward achievable goals and away from the impossible. In the case of the house, this means making the collapse as safe as possible, planning the post-collapse cleanup, and building a new and more appropriate house.

In the case of our social structures, it means looking toward new and different structures that are built on a strong and solid foundation. These new structures are beginning to emerge, and their new foundation is already visible. These structures are entirely new, and their functions are entirely different. The new structures express, manifest, and embody the new potential of the human species—authentic power.

Multisensory perception takes us down to the beach, metaphorically speaking. It reveals a startling vista. Our social structures no longer have a foundation! It is gone. Completely gone! Like the old house, they are hovering over a void, extending into empty space. Only one future awaits them: collapse, and that is what they are doing. They cannot be saved, because the circumstance that brought them to their end is irreversible. Nothing can bring back the cliff under the house, and nothing can reconstruct the foundation that once supported our social structures.

That foundation was external power—the ability to manipulate and control. Our social structures reflect external power, express external power, and perpetuate external power. External power is as inseparable from our social structures as water from a waterfall. Their architecture, infrastructure, and reason for being are external power. External power determined their forms and functions. They were built with external power, by external power, and external power is their foundation. Now the pursuit of external power leads only to violence and destruction. The foundation that once supported our social structures, like the cliff beneath the condemned house, has vanished.

Like the old house, our social structures now lean on the edge of destruction, and they cannot be saved. They cannot be salvaged when they fall. There is no way to lower the condemned house to the rocks below and no way to rebuild it where it is. Our social structures are products of a dying consciousness, and they cannot be saved. Like the old house, they are doomed. So familiar and long in the making, all of them must now be replaced by new and different social structures that are built on a different and solid foundation.

Imagine a steam locomotive thundering down the tracks. It is more powerful than anything before it—brutish, strong, unstoppable. It is a symbol of progress, the concrete presence of a new era. Behind the locomotive is the fuel car, filled with coal. An engineer shovels coal into the massive boiler where water is vaporized, and steam drives the huge pistons that move the locomotive forward. Behind it are cargo and people headed for new destinations. The people do not think about the locomotive that is making their journey possible, except to admire it.

Inside the train, all is wondrous. Countryside moves past—hour after hour—faster than a horse can run. Food is served. Passengers exchange conversation, and cushions comfort their passage. Immovable tracks keep it steady on purpose. Inside and outside, the train is a thing of beauty and inspiration.

Now imagine that the locomotive has run out of fuel, and no more is available. The last piece of coal has been shoveled into the boiler, and the boiler is cooling. No steam is being produced, and the huge pistons are no longer being driven by it.

There is no fire in its belly or smoke in its stack, yet the locomotive moves forward. Its tremendous inertia cannot be interrupted. Its mass and velocity ensure continued momentum, but not indefinitely. The great engine has gone silent and eventually will be cold. The train slows imperceptibly at first and then noticeably. Passengers feel the deceleration and discuss it among themselves. Perhaps the engine has run out of fuel, they speculate, without knowing that no more fuel is available or will be available. Eventually the train comes to a halt. At this point the passengers have no option except to disembark and look for another way to continue their journey.

This is happening to us now. The locomotive is the dying consciousness. It continues to move forward, but only because of inertia. We feel the deceleration. We see increasing dysfunction around us. We see that old ways of dealing with things make them worse. The dying consciousness has run out of fuel. No more is available, and no more will be available. The fuel was external power. Now the pursuit of external power has taken us as far as it can. The train is slowing.

The products of the dying consciousness are disintegrating.

40

# How to Replace Our Disintegrating Social Structures

T he relationship of multisensory social structures to authentic power is the same as the relationship of five-sensory social structures to external power.

It is the relationship of the ocean to wet. The ocean IS wet. Everything in and of the ocean is wet. Everything about, within, and resulting from multisensory social structures has to do with authentic power. Multisensory social structures are the ocean, and authentic power is wet. Everything about, within, and resulting from five-sensory social structures has to do with external power. Five-sensory social structures are the ocean, and external power is wet.

Five-sensory perception is invisible to five-sensory humans. They have nothing to compare it with, nothing to make a contrast that they can see. Therefore, they do not think of five-sensory perception as the defining characteristic of their species, much less its fundamental limitation. The evolution of five-sensory humans requires survival, and their survival requires external power. This is the soil from which five-sensory social structures emerge and grow, the realm of five-sensory perception and external power, the old consciousness—the realm of the personality.

Multisensory humans recognize the difference between five-sensory perception and multisensory perception. They know that multisensory perception is the defining characteristic of their species. Their evolution requires spiritual growth, and their spiritual growth requires creating authentic power. This is the soil from which multisensory social structures emerge and grow, the realm of multisensory perception and authentic power, the new consciousness—the realm of the soul. In other words, five-sensory social structures have no relationship to the soul, its intentions, or its energy. They are obsolete, unworkable, unfixable, and dangerous.

They are obsolete because they are built on external power, and we need to create authentic power in order to evolve. They are unworkable because they create discord, competition, hoarding, and exploitation while we need to create harmony, cooperation, sharing, and reverence for Life in order to evolve. They are unfixable because they are not broken— they served a species whose time has expired. They are dangerous because the pursuit of external power now produces only violence and destruction. In short, our five-sensory social structures have no salvage value. The unimaginable has boldly arrived. It stands before us unapologetic and immovable—*the social structures that are crumbling around us no longer support our evolution.*

Multisensory social structures are sprouting like grass in the spring through cracks in sidewalks. The sidewalks, metaphorically speaking, are five-sensory social structures. The growing grass will eventually break them apart. Nothing can prevent this. Socially responsible investing, benefit corporations, fierce opposition to genetically modified crops, alternative healing modalities, burgeoning markets for organic food and health-care supplements, restorative justice in place of criminal punishment, and patient self-responsibility infiltrating patient-doctor relationships are glimpses of emerging multisensory social structures of the soul.

When I was a boy in Kansas, I sharpened my pocketknife with a wet stone. Every boy I knew did. Then I discovered that a grinding wheel did the job faster, better, and spectacularly. Sparks shot downward dramatically the moment the blade touched the spinning wheel. By analogy, the blade is external power, the spinning wheel is pursuit of it, and the sparks are products of the pursuit.

Science, technology, aircraft, spacecraft, antibiotics, computers, and the internet are some of the sparks. Five-sensory humans fixate on them.

Multisensory humans see other sparks, too, for example, they see insurance companies prioritizing "medical savings" over "treatment expenses," and customers dying while investors and executives profit. They see wealthy guilty individuals safer in criminal courts than indigent innocent individuals. They see public servants (politicians) soliciting bribes (donations) without shame or fear. They see governments recording every email, text, and call they receive and every email, text, and call they send. They see enormous companies recording their every purchase, change of location, and mouse click in order to manipulate them, and then selling that information to other companies that also manipulate them. They see the sparks of oligarchy, dictatorship, nuclear weapons, poverty, slavery, endless warfare, institutional killing, and global pollution flying from the blade.

They see competition for customers, investors, influence, and sexual partners spinning the wheel. They see the sparks of discord, competition, hoarding, and exploitation flying from it. They ask themselves, "Why develop antibiotics for cows on their way to slaughter?" They see that healthy cows are not the issue. Profit is the issue. Exploitation is the issue. Self-gain is the issue. They see corporations striving relentlessly for quarterly profits, and investors relentlessly demanding them. They see that the well-being of employees, customers, communities, and countries is beside the point. Life is beside the point. The point is external power. They see that none of this is healthy, life-giving, or fulfilling.

When you create authentic power, no wheel spins, and no sparks fly. Your experiences change from unconsciously chosen and destructive consequences of fear to consciously chosen and constructive consequences of love. Your creativity no longer supports disintegrating five-sensory social structures of the personality. It flows instead into new multisensory social structures of the soul.

You do not need to decide to do this. Your choices of love contribute to new social structures of the soul. Your choices of fear do not. Love is the direct route to where you want to go. Fear is the direct route to where the frightened parts of your personality want to go. As you choose love, five-sensory social structures of the personality cease to emerge from the old human consciousness, and multisensory social structures of the soul begin to emerge from the new human consciousness.

Creating authentic power requires you to step into the darkness of fear and the fear of darkness, move beyond them consciously, and enter the light of love with your arms open.

This is the only way to replace our disintegrating social structures.

# The Grand Temple of External Power

One social structure is the mother of all five-sensory social structures. Like them, it is premised on the perception of power as the ability to manipulate and control, and it produces the destructive consequences that pursuits of external power now create without exception. This is the Grand Temple of External Power.

All who enter the Grand Temple of External Power worship external power, and there are none who do not enter. Its hymn books sing the praises of external power. Its scriptures explain external power. Its meditations illuminate power as external. Its art reveals the glory of external power—temples of ancient Babylon, pyramids of Egypt, every palace of every monarch, and the skyscrapers of New York City, Shanghai, and Dubai. More are continually constructed, and they are always larger, more impressive, and more expensive. Huge homes, elegant clothing, dazzling jewelry, massive yachts, private jets, and soon private spacecraft, reveal the glory of external power in more limited ways.

The Disciples of External Power pray for external power, even in monasteries and nunneries, schools of science, halls of justice, and hospitals. They recognize one another, even if they have never thought about the Grand Temple of External Power or the idea of power as external. They know one another through their practice, and all of them have the same practice. They assess the value of what they create, what others create, and how to exchange them. They assign meaning in terms of yen, dollars, and pesos. They assign value in terms of bushels of apples, baskets of berries, and shiploads of grain. They assign it in terms of the education they receive and the educations that others receive, the health care they receive and the health care that others receive, and the justice they experience and the justice that others experience.

The Disciples of External Power do not need buildings or places to remind them of what is important. They never forget. Those with more money, education, fame, comfort, food, and safety remind them. Those with less remind them. Those who live in luxury and have everything, those who live in poverty and have nothing, and everyone in between remind them. The symbols of external power are everywhere. Uniforms and weapons are symbols of external power. Money is a symbol of external power. Corner offices on high floors are symbols of external power. Numbers of cows, goats, oxen, and olive trees are symbols. Disciples with less want more. Disciples with more want more. The hunger for external power is insatiable. It is a bottomless hole, a need without end.

Disciples of External Power seek the most they can get for the least they must lose. The more others need what they have, the more they demand for it. The less others need what they have, the less they ask for it. Gain and benefit for themselves is the rule. This rule defines their every interaction, transaction, and endeavor. On the largest scale and the smallest, their intention is the same (self-gain), their energy is the same (manipulation and control), and the consequences they now create are the same (violence and destruction).

I loved airplanes as a child. My room was filled with models I carefully made, gluing balsa wood frames together and then gluing paper to some of the pieces, spraying it with water, and watching the paper dry taut just like the stretched canvas that covered the real flying machines of World War I—the kind that fought the great aerial battles with the Red Baron. I knew every World War II bomber and fighter and all the planes in the Korean War, from our famous F-86 Sabre jets to the almost look-a-like MiGs.

I wanted to fly fighters for the air force or navy fighters from aircraft carriers after I graduated from Harvard, but my limited eyesight prevented me. I made my first solo flight on Okinawa on a weekend while I was in the army. It was in an old canvas-covered two-seater much like my first early models, from a rural landing strip the width of a two-lane road. I thrilled at the beauty of the white beaches and clear turquoise water sliding below me, and immediately headed toward land again, just in case. Then terror flooded me at the thought of landing. No one was with me to help get the plane down, but I was hooked.

After the army I got a private license, a commercial license, an instrument rating, a multi-engine rating, and a ground instructor license. I steadily moved from simple single-engine fixed-gear planes to variable-speed prop planes to multi-engine aircraft with retractable landing gear. I loved flying. I loved doing aerobatics. The old ache to fly a supersonic fighter in combat was still with me. Then I discovered something startling. I had assumed that flying the small, simple aircraft that were available to me was in a different universe of experience from flying the high-performance aircraft I longed for. I discovered that they both fly the same!

*All* fixed-wing aircraft fly the same! They all have the same controls and essentially the same instruments. They all require the same basic skills and knowledge. More complex planes have more complex procedures, and special ratings are required to learn them, but the aerodynamics of small general aviation aircraft are *identical* with the aerodynamics of the largest passenger and cargo planes and the fastest fighters. If you know how one flies, you know how they all fly.

The same is true of the Grand Temple of External Power. The dynamics behind the largest interactions in the Grand Temple of External Power and the dynamics behind the smallest interactions in the Grand Temple of External Power are identical. Some are more complex, such as financing a skyscraper or international trade deals, and special training is necessary to learn the complexities, but if you know how one interaction works, you know how they all work. Street vendors, laborers, multinational corporations, and nations all follow the same rule. Financial markets and commodity exchanges follow the same rule. The rule is maximum gain, maximum self-benefit, and maximum profit. Each time we strive to benefit at the expense of another, we follow this rule.

We hunt for best prices, and sellers entice us with special offers, volume discounts, and free shipping. The largest weapons manufacturers in the world do exactly the same when they sell to governments (including their own)—just as the same aerodynamics enable jumbo jets and made-in-the-garage airplanes to fly. Negotiating the price of a bomber and the price of a watermelon is the same dynamic. Only details differ.

A participant at one of our events, an elder in an aristocratic European family, was describing some of her wonderful art to us—Picasso, Chagall, Monet, Rembrandt—when I exclaimed, "How amazing it must be to live with these paintings!" "They are not in my homes," she said with surprise. "They are in vaults in Switzerland. I hang duplicates on my walls." At first I thought that only the very wealthy hid beauty where it could never be seen, much less appreciated—until I remembered my mother in our small Kansas town storing (hiding) family china safely out of sight.

We are all in the Grand Temple of External Power, and until recently we have not realized it. The Grand Temple of External Power is the domain of the five senses. Disciples in the Grand Temple seek self-benefit without cessation, even for a moment. They do not care what that creates for others. This is the pursuit of external power.

When their interactions involve goods and services, their pursuits create an "economy."

# 42

# Contributors and Consumers

A n economy is an area where goods and services are produced, distributed, and consumed. It can be a large area, such as a continent, or a small area, such as a village. It can be the largest five-sensory area—all nations and cultures, all places and all people. This is the global economy. It is a ruthless, aggressive, fierce, and self-serving product of fear. We usually hear most about this economy, but we are also affected by national, state, and municipal economies. We can even recognize "economies" in neighborhoods, relationships, and families. Self-interest is indistinguishable from the concept of "economy." It is the foundation of every five-sensory economic (mutually exploitive) activity.

Economics is the study of how we use opportunities to benefit ourselves—how we "take advantage," "capitalize," "exploit," and "monetize" them. In 1776 a Scotsman, Adam Smith, described his understanding of an "invisible hand" in the "market." The "market" was (and is) the always dependable intersection of intentions of greed that determines the selling price of anything. A deal is done when a willing buyer agrees with a willing seller on a price.

The seller might be willing to sell her house, for example, because her children are hungry and her dying husband needs medicine, but the buyer is not concerned with this circumstance. In fact, buyers seek out such circumstances. The intention of the buyer (self-interest) is not affected by the intention of the seller (self-interest). Self-gain is the intention of every buyer and every seller in every economy.

No economist has yet found a way or reason to challenge Smith's assertion that rational (unfeeling) self-interest (fear) and competition (fear) lead to (five-sensory) prosperity. Smith built this edifice of fear on the foundational experiences of every frightened part of every personality. They all fear not getting what they want, and they all fear losing what they have. They all pursue external power. Pursuing external power is flight into the fantasy that manipulation and control can produce self-worth and joy. "Consumerism" is another word for that flight.

Consumers are the driving force of every economy. Even owners and directors of companies are consumers. The entire world is their source of consumable goods and services. They consume what they need to produce more consumable goods and services. They decide how much iron ore, wood pulp, computers, office furniture, machinery, information, and investment capital their companies will consume.

Consumers take. They make things inaccessible to others. Whatever it is, consumers use it up—food, water, electricity, gasoline, everything. They deplete, devour, defoliate, and destroy. They suck in what they can, and they use it for themselves. Consumers hoard because they never have enough. They compete with other consumers for the same goods and services. They do not trust the Universe to provide what they want to consume, need to consume, and are desperate to consume. Consumers are like hamsters on a treadmill.

Consumers take no responsibility for what they consume. They are part of a larger system (economy) that takes no responsibility for what it consumes. Consumers even see themselves and their relationships as consumables. They say, "I can't get enough of her." "She is a source of wisdom." "I want more of him."

Consumers buy houses, apartment leases, cars, clothes, and everything they can. Consumers are doubly important to an economy when they are also "workers" who produce the goods and services they consume. Individuals who have no "resources" to consume and do not work to produce consumable goods and services are useless to the economy. They sleep on cardboard, starve on sidewalks, and die under bridges.

Contributors add, augment, and make things accessible to others. They create, innovate, and share. The world is more and fuller because of them. They bring new and beneficial things into the Earth school. Their generosity and compassion, acts of selfless heroism, celebration of others, and constructive creativity bond them. They take the long view, the seventh-generation view. They plant crops for those who will harvest them in the future. They know the seed never sees the flower. Contributors trust the Universe to provide what is appropriate.

My adopted Lakota uncle once asked me, "Nephew, do you know that buffalo calves are always at the center of the herd where they are safe? The older buffaloes move to the outside of the herd where they give themselves to their brothers, the wolves." Then he reflected awhile and said, "I am like those old buffaloes now. My life is all for the people." He meant *all* people.

What is lost when a buffalo gives itself to wolves? Can the Universe be diminished or increased? Is it diminished or increased when fire consumes wood? Physicists say not. They say that fire transforms potential energy in wood into radiant energy (light) and thermal energy (heat). Is the Universe diminished or increased when an engine burns fuel? Physicists say that potential energy in fuel is transformed into kinetic energy (a vehicle moves) and chemical energy (carbon dioxide). Is carbon dioxide consumed by plants and trees? Biologists say that plants and trees transform carbon dioxide into oxygen. Do we consume oxygen when we breathe? Physiologists say we transform it into carbon dioxide (which feeds plants and trees) and forms of energy that cells in our bodies use to grow. In fact, they tell us that every living thing transforms (metabolizes) energy.

A great Hindu deity, Krishna, told Arjuna, the greatest warrior in the world, before the greatest battle of the world, "He who thinks he can kill, and he who thinks he can be killed, are both wrong." He could have been talking about energy (I think he was). Hindu scriptures say, "Fire cannot burn the soul. Swords cannot cut the soul." Does the death of a personality make the Universe smaller? Does the birth of a personality make it larger? The transformation of Energy, of Life, of Consciousness, of Love from one form to another has no beginning, and it has no end. Energy cannot be increased or decreased. (This the first law of thermodynamics.) The Universe cannot be diminished or increased.

"Consume" is an artifact of five-sensory perception, like "chance" and "random." "Contribution" is the reality of multisensory humans.

We contribute (transform) energy with each breath and motion. Every metabolic process uses and produces energy. Chemical energy becomes radiant energy, potential energy becomes kinetic energy, and more. This dynamic has always been a very big part of who we are and what we do.

We unconsciously transform fear (such as jealousy) into other forms of fear (such as anger and resentment) when we pursue external power. We consciously transform fear into love (such as gratitude, patience, and appreciation) when we create authentic power. We are powerful and creative, compassionate and loving spirits. We contribute with each intention of love and each intention of fear. We cannot stop contributing. In each moment we answer the question, consciously or unconsciously, "*What* shall I contribute?"

Contributing love does not increase Love in the Universe. Contributing fear does not decrease love in the Universe. The Universe *is* Love. Our contributions determine *our experiences* in the Earth school. When we contribute love, we experience creativity, meaning, and joy. When we contribute fear, our lives fill with pain and despair.

Now we are becoming *conscious* contributors.

We are taking our place in a new economy.

# 43

# The New Economy

The new economy is as different from the old economy as multi-sensory perception is from five-sensory perception, as authentic power is from external power, and as the new species that we are becoming is from the old species that we are leaving behind. It is as different as love is from fear. The old economy is wholly the product of five-sensory humanity and wholly unsuitable for multisensory humanity.

The old economy requires the pursuit of external power. The pursuit of external power now produces only violence and destruction. This roadblock prevents our evolution. The old economy is not the roadblock. Pursuit of external power is the roadblock. The old economy projects the five-sensory understanding of power as manipulation and control onto the domain of producing, distributing, and using goods and services.

The old economy reduces human activity to gain and loss, removes caring and connection from human experience, and divides participants into haves and have-nots, powerful and powerless, hungry and fed, safe and vulnerable. It is destructive in every way, its foundation is failing, and it is falling.

From the multisensory perspective, the entire structure of the old economy is an unconscious creation of frightened parts of personalities. It is a shockingly simple, utterly accurate portrayal, on the canvas of collective experience, of the dynamics within each of us that are the most painful and destructive.

The old economy is an unconscious confluence of self-interests. It is a terrifying real-time, real-life definition of "unsustainable." It is based on discord, competition, hoarding, and exploitation. It is of the personality.

We contribute to the old economy with each choice of fear and doubt. Everything that obstructs the evolution of multisensory humanity, the old economy is.

Blackberries grow everywhere in Oregon at the end of the summer. They grow by roads and streams. They grow in cities, in the country, and in backyards, including ours. They grow quickly, and they are tough and thorny. We joke here that one enormous blackberry root is growing beneath the entire state. That explains why pulling plants here and there, or tens of thousands of them, cannot eradicate blackberries. The state-size root would need to be pulled.

External power is the species-size root beneath all five-sensory social structures. Until we pull it, our social structures will continue to prevent the evolution of multisensory humans. The only place we can pull this root is in ourselves. This means that our social structures will not change until we change. From the multisensory perspective the world reflects our inner dynamics just as a mirror reflects appearances. The old economy is one of our reflections. It shows us the brutality of the parts of our personalities that exploit instead of contribute.

Competition, discord, hoarding, and exploitation are the stuff of the old economy. They *are* the old economy. In other words, the old economics is the academically approved playbook for frightened parts of personalities that make choices unconsciously from fear—that pursue external power.

Harmony, cooperation, sharing, and reverence for Life are the stuff of the new economy. Multisensory individuals create these things when they make responsible choices—choices that create consequences for which they are willing to assume responsibility. Said another way, the new economics cannot replace the old economics until the understanding of power as alignment of the personality with the soul replaces the understanding of power as the ability to manipulate and control. This is beginning to happen.

Millions of investors that previously sought only monetary gain now seek more. They impose "do no harm" criteria on their investments. For example, they refuse to invest in companies that manufacture weapons, produce unhealthy products, pollute the environment, or disdain humanity, such as companies that seek to control the necessities for life—water and food. This is called socially responsible investing. It is a mainstream investment activity. Students around the world are demanding that their universities divest stocks of socially irresponsible companies, and workers around the world are beginning to demand that their pension funds divest them too.

Now investors are moving beyond passive "do no harm" criteria to proactive "do good" criteria. They demand that companies whose stocks they buy contribute to the well-being of employees, host communities, host countries, and the environment. This is impact investing. It is becoming mainstream. In other words, millions of investors around the world, once unconsciously united in greed, are consciously uniting in support of Life.

A new economy is emerging.

Not only trees make a forest. Each tree is home to many species of insects and small animals. They burrow into its bark and beneath its roots. Small birds eat the insects and large birds eat the small birds. The contributions of a tree do not end when it falls. New contributions begin and continue as the tree decays (transforms) and the new forms of energy that the transformation produces contribute to yet more species of animals and insects and microscopic organisms.

The birth, growth, and death of forests are unceasing. Fires create space for new trees. Wetlands become meadows, meadows become forests, and the ecosystem—the marvelous economy in which birth, life, and death intermingle, mutually contribute, and mutually receive—continues, benefiting all parts and receiving the benefit of all parts.

The new economy is also an ecosystem. It reflects the appropriateness that is everywhere apparent to multisensory perception. When each human experience is a karmic necessity (it is), what is scarce? (Nothing.) What is abundant? (Nothing.) What is appropriate? (Everything.) We build the new economy with each of choice of love and trust.

The new economy is a projection of power as authentic onto the domain of giving and receiving gifts with the living Earth and among ourselves. It is a beautifully simple, always accurate, continuously created portrayal, on the canvas of collective experience, of the most healthy and joyful dynamics within each of us.

To five-sensory humans an economy based on the values of the soul is an impossible ideal. To multisensory humans the old economy is the impossible ideal. It creates more and more violence and destruction as it disintegrates, preventing our evolution, and threatening our survival. It embodies external power while our evolution now requires authentic power. That is why none of our social structures, including the old economy, have a future.

A new wind is blowing, and it is blowing from a new direction.

# 44

# The New Intention of Business

T he economy is one altar in the Grand Temple of External Power. Business is another. The two stand side by side, and worshippers at one easily and often worship at the other. The economy is analogous to an ocean of external power. Businesses are analogous to fishing vessels that ply the ocean of external power.

Some of the vessels are small, and they fish with small nets. Others are enormous, and they drag nets miles-long over the ocean floor. This destroys almost every living thing. Still others are part warship, and they battle with one another whenever possible. The vessels do not drag nets to catch fish. They drag them to make profit. Fish are unimportant to them, except for the role they play in making profit. The more fish the vessels catch, the more profit they make. Profit is so important to them that they destroy myriad forms of aquatic life to achieve it. Yet the captains of the trawlers (executives of the businesses), the crews on the trawlers (employees of the businesses), and the owners of the trawlers (stockholders) are not deterred.

The fish in the ocean, in this analogy, are customers and investors. They pursue external power also. Customers look for deals. Investors search for undervalued stocks, place bets against the well-being of other investors, flock to funds and companies that help them profit, and desert them as quickly when they do not. Just as customers seek bargains and buy them wherever they can, investors have no loyalty except to their own benefit. All the fish in this ocean fish!

For example, vessels on this ocean do not cast nets over empty water, and they do not hunt for fish. A huge industry attracts fish to them. This is the advertising industry. The advertising industry is not interested in the well-being of vessels. It is interested in profit. It is fishing also. Advertising businesses are customers of other businesses, such as radio and television stations, newspapers, internet providers, graphic designers, and on and on. Each of these businesses also is interested solely in profit and, in turn, is a customer of other businesses that are interested solely in profit. *Everything* in the ocean of external power is interested solely in profit. This is the nature of the ocean of external power.

Profit is excess. It is more money than a business needs to pay its expenses, in other words, more than it needs to pay for everything it owes to anyone. It is more than it needs to pay employees, other businesses that sell to it, investors every three months to keep them investing, and in the case of multinational corporations, executive salaries and benefits that are *hundreds* of times greater than other employees receive. Everything left over after all of that is profit! Multinational corporations usually have *a lot* left over. What do they do with their profit? They use it to make more profit. They can never get enough.

Does this sound familiar? Frightened parts of our personalities relentlessly require more—admiration, recognition, appreciation, money. The need for more is intense because the pain of powerlessness beneath it is intense. Frightened parts of our personalities pursue external power to mask that pain. Multinational corporations do not experience the pain of powerlessness because they cannot experience anything. They are not personalities. They are reflections of our destructive interior dynamics.

The frightened parts of our personalities contain no flicker of compassion or trace of wisdom. Therefore, there is no flicker of compassion or trace of wisdom in multinational corporations. Their goals hollow and destructive, their pursuit of profit toxic, their presence despised and feared, they produce the same predatory and combative activities as our own pursuits of external power. Their avaricious executives and investors are our proxy actors. They do not produce these ruthless and rapacious monstrosities. *We* are the origin of them. The enormity of their destructive intention and savagery of their pursuit of external power originate in *us*.

Multinational corporations reflect all that is callous, destructive, and brutal *in us*. We cannot change these reflections without changing ourselves. Mirror on the wall, who is the Most Loving of All? Who is the Cruelest? Which are you?

Ralph Waldo Emerson described a tipping point in this way:

> Each man takes care that his neighbor shall not cheat him. But a day
> comes when he begins to care that he does not cheat his neighbor.
> Then ... he has changed his market-cart into a chariot of the sun.

We are at a tipping point, and we are tipping toward the sun. Hundreds of millions of multisensory humans create authentic power instead of pursue external power. New businesses explore a new frontier where the need for profit meets the requirements of the heart. The merger of spiritual partnership and commerce calls to us. The compass by which businesses set their course is acting strangely. It no longer points toward profit, the old true north. New businesses follow a different polestar. They steer toward a different destination. They participate in a dynamic of serving others that is made possible by profits instead of the obsolete dynamic that is motivated by profits that are generated by serving others. Beyond this dynamic lies the potential of the newest of all business intentions. It is the intention of pure service, just as the oldest of all business intentions is pure profit.

New businesses reverse the direction that business energy flows! They transform taking into giving. They seek connections instead of customers. They contribute to life instead of exploit it. They change the bottom line of business to love from fear!

New businesses are turning business upside down, and for the first time we see that is the way it needs to be. We see for the first time that is the way *we* need to be—that our evolution now requires contribution instead of exploitation, connection instead of consumption, and constructive cocreation in a larger domain of experience than we have been able to imagine.

The new social structure of business is emerging, and we are part of it. Who else could be?

# 45

# Multisensory Governance

E very government, by any name, was created by five-sensory humans evolving by surviving, and surviving by pursuing external power. In other words, all governments are based on external power, no matter where they originated, what they are called, how they are structured, or what they profess. Therefore, all governments are now unstable, unworkable, and destructive.

We are in new territory. Our governments are failing, and they cannot be fixed because they are not broken. They are obsolete, and they cannot be modernized. Previously they supported the evolution of five-sensory humans. Now they prevent the evolution of multisensory humans.

Five-sensory forms of government create and enforce rules that govern collectives, for example, rules that prohibit marrying outside a tribe or inside a clan. Parliamentary democracies and councils of elders are both five-sensory forms of government. The origin of a five-sensory government may be a warlord or an absolute monarch (originally the same). Control flows from the top (warlord or monarch) to the bottom (everyone else). In most such governments resistance ensures prison, torture, and death. The monarchs of medieval Europe, the Russian czars, Japanese and Chinese emperors, and the governments of Saudi Arabia, Russia, and China are a few examples.

In this chapter and the next the government of the United States illustrates the dead-end relationship between a five-sensory government and the evolution of multisensory humans, but this relationship is the same for all five-sensory governments and all multisensory humans.

Some scholars consider cathedrals our greatest collective creations.

Some scientists say space exploration is our greatest. I believe the greatest of all collective creations is our advanced forms of five-sensory governance.

Athens, a Greek city-state (500 BC), was probably the first democracy. The Athenian elite—educated, property-owning males—were its only citizens. Women and slaves were not. The men chose their government by lottery and participated in it. Women and slaves did not. The American democracy two thousand three hundred years later was essentially the same (except for the lottery). The Colonial elite—educated, property-owning (white) males—were its only citizens. Women and slaves were not.

The history connecting these democracies is violent. For example, in 1215 English thugs (barons) warring with a boss thug (king) reached an agreement that was brokered by the thuggish Catholic Church. Thuggery means brute force, the naked pursuit of external power. The thug king gave the thug barons some of the things they wanted. Then all involved discarded this agreement and returned to thuggery, but in the process a new thing had happened. The thug king agreed to limit his activities! This had never occurred before. Thug kings (and thug queens) had claimed to rule by "Divine Authority," which meant their decisions were the will of God.

The agreement between these thug barons and this thug king became known as the Magna Carta. (*Carta* means "charter." A charter is a grant of rights.) The Magna Carta ("Great Charter") was a failed attempt to end a conflict without violence, but it contained the kernel of an idea that eventually became known as the "Rule of Law." Advanced forms of five-sensory government today are designed to end conflicts for external power without violence, specifically, they are designed to transfer external power without violence.

The American government is one of them. The American Founding Fathers (there were no Founding Mothers) created constitutional representative democracy to harness conflicting pursuits of external power for the common good. They incorporated the best ideas about governance they could find from prior and contemporary colleagues.

John Adams venerated Cicero (Roman, 106–43 BC), who championed the republic. Cicero also influenced Thomas Jefferson, who drafted the Declaration of Independence. Thomas Hobbs (English, 1588–1679) advocated equality among certain men (but not equality with women). He proposed "representative" political power (based on consent of the governed) as the only legitimate political power. John Locke (English, 1632–1704) advocated separating governmental powers and declared revolution to be a right—and, in certain cases, an obligation—profoundly influencing the American Revolution, the Declaration of Independence, and the Constitution of the United States. Montesquieu (French, 1689–1755) described a separation of governmental power among a legislature, an executive, and a judiciary, which, together, are the fundamental "checks and balances" of the American government. In fact, the American Founding Fathers cited Montesquieu more than any source except the Bible.

The government these men created, remarkable as it has been, is now doomed for the same reason the house extending over the void is doomed—its foundation is gone. There is no longer a common good to the pursuit of external power. There is no good of any kind to the pursuit of external power. Like the house, it will fall, along with all other forms of five-sensory government.

Democracies—the highest mountains in the range of five-sensory governance—have always been caldrons of conceit, deceit, treachery, and mean-spiritedness, in other words, pursuits of external power. Nonetheless, their advantages were great. Losers of political wars, even the most brutal, could regroup, plan again, and attack in greater force the next election (instead of being killed). Winners entrenched, grew stronger, and attacked again with advantage (as incumbents) in the next election.

All of this is now counterproductive to the evolution of multisensory humans.

No matter how many five-sensory governments we create or destroy, how intelligent, sensitive, refined, and caring or how vile, venomous, crude, and violent are the individuals we elect to them, the five-sensory social structure of governance now leads only to violence and destruction.

This circumstance is permanent. The great American, French, Russian, and Haitian revolutions no longer show us a way forward. Revolutions only turn the wheel. They transfer external power from one set of hands to another, from one set of values to another. Evolution replaces the wheel with previously unimaginable forms and functions.

We are in an Evolution, not a revolution.

# 46

# Multisensory Governance—
# The First Glimpses

The five-sensory social structure of governance is built upon and expresses external power. External power now produces only violence and destruction. This is the general framework with which to approach the changing social structure of governance.

The relationship between those who are governed and those who govern could be looked at as one of unity, that is, there can be no governed without those who govern, and there can be no governing without those who are governed. In other words, there are always those who are governed and those who govern. These are the divisions that are now melting, so to speak—the divisions between "I" and "other," between "other" and "I." These divisions are based upon and anchored in five-sensory perception.

From the impersonal perspective of the soul, which means from the perspective of a multisensory human, those who are governed and those who govern are not separately existing individuals or even entities. *Individual*, as five-sensory humans understand this term, means a personality. As multisensory humans understand it, *individual* means "personality plus soul." When soul enters the picture, the picture changes radically and dramatically.

Each soul has myriad personalities, and from the perspective of the soul, all of its personalities and all of the interactions of its personalities exist simultaneously. This cannot be grasped or appreciated by the intellect, and there is no indication of it to the five senses. Yet as the human species becomes multisensory, this reality becomes more evident. A

victim in one incarnation becomes a villain in another. Roles are reversed. Variations of roles are experimented with. All of this experience
is accumulated, so to speak, in the soul.

Where in this larger picture does the understanding of "governed"
and "governing" appear? It is transient. It is virtually ephemeral, although
it does not feel that way, and it is not experienced that way by a personality in the Earth school. Therefore, when we ask "What is the alternative
to the five-sensory social structure of governance?" the correct answer,
the accurate answer and the overall perspective, is "an emerging social
structure of governance that is built upon the perceptions and values of
the soul rather than the perceptions and values of the personality." Yet
the questions remain, "What does that mean to individuals?" and "What
can individuals do to contribute to the emergence of a multisensory
social structure of governance based upon the values and energy and
intentions of the soul?" Again, the overall answer is "create authentic
power." There is no other way to contribute to the emergence of the
social structures that the personalities of your soul experience and that
multisensory personalities are creating as they create authentic power.

From a five-sensory perspective, however, this answer is unsatisfac-
tory, for the five-sensory perspective is one of changing the physical
world in order to find relief from pain, from insecurity, anxiety, self-
loathing, lack of value, and continual wanting and not having. Therefore,
from a five-sensory perspective, the answer is "*do* something." Something
must be done, and the individual must do it or the collective must do it.
This is the orientation upon which the existing social structure of governance and, indeed, all five-sensory social structures, are built. Therefore,
the first step in contributing to the emergence of a multisensory social
structure of governance that is based upon the values, energy, and intentions of the soul is to release the five-sensory imperative of doing something, of changing the world.

The world is not changed by this imperative. Your experiences of
the world are changed. Your karmic obligations are not changed. They
continue to produce experiences, and those experiences continue to give
you opportunities to choose more wisely and more compassionately.
The frightened parts of a personality, we might say, are the governing

aspects of that personality. They demand of the personality what they feel is necessary for the personality to do, to produce. As you challenge the frightened parts of your personality, you challenge the very division upon which the five-sensory construct of governance—those governed and those governing—is built.

Instead of attempting to change those who govern in the external world or those who are governed in the external world, you change in yourself what is governing and what is governed, yet within yourself that distinction exists only so long as frightened parts of your personality exist and continue to exert control. As the frightened parts of your personality are challenged, they lose the control that they are seeking, and as they are challenged, loving parts of your personality are cultivated. When you challenge a frightened part of your personality that judges, for example, you cultivate a loving part that accepts. The loving parts of your personality do not seek to control. They seek to contribute, and they do.

Five sensory personalities say to themselves, "What good can my contributions do when billions of other individuals in the Earth school are contributing differently than I contribute?" The intellect poses this question, and it seeks the answer in the domain of the five senses. In the domain of multisensory perception, the answer is apparent. The world, including human social structures—and in that group the social structure of governance—is a mirror, a projection, a way of understanding oneself. As you attempt to change the reflection, it does not change except into another reflection, a reflection again of one who is attempting to change the reflection, which means the external world. Yet as you turn your focus inward and change yourself, that changes the reflection in a significant way. It removes from the reflection the pursuit of external power.

In other words, a social structure is an experience in the macro. Yet the macro cannot exist without the micro. The only place that change is possible is in the micro, for the macro reflects the micro, and it is here that the intellect collapses, so to speak, with a great deal of objection.

The five-sensory social structure of governance is based upon external power and who has it. The social structure of governance in which constitutional representative democracy emerged still reflects this circumstance unchanged. Those with the most votes have the most external power. Those with the most influence have the most external power. There is no way to change that by pursuing influence and external power.

This question, in other words, "What can I contribute to an emerging social structure of governance?" goes to the heart of multisensory perception and the higher order logic and understanding of the heart. It puts individuals who are in a state of transition, such as you, in a challenging position, for the frightened parts of their personalities demand that something be done and dismiss as groundless or ridiculous the idea that internal transformation can bring about external transformation. Yet the higher order logic and understanding of the heart sees this clearly, including attempts to bypass this perception, for example, by attempting to change oneself into a better person, so to speak, in order to create a better world. This, again, is a five-sensory perception of the world that separates self and other, self and world, inside and outside. There are no distinctions between these two from the impersonal perspective of the soul.

This challenging circumstance arises because for the first time the entire human species is transforming from one that is limited to the perceptions of the five senses, and that understands power as the ability to manipulate and control, into a species that is multisensory and sees power, and experiences power, as the alignment of the personality with the soul, and sees also the emerging multisensory social structure of governance. Who governs? Who is governed? It is here that a responsible choice is inevitable, is inescapable. Yet from that perspective, you govern, and there is nothing to govern.

If this is the case, then what would happen to social injustice, inequity, racism, bigotry, authoritarianism, brutality? These are all also reflections of internal dynamics, and all of those internal dynamics exist in you, in each individual. From the five-sensory perspective, they are curses or obstacles. From the multisensory perspective, they are signs, or indications, of what needs to be changed. Yet what needs to be changed needs to be changed in you.

These experiences, these insights, colliding as they do with the demands of the intellect and the limitations of the five senses, are themselves the first glimpses of the emerging multisensory social structure of governance.

# 47

# Health from a Deeper Place

"Health care" has four parts—insurance companies, pharmaceutical manufacturers, hospitals, and physicians. Tensions within and between these parts have produced a grotesque consequence in the United States: a health-care system that is more interested in its own health than the health of the patients in it.

Insurance companies, as we discussed, deny treatment to dying customers in order to increase profits for executives and stockholders. The dying customers die.

American hospitals prioritize getting paid. Emergency room patients plead for doctors while employees type names, addresses, and insurance policy numbers into databases.

Pharmaceutical manufacturers charge the most that Adam Smith's invisible hand permits for their drugs, including those that save lives when administered or end them when withheld. When customers cannot pay, they withhold, and the customers die.

Physicians are pawns in this system or entrepreneurs in alliance with insurance companies, pharmaceutical manufacturers, and hospitals.

This is the starkly brutal American "health care." Millions of individuals must choose each month, each week, or each day between rent, food, heat, and medicine. (Which would you choose?)

Whether a health-care system is private, nationalized, or a combination, the five-sensory social structure of health care in which it functions is built on external power. The care that it provides is built on external power.

Five-sensory medicine manipulates and controls bodies at the molecular level (pharmaceuticals) and at the level of organs (surgery). It defines health as physical health and identifies every physical dysfunction as the effect of a physical cause. It asserts that every lack of health is a lack of physical health. From the five-sensory perspective no other kind of health is possible, just as no other kind of power than the ability to manipulate and control is possible.

Mental health, emotional health, psychological health, and even "spiritual health" are reduced to physical causes and physical effects. No cause of disease is deeper than physical, and no cure is deeper than physical. Health before conception and after death are inconceivable. In the domain of the five senses, the brain is the birth place and death place of every experience. All thoughts, emotions, insights, and revelations lead to the brain and dead-end there. Every human experience—transcendence, ecstasy, inspiration—is a by-product of organic chemistry. The death of the brain is the death of consciousness.

Five-sensory physicians dissect corpses in order to understand life, but they cannot understand Life that way. They do not understand their own lives—their emotions and intentions and energies of love and fear within themselves and how they choose between them. They have no thoughts of spiritual growth, supporting others in spiritual growth, or receiving the support of others in growing spiritually. They cannot distinguish between mortal personalities and immortal souls. Therefore, they are ignorant of the relationships between them.

They do not recognize the birth of a personality as the voluntary entrance of a soul into the Earth school, or its death as the return of a soul to nonphysical reality at a time of its choosing. They do not recognize the difference between a cure—manipulation of a physical process—and a healing—movement of consciousness into love. They seek the fountain of youth as kings and conquistadors before them, yet they do not recognize the cause of aging around them and within them—negativity.

Longer lives, better physical health, and less pain are the great gifts of their efforts, but more is now required to create and sustain health, and far greater gifts now offer themselves. Health comes from a deeper place. The origins of physical health and physical illness are not physical. Five-sensory individuals consider acute physical dysfunctions—such as heart attacks—to be sudden emergencies. They rush to emergency rooms with lights flashing and sirens wailing. From the multisensory perspective, five-sensory "emergencies" develop over lifetimes. *Every physical dysfunction is an emergency by the time it appears in the Earth school.* Only the creation of authentic power is long-term preventative health care.

The multisensory social structure of health care supports and reflects the wholesome, constructive consequences of love. It rests upon conscious choices. It identifies the effects of nonphysical causes (intentions) upon physical phenomena (such as diseases and injuries) and nonphysical phenomena (such as emotional experiences). It recognizes physical health and emotional ease as the same (love) and lack of physical health and emotional dis-ease as the same (fear). It recognizes the compassion and wisdom that shape lives into experiences of humbleness, clarity, forgiveness, and Love, and the lack of compassion and wisdom that shapes them into experiences of arrogance, ignorance, hatred, and fear.

The inseparability of health and authentic power is the foundation of the multisensory social structure of health care. Relationships between personalities, souls, and health are its content. It requires self-responsibility. It understands health as love (the absence of fear) and illness as fear (the absence of love).

Cocreative patient-physician relationships, multibillion-dollar supplement and vitamin markets, and spiritual partners supporting one another in creating health are glimpses of the multisensory social structure of health care that is emerging around us. It serves the stabilized, ongoing, conscious experience of Love and nothing else.

How strong is your conviction that a social structure of health care that serves the stabilized, ongoing, conscious experience of Love is impossible?

How strong is your conviction that it is inevitable?

# 48

# The Coronavirus Miracle—Why?

As I write this in spring of 2020, this is where we are, and this is what I see. The corona virus is symbolic, as is everything in the Earth school, but the coronavirus is an experience in the Earth school that is touching virtually everyone on the Earth at the same time. Therefore it is worth learning from.

Five-sensory humans are learning the physical aspects of a coronavirus infection and how to contain it. Multisensory humans can learn from the coronavirus in ways that five-sensory humans cannot. We can look at our experiences of it. We can use our emotional awareness and our responsible choices to challenge the fears that it is activating in us, and while those fears are active, we can respond from healthy, loving parts of our personalities. We can apply this to what we say and what we do. We can look at our intentions in all that we say and all that we do.

For example, do you keep yourself separate from others because you fear being close to them and becoming infected? Or do you keep yourself distant from others because you care for them, your love reaches out to them, and you intend to protect them from infection? When you speak or act are you speaking from fear and lending agreement to the fear of others? Or are you speaking from a loving part of your personality and modeling for others an alternative way of speaking and acting and interacting during these times? That is what the coronavirus can teach you, and it is also teaching others at the same time, if they are willing to learn.

It is fear in the human species that has produced the coronavirus. All of the behaviors necessary to contain it are graphic and unmistakable expressions of the behavior of fear—separation, distance, physically taking care of yourself alone. Yet these same behaviors can be taken in love. Looking at the behaviors that are necessary to limit the spread of the coronavirus, and seeing that without the intention of love behind them, they perfectly express the intentions of fear, allows you to focus on and recognize within yourself the difference between love and fear, and choose love. This is the difference that you can make in your contribution to the eradication of the coronavirus.

The only way to eradicate this virus and all other expressions of fear in the human species is for the human species to use its emerging multisensory perception and understanding of power as authentic to create with love instead of with fear. What would a world be like that is created with love instead of with fear, that is created consciously with the parts of your personality that are aligned with your soul instead of with the parts of your personality that you incarnated to experience and move beyond the control of? It would be a world of harmony, of cooperation, of sharing, and of reverence for life. All these are quite different from fear, and the experiences of all these are quite different because they are all quite different from the experiences of fear.

Keep your distance from others, but make it a social distance. When it is from fear it is not a social distance. It is a selfish distance. Keep yourself clean. Wash your hands frequently. Look at these acts symbolically as well. Imagine that clean means free of fear. Imagine that washing your hands means putting down all those activities and thoughts of fear, sanctifying your hands, making them instruments of love.

The coronavirus pandemic is a powerful learning opportunity. What will you learn from it? Will you learn to indulge further your fears, to sink deeper into their limitations and their pain until you sink all the way to the primal experience of the pain of powerlessness and it's unbearable, excruciating pain? Or will you use your experience of the coronavirus to begin to lift yourself above the magnetic fields of fear in yourself and around yourself, which are ultimately the same, and to challenge them by creating with love, acting with love, thinking with love, giving your life to love?

That is the alignment of your personality with your soul. It requires creating authentic power. Use all that you are experiencing in this time of the coronavirus to create authentic power. Enjoy yourself. Does that sound shocking, that you can enjoy yourself? Ask yourself the origin of that thought—the inappropriateness of joy at any time in your life, even while others are in fear. That thought itself comes from fear in you. That thought itself contributes to the coronavirus, as does all thought and energy of fear contribute to the manifestation of fear and the products of fear in the Earth school.

Doing these things requires becoming a spiritual person. It requires becoming a spiritual person in a world that does not yet recognize spirit, yet you recognize spirit, and you are part of the world. Allow your presence in the Earth school to be a part of an emerging world that not only recognizes spirit, but that is built upon spirit and the intentions of the soul, that creates individuals of humbleness, clarity, forgiveness, and love instead of individuals of arrogance, self-loathing individuals whose perceptions are contaminated continually with fear, individuals who do not forget and do not forgive, individuals who strive to use other individuals, individuals who exploit instead of revere, individuals who take instead of contribute, individuals who do not value Life except from the perspective of fear.

The transformation of human consciousness from five-sensory perception, and the understanding of power as external, to multisensory perception, and the understanding of power as alignment of the personality with the soul, enables this understanding. This understanding was not available in times of earlier widespread infections. It was not available in the time of the bubonic plague. It was not available in the time of smallpox. It was not available in the time of polio. All those were manifestations of fear in the Earth school. It does exist now, and your awareness and the new human consciousness can be brought to bear upon this manifestation of fear in the Earth school. That is what it is here for.

There has always been the symbolic power and substance of all manifestations of fear in the Earth school. Yet five-sensory humans are blind to them, and so five-sensory history is a chronicle of warfare, of suffering, of disease. Now we are in the process of creating a new history, an ourstory of love.

The time of the coronavirus is a good time to begin this process.

# 49

# The Coronavirus Miracle—
# The Pandemic

The coronavirus is raging around me. Fear of it, talk of it, and the reality of it are everywhere. Millions of jobs are disappearing daily, the world economy is teetering, and hospitals from Rome to Shanghai to New York City are understaffed, unequipped, and impotent as tsunami after tsunami of individuals infected with the coronavirus sweep over them. Many have died. Many are dying. The most difficult circumstances are yet to come in economically undeveloped countries and collectives. Yet profoundly positive effects of the coronavirus are already visible.

The coronavirus is giving us opportunities to discover how we have been creating and how we can create differently if we choose. Every painful emotion gives us this opportunity, but the coronavirus is different. One generation after the birth of the new consciousness, the coronavirus is offering *every* human from *every* culture, religion, ethnic group, and economic circumstance *at the same time* and *in the same context* opportunities to become aware and responsible or implode under the fear of the collective. The potential to implode is great when so many individuals fear as they fear now. So also is the potential to love.

From the perspective of the new consciousness, the coronavirus pandemic is a great beginning and a great ending, a great gain and a necessary loss. It can be seen as the beginning of an aware life and the end of a complacent life, the beginning of gratitude and the end of superficial interactions, the beginning of deep feeling, insight, appreciation, and love, and the end of indifference.

In other words, the coronavirus pandemic can be perceived as the biggest emergence of love into the awareness of the human species ever seen, and it can be seen as a disaster of hundreds of millions of individuals sinking into fear of one another and the future. How we see it depends upon how we choose to see it. If we choose unconsciously, we see it through the filter of our fears, with contraction, competition, disinterest, and apathy, rather than using our experiences to learn about ourselves and apply what we learn to create authentic power. These perceptions— loving and frightened—teach us, each in our own way, what we need to learn about ourselves to create joy, meaning, and love in our lives.

I see the coronavirus as love raging. When you open to the possibility that the coronavirus is raging love, you open to the possibility that everything, every experience, every circumstance in the Earth school, is love. A new reality becomes visible, faintly at first and then more substantially: The Earth school exists to support you in aligning your personality with your soul—with harmony, cooperation, sharing, and reverence for life.

It is possible to misinterpret the coronavirus because the behaviors that are necessary to contain it mirror behaviors of fear. These are isolation, separation, and distance. Yet the coronavirus is not merely a virus. It is an unprecedented all-encompassing species-wide experience that offers *every* human *simultaneously* the opportunity to *choose love* while experiencing fear. This is the ongoing, never-ending offer of the Earth school, but this version of it is coming to all of us at the same time in the same clothing.

The coronavirus is not as lethal as smallpox or the bubonic plague (except to those who die of it), but it kills. It cannot be trifled with. Individuals who feel healthy, vital, and creative can be infected without suspecting it, and they unknowingly infect others, who also unknowingly infect others, and so on. In other words, the coronavirus shows each of us that the well-being of others and our well-being are not different.

In this time of fire and hope hundreds of millions of humans are beginning to recognize that "we are one" is more than a slogan. The five-sensory social structure of health care is blind to this, yet it is the essence of health. The five-sensory social structure of health care conceives the coronavirus as a consequence of physical circumstances in the same way that it conceives all health and illness as consequences of physical circumstances. It does not recognize that all experiences in the Earth school, including the coronavirus, have value and serve a purpose. That purpose is to show us on the screen of our collective experiences the behaviors of fear, and that the only remedy for fear is love. In other words, the purpose of the Earth school is to teach us to love.

The emerging multisensory social structure of health care explores every physical dysfunction and its remedy in this new context—the cause of every physical and nonphysical dysfunction is fear, and the remedy for it is love. Yet love is not a substance that can be bottled, labeled, and prescribed, or needs to be, for it is given freely, consciously, by all who experience love in themselves. In other words, it is given by individuals who are challenging the frightened parts of their personalities by reaching for the loving parts of their personalities and acting from them instead. Those are individuals who are creating authentic power.

The magnetic field of fear on the Earth is immense as I write. All individuals feel it. That fear exists in themselves, and they are seeing it projected onto the screen of their collective experiences. The coronavirus pandemic provides us opportunities to project care, compassion, patience, sensitivity, and love upon the screen of our collective experiences. It shows us the only way we are now able to evolve. Human evolution now requires proactive kindness, proactive caring, proactive contribution, especially when frightened parts of our personalities are active—when we feel inadequate, unworthy, superior, inferior, righteous, angry, or any other form of fear. It requires the conscious intention of love and actions that express it. Each action that expresses love is great, no matter how small it appears—a phone call, a text, an email, a smile at a neighbor, or a wave from a window.

The coronavirus pandemic is different from all previous global experiences in a fundamental way. It is different from the world wars, different from the plagues that decimated our species, and different from our countless experiences of deprivation, suffering, and starvation. All these were viewed by five-sensory humans as physical circumstances that were created by physical circumstances. Multisensory humans see the coronavirus as a spiritual circumstance that is created by spiritual circumstances.

They see everything as spiritual.

# 50

# The Coronavirus Miracle—
# The Protest

Protests in every American city, protests in European cities, protests in Asian cities—protests around the world—fill headlines. Three months after the coronavirus broke upon us hundreds of thousands of individuals are marching in protest, day after day, night after night, leaving the safety of their homes in the midst of a global pandemic to make a statement. Within weeks the protests have spread to *two thousand* American cities and towns and far beyond them to many countries and most continents. They are protesting brutality.

Five-sensory humans moved from one era of turbulence to another, from massacres to starvation to warfare to domination to destruction on ever-more massive scales. This turbulence is different. It is purposeful, and many individuals sense it as purposeful. The pandemic gave individuals around the world a mandated pause in their lives, away from activities they used to obscure their painful emotions and the frightened parts of their personalities that generate them. It disrupted established patterns of distraction, familiar refuges of mindlessness—going to work, returning from work, taking children to playdates, shopping, discussions at the office, in the classroom, the game of cards, the game of ball, the game of chess, the game of finance, the game of fashion, walking through the park, walking through the countryside, traveling, and vacations that distract from distractions. All these and more were broken by the coronavirus and in many cases shattered.

It is a result of this that the public, unapologetic murder of a defenseless black man by a white policeman in an American city ignited a global protest. Violence of this type is not new to Americans. It is writ large in American history, from Colonial slaveholders to the slaughter of Native Americans by the United States Cavalry to the hideous hanging of black people by countless white people. There were no protests then. Why is there a global protest now?

There is a global protest now because our species has entered a new consciousness. We were a five-sensory species then that evolved by surviving, and survived by pursuing external power. Now we are a multi-sensory species that evolves by growing spiritually and grows spiritually by creating authentic power. The difference is beyond measure. It is the difference between love and fear. It is the difference between a fear-based species and a love-based species. We were the fear-based species. Now we are becoming the love-based species. That requires choices of love instead of fear, and multisensory humans are making them. Their protest is peaceful and purposeful. They model peace and purpose consciously. All of this is happening now, and individuals have found it important enough to risk their health and their lives for. "I brought my children to see this," said one father. "I want them to be part of history in the making."

The protest began against police brutality because that brutality was the most evident. Then millions of white Americans, most for the first time, recognized the reality of systemic racism—the gruesomeness of it, the horror of it, the weight of it on their Afro-American brothers and sisters—and the protest expanded to include systemic racism. Then it expanded again to include the genocide of Native Americans by white invaders (settlers), and more Americans glimpsed, also for the first time, the American caste system. Like slabs of ice and snow fracturing under stress, breaking loose, and sliding down a mountain, huge slabs of ignorance and unconscious slumber began to break loose and move. Individuals around the world joined this movement, and a great avalanche was in motion. It still is.

I have seen avalanches. They break tall trees like twigs, bury everything beneath snow and ice, and permanently change the terrain around them. Nothing is left as it was before. We are already seeing some of the new terrain—individuals facing violence without becoming violent;

protesters locking arms to protect a policeman separated from colleagues; protesters guarding stores against looters; National Guardsmen
atop buildings waving to protesters below; and the world responding to
these soul-to-soul connections with fullness of heart as they dissolve all
differences.

This avalanche is global. The entire mountain is moving. Protesters
are marching in Paris, Karachi, and Tokyo. They are seeing the brutality
of the old consciousness for what it is—the pursuit of external power.
They say to one another, "We are all in this together." We have always
been, and now are we waking to it. These individuals intend to replace
obsolete, destructive systems built on external power with new, constructive systems built on the intentions of the soul. They are walking the path
that Gandhi, King, Jesus, and countless saints, known and unknown,
walked before them.

We can view all of this in terms of authentic power, in terms of what
these circumstances look like in our lives and our experiences as humankind evolves rapidly into multisensory perception and the recognition
that external power now produces only violence and destruction. The
choice between love and fear has always been graphic, but now more
individuals are aware of that. As they are brutalized by police and neighbors who disagree with them, will they react in fear or will they respond
in love? There are countless examples of police brutality without reason
or reservation. There are also examples without number of loving connections, loving support, and different ways to interact.

A supportiveness is emerging in individuals who once separated
themselves from others with different experiences, appearances, and
beliefs and within groups that were previously divided, among them
ethnic groups. A thirst has emerged in white students in the Earth school
to understand what black students in the Earth school experience in the
United States and minorities everywhere have experienced at all times.
The pursuit of external power *is* brutality. They cannot escape this brutality by becoming brutal themselves. If they permit their experiences of
brutality to brutalize themselves, they step into a pit of pain that deepens
continually. Yet in contrast to that are emerging experiences of connection, oneness, and the desire to be together and to assist one another, all

in the context of individuals who are forced to be apart for the well-being of one another.

This is a rich time. It is a time to be aware of the events around you and your experiences of them from the perspective of the evolution of our species, from the perspective of the new context in which *everything* is now occurring—the transformation of human consciousness itself.

# The Coronavirus Miracle—
# The Symbol

The coronavirus will be seen as a turning point in human behavior and evolution. The initial turning point, the emergence of multisensory perception and the understanding of power as alignment of the personality with the soul, went virtually unnoticed. This turning point is unmistakable and will not be forgotten. The pandemic and electronic communication have made it part of every human on the Earth, from those remote from the suffering and dying to those who are dying and suffering. It is an invitation from the Universe to grow spiritually. It is an invitation that we can refuse, but not one that will disappear.

The coronavirus offers us opportunities to see our individual experiences and our collective experiences from the expanded perception of the new consciousness. Five-sensory humans attempt to see them from the limited perception of the old consciousness, but the magnitude of the coronavirus, the timing of it, the omnipresence of it, the energy of it, are much larger than the five senses can perceive and the intellect can conceive, deduce, or conclude. It is beyond the range and the limitations of five-sensory humans, yet many individuals in the Earth school are five sensory. Therefore, this event, which is quite large in relationship to all other contemporary human events, is creating turmoil. This turmoil is providing learning opportunities for all involved.

This event is as large and impactful as the Ice Ages or the extinction of species that eliminated dinosaurs from the Earth. It affects all humans, but it affects them in ways that are not as final as Ice Ages and species extinctions. A major species extinction is in process at this moment. However, that alone is not sufficient to awaken individuals in whom multisensory perception has emerged to the relationship of the coronavirus and all that it brings to the evolution of the human species. The coronavirus does this with inclusivity that matches the largest global events of human past, but without the immediate threat to the survival of the human species. Multisensory individuals are beginning to sense this, the magnitude of it. It is not something that comes and goes quickly.

Five-sensory humans are striving for a five-sensory remedy, and they will create one that will profit its creators more than most organizations and individuals in the history of humanity have profited from a single endeavor. Yet all of that is and will be the pursuit of external power. There is no vaccine for fear. A deeper remedy for this circumstance is the creation of authentic power, and that deeper remedy is the only remedy. That is the message the coronavirus pandemic presents us gently. The coronavirus itself is not gentle. It has infected millions of individuals, and many of them are suffering greatly. It has killed a great many individuals. Yet most of the individuals on the Earth are uninfected. Therefore, there is learning, but learning that is not deadly to the entire species of humankind.

As individuals away from other individuals have time to reflect, even if they do not desire to reflect, they are beginning to appreciate this circumstance. The coronavirus pandemic is a compassionate gift from the Universe, an event that supports the entire human species in moving toward its new evolutionary path. It is not meant to punish or frighten us. It is designed to support the awakening of love in the human species—the creation of authentic power.

As we have discussed, the death of a personality is determined by the soul of that personality. It is a decision made by the soul to return home to nonphysical reality. This has always been so, even when the number of deaths has been large, such as in World War II or the Holocaust within World War II. Yet those were experiences of five-sensory humans inflicting pain and destruction on five-sensory humans. It is not destruction that is being inflicted now upon the human species.

The coronavirus pandemic provides us countless opportunities to grow spiritually. It provides them to multisensory humans who have declared they will no longer contribute the brutality that has characterized the human experience. What shall they do when fellow students in the Earth school do not take them into consideration, for example, refuse to wear a mask? Will they react with judgment and anger? Or will they respond with love?

Resistance to wearing a mask has nothing to do with the act of wearing a mask. It is a reaction of fear. It is an objection to the world being the way it is. The individuals who refuse to wear a mask refuse to acknowledge changes in the world that are real, and rather than experience the pain of those changes, they choose an issue such as this one to distract themselves from what they feel. All of these opportunities are gifts within gifts from the Universe, each tailored to the spiritual needs of those who receive them. By spiritual I mean having to do with the soul.

Withdrawal into seclusion is not an answer, although it is required for containing the coronavirus. Withdrawal is not possible because all individuals are beginning to see how dependent they are upon one another. Yet that dependency, that closeness, cannot be expressed physically. So it is presented to each individual from within, to be recognized, acknowledged, and appreciated.

The coronavirus is eliciting the most constructive and fulfilling potentials of the emerging human species—loving responses instead of fearful reactions, appreciation of others and life instead of exploitation, and countless cocreations that bring us together again and again.

This is a special time, to be appreciated. Five-sensory humans cannot understand how death and suffering can be appreciated, yet from the larger context it is visible. From the higher order logic and understanding of the heart, it is felt and understood.

Pierre Teilhard de Chardin, a Jesuit priest, followed his heart to a place that his order would not permit him to share while he lived, but hundreds of millions of multisensory humans are now exploring that place. "Someday," he wrote, "after mastering the winds, the waves, the tides and gravity, we shall harness for God the energies of love, and then, for a second time in the history of the world, we will have discovered fire."

How many more gifts such as the coronavirus will the Universe provide us?

As many as we need to cocreate on our journey toward Love.

# 52

# The Multisensory Social
# Structure of Education—Joy

ultisensory education is one of the most joyful parts of being human. It is a spiritual partnership. You freely share with others, and you openly receive from others, and this continues. As you cocreate, loving guidance and insights come to you from nonphysical Teachers. You are a learner and a teacher for the benefit of all. That is multisensory education.

The operative word is joyful. Education proceeds most effectively, most helpfully, and most thoroughly when it is joyful. Without joy education becomes a task that is not wanted. The difference between joyful learning and learning that is not joyful is the intention. It is one experience to learn history because it is required, and it is another experience to learn history because you are deeply interested in it.

Why is it that some individuals have little interest in a certain period of French history and others are keenly interested in it? Why is it that some individuals have a desire to learn about healing, and others have a desire to learn how to work with their hands? All experience in the Earth school is influenced and in many cases determined by karma. That means it is often determined by experiences of other personalities of the soul, which are sometimes referred to as other lifetimes. These considerations are absent from five-sensory education.

A broad range of subjects is necessary for the balanced well-being of an individual, such as ability to write, speak, calculate, and communicate unambiguously. Yet these are not life-satisfying activities. They open the door to new ways of learning, and those new ways of learning open the door to passion. Being a mechanic because working with tools and devices satisfies you is a different experience than being a mechanic because that is the only way to support yourself and your family. The first has passion in it. The second has none.

Passion and previous lifetimes often go together. That is why some individuals feel comfortable working with their hands and uncomfortable working with concepts, and some individuals are so attuned to words and language that poetry becomes their passion, and their poetry moves others deeply. It is also why some individuals have a passion for manipulating concepts, such as mathematical formulations, and others do not.

Multisensory education is as broad-based and specific as it needs to be given the needs of the student. One of the first aspects of multisensory education is to begin the process of exploring what brings passion for the student. If a student does not have a broad-based foundation, he or she will not be able to master or express all that is required. Yet no matter how broad-based and thoughtful the education, if it does not call to his or her passion, it will remain limited.

It is often the case that learning must be done or is done without passion because it is considered necessary. This is a common experience of students in the five-sensory social structure of education. They care not for what they learn, yet they feel that they must learn it or are told that they must learn it. But when there is a desire to learn because what is learned offers a channel for the passion that they feel, that transforms education and the experience of learning. That passion is always an indicator of an interest that satisfies the soul.

It can be in music, in art, or in drama. It can be in mathematics or in history. It can be in languages, cultures, or the development of communications technologies. It can be in carpentry or plumbing. The content itself provides a doorway, a vehicle, for passion. Without the passion, there is no interest in going through the door. Therefore, the multisensory social structure of education is based on joy. That means it is based on passion, and that means it is relevant to the needs of the personality that the soul has chosen for its journey though the Earth school.

The social structure of multisensory education, like the five-sensory social structure of education, is not limited to buildings or campuses. It exists everywhere. The five-sensory social structure of education is the human experience of pursuing external power and the fear that drives that. In the same way, the multisensory social structure of education is not limited to buildings or campuses. It exists everywhere. It is life in the Earth school as revealed by multisensory perception. It is exploration of the miracle that some individuals are drawn to interests that are so different from the interests that attract others.

The multisensory social structure of education begins with this and provides the necessary foundation that allows individuals to learn through reading, express themselves through writing, and support themselves through arithmetic and mathematics, but most importantly allows them to sense the passion that fills their lives as they find those endeavors that allow them to give the gifts they were born to give. Those gifts will always have to do with other individuals and with Life, for how can they be gifts to give if there is no desire to give them, and if there are not others to receive them?

Students cannot experience their passion while they create with fear. Therefore, authentic power—learning how to create with love rather than fear—is the basis of multisensory education. Without the creation of authentic power in education there can be no passion.

If there is no consciousness of the difference between love and fear, fear will be the intention behind the actions of students in the Earth school. Fear is an unconscious intention. Individuals do not need to think about intentions of fear in order to act upon them. For example, they do not need to think about being jealous or angry or feeling superior or inferior in order to feel these ways. They do not need to think about exploiting others or using others for their own benefit in order to find themselves doing these things.

The creation of authentic power is the challenge to all of that, which means it is the challenge to fear. Creating authentic power provides the tools—emotional awareness and responsible choice—that allow the experiences of creating authentic power, which are intimate, often painful, and fulfilling. It brings the heart into the awareness of a life in the

Earth school. It brings emotions—consciously chosen and cultivated emotions—into a life in the Earth school. The desire for meaning and purpose is always the desire for harmony, cooperation, sharing, and reverence for Life.

It is always the desire for the soul.

# 53

# The Multisensory Social Structure
# of Education—Fulfillment

Creating authentic power allows a distinction between love and fear. Creating authentic power brings meaning to emotional pain and the ability to use it to move beyond the control of frightened parts of the personality. It is in moving beyond the control of the frightened parts of the personality that the meaning of passion emerges. Passion is why some individuals are drawn to speaking Chinese, others to studying the ocean, and others to educating children. These are part of the gifts that they incarnated to give.

None of this fits into the framework or understanding of the five-sensory social structure of education. The soul is not recognized because five-sensory education is based upon the perceptions of the five senses. Intention is not recognized because the intention of love does not further the pursuit of external power. It prevents it. Emotional awareness is of no importance in the five-sensory social structure of education because emotions are seen as hindrances to the pursuit of external power.

The term "emotional intelligence," when it refers to the use of emotions and the ability to suppress them or repress them in order to pursue external power, has no part in the multisensory social structure of education. In the multisensory social structure of education the heart is central, which means emotions are central, to the creation of authentic power.

Significant choices are choices of intention, and in the Earth school the only two significant intentions are love and fear. As an individual creates authentic power, these intentions become clear and also the relationship between them and the consequences they create, until there is a passion to move beyond the control of fear and into the freedom and fulfillment of love. All of this is of the same fabric, for an individual in the multisensory social structure of education discovers that those things that are natural attractions, such as this language or that language, this culture or that culture, working with hands or working with the mind, are all means of expression and giving.

When there is no passion and there is no joy, all that a social structure of education can provide is meaningless. That is why there is often so much resistance to education, because it has come to mean the pursuit of external power, becoming more effective in pursuing external power, and becoming a more useful tool for others who are pursuing external power, for example, becoming a worker that is needed for an assembly line or a programmer that is needed for developing software.

The same action, as we have discussed, can have different intentions. If the intention is fear, it produces a false excitement, the excitement of the possibility of moving beyond a limitation, such as a disadvantage or lack. Moving beyond that kind of limitation leads to temporary happiness, the illusory fruit of external power, and then to a free fall into fear again when you lose what you gained or someone takes it from you.

When the limitation the action is moving beyond is a constriction imposed by fear, that produces spiritual growth. It may take a long time without knowledge of the creation of authentic power. When an individual is constrained by a karmic circumstance, for example, poverty or prejudice, moving beyond those constraints often begins with resentment against what appears to be the origin of them, which is the world, which is the ignorance of other people. Yet eventually the strength that can emerge is the strength of the experience of moving beyond constrictions of fear, drawing upon one's own resources but without judgment of others. That is genuine power. The other is external power.

Authentic power is the content of the multisensory social structure of education, and with that comes all that we have discussed—access to the heart, the higher order logic and understanding of the heart, the fulfillment of contribution, the fulfillment of belonging. Without these things there is no joy, and there is no passion. All these things are offered by the multisensory social structure of education. It does not function by imposition. It functions with love. It honors love. It honors passion, passion to give the gifts that one was born to give, passion to raise a family, teach, write, build with one's hands, create art, or passion for healing.

As a student finds passion, she or he begins to see that what she or he learned through the five-sensory social structure of education is helpful, but that it was presented in fear. It was learned in fear, and it does not lead to the satisfaction of giving and of contributing, because those things are not part of the five-sensory social structure of education.

This is why kindness is not in the curriculum of the five-sensory social structure of education, and indeed it cannot be studied as a subject is studied in the five-sensory social structure of education. The multisensory social structure of education goes directly to the creation of those experiences that will clarify what leads to passion in different individuals, and that is always the creation of authentic power.

The process of creating authentic power—the tools of creating authentic power—remains the same, but the frightened parts that arise are different. The passions that arise are different. The satisfaction that comes with learning a new language or the satisfaction that comes with teaching or expression through writing are different. Multisensory education utilizes those differences because those differences are fundamental. For each student in the Earth school they express interests and aptitudes that reflect prior experiences, and those experiences are often prior to the incarnation of the soul of the personality.

The creation of authentic power is the focus of multisensory education, yet that itself cannot be learned if there is no openness to it, for if there is no openness, there can be no passion. As the human species becomes multisensory, its interests change. Its paths to meaning and fulfillment change. Its content changes, and that change of content is the change from fear to the appearance of love, and then the cultivation of love and the challenging of fear.

The horizon of students in the multisensory social structure of education offers different destinations for different students, but these destinations cannot be reached without the creation of authentic power. They take shape, or form, as students reach toward them. For example, a young child who is drawn to play a musical instrument cannot know where that interest will lead. A young child who is forced to learn a musical instrument does not care about the instrument or where learning it will lead. It knows intuitively that it will lead nowhere. The other child knows intuitively that it will lead to richness, although the child does not think in those terms.

We are each a teacher as well as a student. Teachers in the five-sensory social structure of education teach fear. They do not know how to distinguish fear from love in themselves. They are expected to teach fear. The pursuit of external power is the curriculum of the five-sensory social structure of education. Everyone in the five-sensory social structure of education teaches it, not only those in schools or on campuses. Parents teach it. Colleagues teach it. Peers teach it.

What you teach as you create authentic power is very different, and what those around you learn is very different. You teach what is longed for, what is necessary, what is desired. In the domain of the five senses that is the pursuit of external power, the product of fear. In the multisensory social structure of education that is the creation of authentic power, and that leads to appreciation of emotion, the necessity of responsible choice, and fulfillment, meaning, and joy.

What are you teaching?

# 54

# Science of the Soul

Five-sensory science explores physical phenomena. Multisensory science explores the dynamics that create and sustain the physical world. It explores a larger reality beyond the fence of the five senses. This larger reality is the new frontier of science.

Multisensory science explores the soul and its relation to the Earth school. From the perspective of five-sensory science, the soul does not exist, and life is an anomaly. In other words, five-sensory science is irrelevant to this frontier. Five-sensory science is "empirical" science. It is a product of five-sensory perception. Multisensory science is the science of the soul. It is a product of the new consciousness.

Impressive as five-sensory science was, and still is in the realm of physical phenomena, it has a central, fundamental, embarrassing-to-five-sensory-scientists hole in the middle of it. In the years since Newton created physics to now, this embarrassment has continued unabated. Despite supersonic transport, moon landings, landings on other planets, and capability to destroy life on the Earth countless times, the embarrassment, the hole-that-cannot-be-filled, persists and grows ever larger.

The one thing that five-sensory science cannot explain, the most significant thing that five-sensory science cannot explain, the elephant in the room, so to speak, that five-sensory science cannot explain—and the room is the Universe—is CONSCIOUSNESS. From the perspective of five-sensory science, consciousness does not exist. This is absurd, of course, because I am thinking about consciousness, writing about consciousness, and now everyone who is reading this book is conscious of my doing these things. Five-sensory scientists know this, which is why they are embarrassed.

What an amazing embarrassment!!! Five-sensory science cannot measure, weigh, or locate consciousness. Electron microscopes cannot find it in the realms of the very small. Radio telescopes cannot find it in the realms of the very large. Five-sensory science cannot even define consciousness except in terms of things and processes that are not conscious.

The way that five-sensory science approaches this embarrassment is even more embarrassing. Five-sensory scientists explain the origin of consciousness the same way that humans four hundred years ago explained the origin of maggots on rotting meat, i.e., "spontaneous generation." According to the four-hundred-year-old explanation, at some point in the process of meat rotting—Poof!—maggots appear. According to the current explanation of consciousness, at some point in the process of increasing complexity—Poof!—consciousness appears. (Really.)

This embarrassment does not exist for scientists of the soul. The premise of the science of the soul is that Life is and permeates all that is. In other words, the premise of the science of the soul is that the Universe IS consciousness. *Everything* is consciousness, although not necessarily as five-sensory humans recognize it. The stars and galaxies are consciousness. Mountains, planets, and space are consciousness. The Universe is a spiritual enterprise, not a material one. *Spiritual* means "having to do with the soul."

Love, fear, emotion, intention, and choice are central to the science of the soul. It explores the soul, its relation to the physical world, and the relation of emotions, intentions, and choice to the evolution of the soul. Five-sensory science explores the physical world and how it works.

Five-sensory science has come to its end. The science of the soul has begun. It addresses the most important questions of five-sensory humans, "Why am I here?" and "What is my purpose?" It also addresses the important questions of multisensory humans, "What is my soul?" "What does my soul want from me?" and "What can I do for my soul?"

The science of the soul is different from everything you have read, experienced, or thought about five-sensory science. We are the new scientists of the soul. As we develop emotional awareness and practice responsible choice, we become scientists of the soul. When we create authentic power, we are scientists of the soul.

Your life is your laboratory. You enter it in the intimacy of your experience. You experiment continually (choose intentions) and learn from consequences they create. Your spiritual partners are scientists of the soul, also.

The science of the soul explores the incarnation and reincarnation of souls into the Earth school. Without knowledge of this, we cannot recognize the far-reaching effects of our choices or appreciate them, accept them, and learn from them. We cannot comprehend the power of our creative capacity and the extent to which we are responsible for how we use it. We cannot grasp the beauty, perfection, and immensity of the dynamic in which we play a central role.

The science of the soul studies karma. Without knowledge of karma, we fantasize that our actions do not create consequences. The Universal Law of Cause and Effect, the impersonal Universal teacher of responsibility, shatters this fantasy.

The science of the soul studies intuition, the voice of the nonphysical world, the primary decision-making faculty of multisensory humans. Guidance and assistance of nonphysical Teachers flow through the doorway of intuition. As Rumi beautifully described it, the door is round and open.

The science of the soul studies intention, the quality of consciousness that infuses a word or a deed. Love and fear are the two fundamental intentions in the Earth school.

The science of the soul studies authentic power, choosing love no matter what is happening inside you or outside you.

Scientists of the soul cocreate the literature of the science of the soul. Five-sensory scientists compete to create the literature of physical science.

The laboratories of five-sensory scientists are in buildings. Their experiments require apparatuses or imagined apparatuses. Their results must be verifiable by any scientist anywhere. For example, the result that an experimenter obtains at the Stanford linear particle accelerator in the United States must be verifiable by an experimenter at the CERN particle accelerator in Switzerland. These experiments do not change the experimenters. If an experimenter is angry or ambitious, caring or competitive before the experiment, he or she will be the same after it.

Experimental results obtained by a scientist of the soul in his or her laboratory (life) must also be verifiable by any scientist of the soul anywhere. For example, if the consequence of an intention of love is constructive in the laboratory (life) of one scientist of the soul, this result must be verifiable in the laboratory (life) of any other scientist of the soul. If the consequence of an intention of fear is destructive, it also must be verifiable. These experiments change the experimenters. They become aware of their internal dynamics, their responsibility for how they use their awareness, and their relationships with one another as personalities and as souls.

Five-sensory scientists study the countless physical interactions in the physical world. Scientists of the soul study the countless physical and nonphysical interactions among personalities, among souls, and among personalities and souls.

When will you become a scientist of the soul?

# 55

# The Law

Five-sensory law is external power. Five-sensory laws tell us what we can do and what we cannot do. They manipulate and control our behaviors with brutality and violence. For example, we drive (approximately) within a speed limit in order to avoid a fine (manipulation). If we refuse to pay the fine (and we were speeding), it increases. If we physically resist the officer who gives us the ticket, the consequences quickly become brutal and violent.

Ancient Egyptian (3000 BC), Sumerian (2200 BC), and Babylonian (1760 BC) laws, ancient Indian and Chinese laws, Catholic law (canon), Islamic law (Sharia), Roman law, European laws, and American laws are all five-sensory. Taboos that govern tribes and clans are five-sensory laws in practice. Religious demands are five-sensory laws to those who are forced to obey them (think Crusaders and "Holy" Roman Inquisition). They are conspicuously naked pursuits of external power.

Dictators use five-sensory law. They create laws they want and enforce them with brute strength. This is rule *by* law. They are not constrained by their laws. Their laws criminalize behaviors they do not approve, such as protests, elections, travel, dancing, voting, journalism, and more. Dictatorships such as China, Russia, and Saudi Arabia, among others, are examples of rule by law.

Democracies also use five-sensory law. Elected legislatures create laws that confine behaviors of the governed. All individuals are constrained by the same laws, including lawmakers and law enforcers. This is rule *under* law.

The earliest discussions about law in the West were about this difference. Plato (428–348 BC) (approx.) advocated rule by law. He liked the idea of a benevolent monarch, or a "philosopher king." Aristotle (384–322 BC), his student, advocated rule under law. He believed the same law should govern everyone. Aristotle's idea is usually considered better. (Dictators can be vicious murders. Philosopher kings are hard to find.)

This distinction is not always clear. For example, nations that govern themselves with rule *under* law often impose rule *by* law on cultures and countries they invade or colonize (think Britain and the American colonies; Britain and India; Spain and the Americas; France and Algeria; etc.). The American colonies violently rejected British rule by law ("taxation without representation"). Their famous Declaration of Independence and Constitution proclaimed rule *under* law for themselves. At the same time they imposed rule *by* law on women, slaves, and Native Americans who survived their genocide. The French, Bolshevik, and Haitian revolutions also violently rejected rule by law.

Sometimes rule under law metastasizes into rule by law. Nazis (rule by law) were elected in Germany (rule under law) between World War I and World War II when discontent with the economy was high. Today frightened individuals and their political parties (rule by law) are being elected to governments in the West (rule under law) as discontent rises, for example, with immigration. In both cases the issue is fear, not economics or immigration.

Multisensory individuals see this, and they also see the inadequacies of five-sensory law. Love cannot be legislated into existence, and fear cannot be legislated out of existence. They see that love and fear are choices that millions of individuals now can identify as the new human consciousness emerges within them. They see that their evolution now requires choices of love within themselves, even while fear within themselves painfully demands expression and action.

The new human consciousness has brought five-sensory law to the end of its usefulness—including rule under five-sensory law—as it has brought every five-sensory social structure to the end of its usefulness. We are witnessing the dissolution of one of the pinnacle achievements of five-sensory humanity.

In my opinion, rule under law is one of the two greatest collective

creations of five-sensory humanity. The other is representative constitutional democracy. They are closely related. Both developed slowly
and were perfected—as much as they could be perfected—relatively
recently. Representative constitutional democracy embodied rule under
law and was the crucible in which rule under law was stirred, distilled,
and refined. Now the five-sensory social structure of law and the five-
sensory social structure of governance are both disintegrating.

Rule under law gives most individuals protections that are precious to
all individuals, such as presumption of innocence, fair and speedy trial,
and equality under the law, but its inadequacies have become undeniable. It is unequal in application—indigent individuals cannot afford it,
wealthy individuals can. It is adversarial—attorneys combat one another
with arguments in courtrooms as gladiators once did in coliseums with
swords. It produces verdicts, but not always justice. DNA analyses often
exonerate individuals after their incarceration, sometimes after they die
in prison, and sometimes after they are executed in prison.

We say that justice is blind, but the social structure of five-sensory law
is not blind to skin color, wealth and lack of wealth, education and lack of
education, influence and lack of influence, and much more. It is not blind
to external power, and it cannot be, because it *is* external power. It is the
best social structure of law—the very best—that five-sensory humanity
could create, but it is insufficient for the multisensory humanity that is
being born. It is insufficient for us.

Five-sensory law—under it as well as by it—is devoid of relationship.
Victims and villains in the Earth school are souls learning together the
great lessons of all personalities—harmony, cooperation, sharing, and
reverence for Life. The inadequacies of five-sensory law are already producing alternatives, such as restorative justice. Restorative justice brings
victims, offenders, and affected individuals together, sometimes in a
circle, to uncover and utilize the depth of their connections.

Victim and offender, arresting officers, parents, families, and friends
of families ask themselves and one another: who has been hurt; what are
their needs; whose obligations are these; and how can things be made
right. If their efforts do not satisfy all involved, do not appear just to all
involved, and are not successful for all involved, all involved are thrown

back into the arena of five-sensory law, where questions are simpler and answers never satisfy all involved: what laws were broken, who broke them, what does he or she deserve.

Restorative justice, which is sometimes called circle justice, emerged in Native American, Canadian First Nation, Maori, and Hawaiian cultures, among others. Hawaiians call it *ho'o pono pono* (for the first part, say "ho," pause your breath briefly, and then say "oh" as you finish exhaling). *Pono* (sounds like "pony") means "right" or "correct." *Pono pono* means "*really* right." *Ho'o* means "*do* it." Together they mean "*really* make it *really* right!" This is the heart of truth and reconciliation everywhere.

Restorative justice uncovers connections. It reveals love. It is a new beginning at the time when the social structure of five-sensory law has come to its end. Other beginnings will emerge. Multisensory humans have the privilege and responsibility to cocreate them, explore them, experiment with them, and develop them in consultation with intuition and one another.

Justice in the Earth school is nonjudgmental justice. The Universal Law of Cause and Effect ensures without judgment that students in the Earth school experience what they create. Jesus put it this way: If you judge, you will be judged. Many five-sensory individuals believe this. Multisensory individuals see it.

The simplicity of nonjudgmental justice is unmistakable to them:

- Intentions are causes; experiences are effects.
- Each of us chooses the intention of love or the intention of fear each moment.
- The intention of love creates joy; the intention of fear creates pain.

We can honor nonjudgmental justice or we can ignore it, but we cannot change it. When we ignore it, we do not change. When we recognize it and honor it, we bloom (not comply), contribute (not conform), celebrate (not submit), include (not exclude), and the world that we create does the same.

This is the law.

# 56

# The New Mission of the Military

The five-sensory social structure of the military has no future. The same decay that is destroying the foundations of other five-sensory social structures is destroying the foundation of this one, also. This decay cannot be removed, and it is growing. Everything about a five-sensory military organization expresses external power. Its hierarchical structure. Its blind obedience. Its inability to consider contexts beyond its limited mission.

My mission as an infantry officer in the US military was to "close with and kill or capture the enemy." This is the mission of every five-sensory military without the details. Everything in every five-sensory military supports this mission. To be in a five-sensory military—and they are all five-sensory—is to commit to this mission. Clerks, medical assistants, computer technicians, truck drivers, and engineers in a military may be less aware of this mission, or imagine that they are not part of it because they never touch a weapon, but that is a delusion. This mission pervades the entire five-sensory military endeavor. Every branch of every five-sensory military—land, sea, air, space, cyber—is committed to this mission. This mission is the pursuit of external power.

The pursuit of external power is now counterproductive to our evolution. Offensive or defensive in posture—which are different labels on the same poison—five-sensory military organizations require adversaries or create them. A military is not only an organization that is structured, trained, coordinated, and equipped to pursue external power, it is also the enormous interconnected web of companies and their employees that supply the vehicles, weapons, printer cartridges, and clothing of the people in the military, plus their food, building materials for their hous-ing, and all else. They are also part of the military and its mission. General Dwight Eisenhower, the supreme commander of the Allied Forces in Eu-rope and president of the United States after World War II, observed— and then lamented—the emergence of the "military-industrial complex" that by the end of his presidency had grown beyond his control. Beyond anyone's control. The allegiance of this self-serving aggregate is to profit.

This aggregate has no nationality. American multinational corpora-tions are American in name only. German multinational corporations are German in name only. Japanese multinational corporations are Japanese in name only. They search the world for the least expensive labor, and they hire (exploit) it wherever they can. They build factories where they are able to pay the lowest salaries and taxes, except when they are pro-hibited by law, such as manufacturers of classified weapons and classified components. These multinational corporations have no "home" country. They operate, manufacture, market, sell, and profit around the world. They transfer money through multinational organizations (banks) that do the same.

The "military-industrial complex" exerts tremendous influence over the political systems that attempt to govern it. It spends startling amounts of money to elect (bribe) politicians favorable to its profits. *Every* multinational corporation does these things, but corporations in the "military-industrial complex" bring these practices directly into the arena of "national security." Multinational corporations are not concerned with "national security" above all else, because they have no nation to secure, except in defense of their assets and profits.

Americans think of their military as American. The only thing en-tirely American about it is the people who die when combat comes or is created by politicians financed by the "military-industrial complex." Brit-ish think of their military as British. The only thing entirely British about their military is the people who die when combat comes, and so on. This is not lost on people in uniform. They see their jobs "outsourced" to "contractors" (mercenaries) who, unlike themselves, put paycheck above patriotism. They wonder who and what they are fighting for, and the answers disturb them.

An archetype is an energy dynamic. For example, the archetypes of mother, father, and grandparent shape the experiences of individuals who have children or grandchildren. Individuals who participate in militaries participate in the archetype of warrior. They fall into its gravitational field, so to speak, and their experiences are shaped by it. They are committed to protecting their collectives with their lives if necessary, and they do. Five-sensory warriors protect their tribes, cultures, or nations.

Multisensory warriors see only ONE collective. That is the collective of Life.

They have no interest in protecting borders. They have no interest in defending nations, cultures, countries, cities, towns, tribes, or any of the collectives that five-sensory warriors protect. They focus on Life. They never take their focus off Life. They are committed to protecting Life in every way, including with their own lives. They serve a cause higher than nation, culture, or tribe. There is no cause higher than theirs. They serve Life.

They do not need weapons or war rooms, bullets or ballistic missiles, nuclear-powered aircraft carriers or stealth bombers. Multisensory warriors are motivated by love—love of Life. They are guided by love—love of Life. They are fulfilled by love—love of Life. Multisensory warriors honor Life the way the great Navajo prayer honors Beauty (which, I think, is Life).

- With Beauty before me I walk (Navajo)
  With Life before me I walk (multisensory warrior)
- With Beauty behind me I walk (Navajo)
  With Life behind me I walk (multisensory warrior)
- With Beauty below me I walk (Navajo)
  With Life below me I walk (multisensory warrior)
- With Beauty above me I walk (Navajo)
  With Life above me I walk (multisensory warrior)
- With Beauty all around me I walk (Navajo)
  With Life all around me I walk (multisensory warrior)

Courage in compassion replaces courage in combat. Multisensory warriors have no care for conquests. Their goal is to protect Life, and their tools are harmony, cooperation, sharing, and reverence for Life. They use their courage in the new way—to create authentic power—instead of the old way—to pursue external power. They say from their hearts what needs to be said, and they do with their hearts what needs to be done. They have no interest in the means and end of five-sensory militaries—external power.

The tsunami of suicides in the US military as I write is not caused by length of tours, frequency of rotations, or even traumas of combat. It is caused by a monster realization that is emerging in the psyches of millions of five-sensory warriors. It is a realization they never dreamed or imagined could exist. They are beginning to see the shallowness, inherent worthlessness, and poisonous nature of the mission they are serving. They are willing to give their health, blood, and lives if necessary to support Life. They are not willing to give them to destroy life. They are becoming multisensory warriors.

Multisensory perception is emerging around the world. It is not limited by geography, age, culture, ethnic group, or gender. It is not limited by anything. It is emerging species-wide. It reveals new perspectives and potential. It offers new paths to new destinations. Multisensory perception requires new choices, and multisensory warriors are making them in the depths of their hearts, in the places where they long to shine light instead of grope in darkness.

Nuclear weapons and climate change have long made it impossible, even for five-sensory warriors, to ignore the futility of protecting collectives less inclusive than Life. The largest militaries in the world watched helplessly while fallout from Chernobyl descended on their cities and crops as radioactive rain. What military can prevent radioactive air and water from Fukashima from reaching California and China? Aircraft carriers and stealth fighters cannot protect coastal cities from rising seas. What military can prevent soot from firestorms following a nuclear war from rising into the stratosphere, blocking the warmth and light of the sun, and creating a deadly nuclear winter of famine and cold for all?

The US Pentagon has decreed climate change a national security threat. It is only a small step from there to realizing that failure to protect the most inclusive collective in which we all participate—the collective of Life—from this threat creates a lethal threat to the existence, much less security, of every nation, military, and collective.

Multisensory warriors *experience* this new reality. They *see* the need to transform their military, not only its mission, from a fear-based destructive presence in the world to a love-based constructive presence that supports Life. They recognize the necessity of protecting the all-inclusive collective of Life in order to ensure human survival and evolution and the well-being of all life on planet Earth.

This is the new mission of the military.

# 57

# Art and the Soul

Aconscious life is a work of art. It unfolds as an image on canvas, or a shape from stone under the sculptor's chisel. It is not random. It expresses the power of the artist who creates it.

Art requires intention, but intention is not sufficient. A carpenter has intention when he builds a house. A plumber has intention when she remodels a kitchen. Skill also is necessary, but skill is not sufficient. A skilled lawyer crafts convincing briefs, but her briefs are not art. A neurosurgeon uses skill when she cuts into the brain, but her incisions are not art. Art comes from a place that is beyond intention and skill. Intention and skill are necessary, but art requires more.

Without his soul, an artist cannot make art. Without the deepest part of herself, her creations are artless. Art comes from and calls to the same place in all humans—the nonphysical realm of meaning in which all humans have their home. Art and meaning cannot be separated. Without meaning, there can be no art. Art connects souls with souls. It is a conscious creation that bridges the gap that appears to exist between five-sensory humans within the Earth school.

The intellect cannot recognize art. Art generates a deeper response than analytical processes can produce. It fills needs that the intellect cannot satisfy. Art touches the same place that a golden sunset touches, or the sky lit with pink at dawn. A mountain reaches farther into the interior of the psyche than a thought can penetrate. The ocean calms in ways that concepts cannot. The Earth expresses unbound beauty. Art touches that beauty in us. We expand beyond all that we think when, for a moment, everything disappears but the lightning, the raging ocean, or the mountain alive with a stillness that our lives do not permit. The Earth is art. What is required is provided. What is provided is required. It shows us in every moment that we are living strands in a web of Life.

Art does the same: It reminds us of a greater self. That greater self is the soul. Art touches the soul because it comes from the soul. It illuminates the deeper meanings of every circumstance. In other words, art calls attention to more than itself. The multisensory artist sees the experiences of the Earth school as symbols. The power, depth, and grace of them delight the soul. This perception—shared through the medium of matter—is art. A craftsman shapes matter. An artist shares meaning.

To five-sensory perception, a hammer is a tool. To an artist, it is a symbol of new construction, an amalgam of intention and matter. To five-sensory perception, a carpenter is a craftsman. To an artist, a carpenter represents an archetype. Four workmen by a roadside were asked, "What are you doing?" The first answered, "I am piling rocks." The second said, "I am making a wall." The third replied, "I am building a cathedral." The fourth shared, "I am creating a place of peace and beauty for the soul." The fourth was an artist.

Art requires choice. Each frame in a film is chosen. Will the action be set in a garden, by a river, or on a sidewalk? Will actors speak? What will they say? Every detail conveys meaning. If the director cannot see it, his or her film is not art. Each character in a book appears for a purpose. What is it? Which details shall be described? Which shall not? Does the story span a day, a year, or a century? The author decides. A sculptor shapes stone stroke by stroke. Shall the grain flow this way or that? Shall the surface be rough or polished? There are no manuals for creating art as there are for building cabinets and bridges.

Art requires trust. A painter may know in advance how to start a painting, but not always how to finish it. Intellectual constructions are engineering projects. Art is collaboration with unseen sources of creativity and intention.

Art is healing. The well of thought is not deep. Emotions come from a deeper place. Art comes from a place deeper still. Art reaches beyond the joy and pain of the personality. It comes from and goes to the core.

That is the soul learning through the experiences of its personality. Art is the response of the soul to those experiences.

Art depends upon the interior guidance system of meaning. In other words, the intellect informs craftsmen. The heart informs artists. The excitement of a new color, the exhilaration of a new idea, and the fulfillment of a new path guide the artist step by step. The product of her or his process reveals the plan.

We are all becoming artists, and the art that we are creating is our lives. A life in the Earth school begins with the birth of a personality and ends with its death. Between these events, the personality creates at each moment. When it creates unconsciously, its life is stifled, stilted, and stagnant. Proportions are off, and perspective is distorted. Spontaneity, vitality, and balance are diminished or absent. Events unfold by chance, good or bad. This is the perspective of a victim.

A consciously created life unfolds as an emerging whole with its own intelligence and goals. Friends and fulfillment flavor it. It is flexible and dynamic, satisfying and rich. The unexpected is welcomed. Coherency emerges. Cocreation flows. Five-sensory artists produce sculptures, symphonies, paintings, and books. Seldom do their lives express the beauty or wholeness of their works. Their visions are confined to canvas, stone, words, and sound. The art of a multisensory human fills a larger arena—the span between the birth and death of his or her personality.

To multisensory humans, the chasm between art and other creations of the personality does not exist. Artistry does not lapse beyond the studio. The Earth school is the studio, and the life of the artist is the work. The criteria of great art are humbleness, forgiveness, clarity, and love. Harmony, cooperation, sharing, and reverence for Life are its expressions. Great artistry occurs in conversation, in the grocery store, and at school.

Great artistry is conscious confrontation with parts of the personality that create destructively. It is the conscious choice of contribution instead of exploitation, self-love instead of self-hatred. Great artistry is alignment of the personality with the soul through responsible choice, with the assistance and guidance of nonphysical guides and Teachers. Shaping sounds, images and words are small accomplishments compared to shaping a life.

There are no random elements in art. Artistry begins with this understanding. Great artists know themselves as immortal souls. Like directors, their choices are purposeful. At the same time, art cannot be predetermined. It moves continually toward its own wholeness. It expresses its own intelligence. It surprises.

So does a conscious life. A conscious life cannot be postponed until retirement. Words stop flowing. Vision fades. The book that longs to be written decays. The power of what you can become does not disappear when you ignore it or cover it with concerns that rationalize lesser goals. Creativity emerges unconsciously and therefore destructively. The decision to follow inner meaning is great artistry—the difference between life as art and life as drudgery, between life as an experience and life as an experiment.

Multisensory artists do not create alone, because it is not possible to be alone. When an artist opens to her creativity, her nonphysical guides and Teachers participate in appropriate ways. Their cocreation is the product of all, but it cannot be born without the artist. She is the pencil, and her life is the paper. Without her, neither the work nor nonphysical guides nor nonphysical Teachers can impact upon the Earth.

Each personality is born to give gifts that its soul seeks to give. Alignment of a personality with its soul and the transformation of a life in the Earth school into a work of art are identical. This is our new evolutionary modality. Five-sensory artists strain against the boundaries of five-sensory perception. When they penetrate them, a work of art is born. Multisensory artists live beyond the boundaries of five-sensory perception.

They cocreate in the context of spiritual development. The intentions of the soul flow unimpeded into their activities. When they do not, multisensory artists find and change the parts of themselves that obstruct the flow. Each multisensory artist contributes to the collective that is longing to be born. This is the grand cocreation that now pulls us toward it—Universal Humanity.

We are all being called to the realm of art. There are no precedents for the birth of a new humankind. Each human life, and the collective experiences of humankind, are becoming conscious works of art. The artist in us awakens the artist in others, and the artist in others awakens the artist in us. The human experience is changing inwardly and outwardly. As our lives become artful, our world becomes artful. As our world becomes artful, it expresses the power, compassion, and wisdom of the Universe. This is the birth of Universal Humanity. This is the grand event of our lives. This is the show that we have come to produce, experience, and enjoy.

The curtain is rising.

# UNIVERSAL HUMANS

# 58

# The Origin of the Universal Human

We have been longing for the Universal Human since the origin of our species. We longed for it when we lost ourselves in the night sky. We longed for it when the stars without number called to us, when the Milky Way awed us. We knew from our beginning that we belonged to it, and it belonged to us. We longed for the Universal Human when the great plains stretched before us to the horizon, prairie grasses bending in the breeze. The Universal Human touched us when the deserts appeared to us without end, dune after dune, seas of ever-shifting sand, rebuilding themselves anew. The mountains showed us the Universal Human, touching the sky, alive with ice fields, snow-covered summits, crevasses and pinnacles, gales and sunny afternoons. The oceans brought the Universal Human to us, deep beyond measure, life beyond understanding, power beyond comprehension, currents and winds, storms and calms, caressing beaches and attacking cliffs.

The Universal Human has never been distant from us, like the air we breathe. It has never been separate from us, like our heartbeats. It is older than human thought. It is as old as wonder. Wonder at the Universe and the potential of the Universal Human are the same. Millennia after millennia we have wondered at the Universe without seeing, sensing, or even imagining that it shows us our own potential. The very things that awed us—its total inclusiveness, its unfathomable depth, its beauty beyond words, its endless creativity, and the unity of its countless parts, all moving, combining, separating, and re-forming without end—were the very things we had yet to recognize in ourselves. We were awed by the Universe as an endless symphony of sounds, flow of fragrances, cascade of colors, tastes, and sensations—the ever-new array of five-sensory experiences—forever presenting itself to us every moment without cessation.

It never occurred to five-sensory humans who evolved by surviving and survived by pursuing external power that THEY could be THAT. Now we are becoming a multisensory species that evolves by growing spiritually and grows spiritually by creating authentic power. Now we are entering new domains of experience and understanding. Now we are glimpsing for the first time the most magnificent vista possible to the human species. WE ARE THAT! We are not separate from Life, and Life is not separate from us.

Two thousand two hundred years ago a freed Roman slave named Terence (Publius Terentius Afer) wrote: "I am human. Therefore, nothing human can be alien to me." A young black man, his great heart reached beyond his history, culture, and circumstance to encompass every human thought and experience. This is the greatest five-sensory comprehension of humanity possible—the totality of human thoughts and five-sensory experiences.

Five-sensory humans identify with their personalities—with their minds and bodies. They pursue external power. The world is larger than they. They resist, fear, or live in terror of death. They have no explanation for their births and no understanding of their deaths. Their experiences are partitioned into inside and outside, I and others. This divide is unbridgeable, rending them apart, leaving them longing for the closeness of others and yet so very far away from them. They ache to touch one another and be touched, and they die that way. This great pain is inherent to five-sensory perception.

Multisensory humans identify with their souls. They create authentic power. They experience the Earth school without the limitations of the five senses. They distinguish between Earth suits and the souls that wear them. They do not blame or credit others for their experiences or expect others to change their experiences. They challenge fear in themselves and cultivate love in themselves. They consult nonphysical Teachers and guides. They use the Universal Law of Cause and Effect to create lives of meaning and joy and the Universal Law of Attraction to draw loving companions to themselves. They contribute to the evolution of their souls with their intentions of love.

Universal Humans identify with Life. They see Life everywhere and not only in humans, animals, and plants. They see Life in soil and stars, streams and rivers, sand at the shore, and mud after the rain. They see Life in rocks and crystals. They see Life in space, galaxies, supernovas, planets and the rings around them. Insects, snakes, sages, gold, and excrement are equally precious to them. A gnat is as precious as an elephant. A carcass is as precious as a flower. All that the five senses can detect, with or without assistance, is Life to Universal Humans.

They see Life in all that the five senses cannot detect. Souls, nonphysical Teachers, and Angels are Life. Peoples with different appearances, customs, languages, and ourstories that are living in the very places we now stand, all evolving in their own ways, invisible to us and we invisible to them, are Life. Universal Humans see every experience, no matter how small, as necessary to the compassionate unfolding of the Universe. They are committed to Life and fulfilled by Life. Life is the name of a Universal Human. Life is the address of a Universal Human. Life is the love of Universal Humans.

Never before has human evolution moved so quickly, so transparently, so dramatically toward new destinations. Never before have single words marked so clearly, like signposts along a path, the stages of human identity and potential:

> PERSONALITY—five-sensory human
> SOUL—multisensory human
> LIFE—Universal Human

# 59

# What Is the Universal Human?

The Universal Human is a step beyond an authentically empowered human. A Universal Human identifies with Life—Life in its countless forms. It identifies with all that is, for Life is all that is. It is a focus that allows it to access depths of creativity and awareness, comprehension and insight, all brought to bear for the benefit of Life. Everything that the Universal Human does, the Universal Human does for Life.

This is a richer picture than the intellect can present, for the Universal Human is all that is, because the Universal Human is Life, and Life is all that is. The Universal Human is one whose understanding of what is constructive and appropriate and beneficial is identical with an understanding of what is constructive and appropriate and beneficial for Life. Here again the intellect fails to travel, for the Universal Human cannot benefit Life, because Life itself is all that is beneficial.

The Universal Human can contribute to Life one individual—one aspect of Life that is self-aware, so to speak—that lives in joy, that reflects the radiance of Life itself, that is aware of the complexity of Life itself, of the obscuration of love by fear in the Earth school, and begins to become aware of many processes beyond the Earth school. These processes do not make it otherworldly or take it beyond the Earth school, but more into the Earth school in ways that are more substantial and connected.

The Universal Human knows that by supporting others in creating authentic power in spiritual partnership it contributes to Life itself—not that it makes Life itself better or more than it is, for those are meaningless ways of looking at Life, but that it accesses in its own individualized framework, so to speak, the joy and immensity of Life, the wonder, the healing of it, although here again, Life itself cannot be healed for Life itself does not require healing.

The best way to express the Universal Human is in terms of love, for Love, Life, Consciousness, and Universe are all different ways of approaching the same thing. More accurately, they are different ways of becoming aware of the same thing, and even more accurately, different ways of becoming aware of oneself.

The Universal Human cannot be explained in the way that a personality can be explained. A soul cannot be explained, but it can be described by some of its activities. Life cannot be explained because it is all activities. It is all explanations. It is all lack of all explanations. It cannot be defined, it cannot be described, but it can be experienced, and the experience of Life takes one beyond the limitations of any particular aspect of Life. When the Universal Human walks among humans, it walks among humans as a human—a human expressing love, caring for others, contributing all that is appropriate in that moment, in that circumstance, yet with an appreciation of much more.

The Universal Human is the potential of multisensory humanity as it evolves through creating authentic power. It is a potential that is not yet as fully explainable or demonstrable to multisensory humans as authentic power and multisensory perception are to five-sensory humans. Universal Human is another step, yet it is a step that has already been completed from a perception that will become available to humans as they continue to evolve.

From the perspective of the intellect, these words are unsatisfying and in many cases meaningless and in several cases self-contradictory. Relax into this process. Do not feel that you need to tie up all the loose ends or clarify all the explanations, for they all lead to experience that is now beckoning to the new multisensory human species as it creates authentic power. An openness to the Universal Human is an appropriate approach to the Universal Human.

Is there anyone in human form now that is a Universal Human or have there been others? Yes. There are also those who reach toward the Universal Human. They have some qualities and characteristics of a Universal Human, some more pronounced than others. All of them feel the call, feel the attraction of the Universal Human. They feel it in their lives in meaningful ways, and they act on those meaningful ways.

Universal Humans emerge and begin to take shape as authentically powerful individuals in the Earth school begin to occur. Multisensory perception has emerged and is emerging. Authentic power requires conscious creation, and in the process of creating authentic power the potential of the Universal Human begins to emerge. The emergence of the Universal Human in the Earth school in this way points toward future evolution.

Just as all that was experienced while humanity was five-sensory and evolving through the pursuit of external power was not lost, but now comes into a richer and deeper understanding that allows compassion and clarity and love to become part of the human experience and the creation of authentic power, all that is being experienced and will be experienced in the creation of authentic power as a multisensory human species evolves by growing spiritually will be used in its further development, will apply to its further development, will point it toward its further development, will open it to its further development. That further development is the Universal Human.

We are on a magnificent journey. Statements such as this are already confined by words such as "we." Said another way, a magnificent journey is unfolding, and you are part of it. As you evolve, you will continue to be part of it. There is nothing, and can be nothing, that is not part of it. As you evolve, you begin to sense that the journey and the destination are identical. This perception you can bring with you, and will bring with you, back into the Earth school, so to speak, the Earth school that you have never left as a personality.

As you bring that perception into the Earth school, into your personality, you move ever toward the Universal Human.

# 60

# Adult Citizens of the Universe

Adult citizens of the Universe are aware of their creative capacity and responsibility for how they use it. They do not wait for others to do what they themselves need to do. They love without limits, explore without fears, and create with wisdom and compassion. They do not blame, judge, or condemn. They are not spectators, backseat drivers, or armchair experts. Adult citizens of the Universe are servants of Life, self-responsible advocates of Life, protectors of Life, and lovers of Life. In short, Universal Humans are adult citizens of the Universe.

Children do not see their experiences in the context of spiritual development. Adult citizens of the Universe do. Children blame the world around them when they do not feel safe or valuable. Adult citizens of the Universe change the parts of their personalities that feel threatened and worthless. Children are helpless. Adult citizens of the Universe are helpful. Children do not know when snow blows against the window. They know only that they are cold, and they cry for help. Adult citizens of the Universe close the window, turn up the heat, or put on a coat.

Snow blows against the window in many ways in the Earth school, such as grief, loneliness, despair, righteousness, and vengefulness. Children react to these experiences. Adults respond to them. Children do not understand responsibility. Adults are response-able. Children rage or cower when the world disappoints them. Adults create in themselves what they want to see in the world. If they want a generous world, they become generous. If they want a world with less anger, they become less angry. If they want a loving world, they become loving.

Now we are becoming adult citizens of the Universe. "Children of the universe" no longer describes us. It retards us, impedes our development, and deprives the world of our gifts. It is the perception of a child declaring itself helpless and dependent and determined to remain so. It is the declaration of a sheep demanding a shepherd.

I went to the old cabin-like community center in Mount Shasta, California, a small community that was my home, to hear a Hopi elder, Thomas Banyanca. I revered his name, and I looked forward to being with him. He sat on a rusty metal folding chair in a circle, and we sat on others in the circle with him.

He looked like he had just come from the reservation—a flannel shirt, jeans, and dusty boots. I imagined him in a cornfield the day before. Then he began to speak, humbly and clearly. He said many things and told us that they were the words of the Hopi elders, and that the Hopi elders told him to tell us that now was the time to hear them. Here are a few I remember:

> Be good to each other, and do not look beyond yourself for the leader.
> Banish the word "struggle" from your attitude and your vocabulary.
> All that you do now must be done in a sacred manner and in celebration.
> This could be a good time.
> We are the ones we've been waiting for.

Now is the time. We are the people. Courageous individuals have always known this and acted on it. Adult citizens of the Universe are more than courageous. They are authentically powerful and unstoppable in their love for Life.

As independence for India neared, the British viceroy, on orders from London, summoned Gandhi from a British prison to his palace. Entering in dirty prison clothing, Gandhi said immediately, "Your Excellency, I know I have done things that have been irritants to you, but I hope that will not stand between us as men." The viceroy ordered the beatings, killings, and imprisonments in India, and Gandhi fought them all, but his fight was not with the viceroy. It was with a policy that exploited all Indians. Gandhi never confused the two. The difficulties of his struggle, the extent of his sacrifices, and the sacrifices of the Indian people never distracted him from his love for Life—the Life of the British viceroy or the life of the young people tending goats in the ashram where he lived. Gandhi was an adult citizen of the Universe.

I watched a video of Martin Luther King Jr. locked in a jail deep in the South of the United States, as a white reporter tried to extract a criticism of white people from him. Martin did not provide one. I suspect that he did not feel one. He who crossed the bridge in Selma and marched in Montgomery into vicious dogs, head-bashing clubs, and fire hoses blasting people across streets like rag dolls did not forget his love for Life. Martin Luther King Jr. was an adult citizen of the Universe.

The world we have inherited from five-sensory humanity is filled with painful consequences of pursuing external power. Pursuit of external power has destroyed entire species and is destroying more. Seas surge through coastal cities, inextinguishable fires burn huge forests, air is foul, water is worse, glaciers melt, and ice disappears from the Earth's poles. Hurricanes are more frequent and intense, temperatures skyrocket or plunge. Food supplies shrink. Wars proliferate. Poverty, disease, starvation, and thirst are everywhere and spreading. Nuclear war looms. All because of pursuing external power. Callousness covers the land. The rich take refuge behind police, and the poor despair or revolt.

Universal Humans see these things clearly and address them directly. They replace callousness with compassion, conquest with cocreativity, and despair of distance from one another with the joy of uniting. They commit themselves to Life. They commit their actions to Life. They commit their lives to Life. They create social structures to support Life. They act and speak with beneficence and the unlimited power of their intentions of love. They cultivate their love of Life, focus their love of Life, and consciously apply their love of Life to the flowering of the human species.

They *are* the flowering of the human species.

# Beyond Culture

Universal Humans are beyond culture.

A culture is a form of limitation. It is a large community. Communities are collectives that are formed by fear. The cohesive element in a community, the glue that holds it together, is fear of those who are different in significant ways and often in insignificant ways. Therefore, discussions of culture are the same as discussions of community. They are discussions of collectives that coalesce out of fear.

Cultures are communities that retain their form through generations of humans, and those generations pass them on to other generations of humans. Therefore, they acquire a rigidity that, for example, a community of individuals who enjoy the same sport do not experience. Theirs is a transient community. It forms around a shared interest, and it disappears when that interest disappears. In other words, some communities are older and more rigid than others. Cultures are very old. They predate most collectives. They predate even religions. Therefore, they are among the most rigid communities. Like all communities, the fundamental function of a culture is the safety of its members from potential threats, which means from others who are different.

Participating in a culture—dress, speech, values—does not prevent you from becoming a Universal Human, provided that you are not attached to it or limited by it. For example, you could wear a hijab as an expression of your understanding of Divinity without needing others to understand Divinity as you do, for if Divinity is that which includes all, so also will you include all.

You can be Chinese, enjoy speaking Chinese, eating Chinese food, and the company of others who are Chinese, but if you are identified with these things and feel that others who are not Chinese are not as good as you, you are experiencing frightened parts of your personality. If Farsi is the only language that you know, then your poetry and love songs will be spoken and written in Farsi, but they will reach far beyond those who speak and read it. Rumi, for example, spoke his poems in Farsi eight centuries ago, yet that did not limit his love or his influence, which are the same. The domain of the five senses is a domain of differences. At issue is how these differences are experienced and shared—with love or with fear.

The only community to a Universal Human, as we have seen, is the Biggest Community. It is the only community that is not based on fear, but on love. It is the community in which there are no subcommunities. A culture is a community of subcommunities. For example, the culture that is French is a community that has numerous subcultures—French athletes, French intellectuals, French artists, French accountants, and so on—and all the individuals in each of these subcultures and the subcultures themselves identify with the larger culture, which is French, and the energy of that influences French language, history, cuisine, and all else French.

The Universal Human is beyond all of that. None of it appeals to the Universal Human. None of it is of interest to the Universal Human. None of it touches the Universal Human. The Universal Human is touched by Life and Life alone. The Universal Human sees no distinctions between this culture and that culture, for example, between Chinese culture and French culture, or between American culture and the culture of Ghana. The Universal Human sees only Life.

We can say that the Universal Human is beyond culture; however, it is more accurate to say that distinctions such as culture have disappeared for it. It is not that a Universal Human is beyond culture in the same way that a point on a highway is beyond a previous point. The Universal Human is the embodiment of a consciousness in which cultures and communities do not exist. The only community is Life. Therefore the distinctions—all five-sensory in nature—that separate collectives are not distinctions that a Universal Human makes. A Universal Human makes no distinctions, for all is Life.

Cultures are magnetically attractive to frightened parts of personalities, for they lend an identity that is older than the personality, an identity that is reenforced by others in the culture, by the history, language, stories, perceptions, and the values of the culture. All of that solidity, or stability, comes from identification with a culture, and all identification with a culture comes from fear. No culture is open to every other culture. The energetic of culture, like the energetic of every community, is to offer the illusion of safety and value to frightened parts of personalities that feel neither safe nor valuable.

A Universal Human is authentically powerful. It has no need for such validation. Its validation comes not from external circumstances, history, or any collective, for attachment to any of those expresses fear. Its validation comes from recognizing its nature, from recognizing that it is a compassionate and loving, powerful and creative spirit, that it is responsible for what it chooses, that it can distinguish between love and fear, and that it can choose love. That is, it can distinguish when frightened parts of its personality desire the safety of sameness and choose instead the unlimited love that it is.

Cultures are small. Humans are large. Frightened parts of personalities keep humans small in their behaviors, thoughts, values, actions, and goals. Creating authentic power allows them to move beyond the frightened parts of their personalities into the largeness of who they are, to recognize the largeness of what other personalities are, and the largeness in which all of this occurs, and that largeness is Life.

The creation of authentic power is the alignment of the personality with the soul. The soul does not see largeness or smallness. It does not see black, yellow, red, white, or brown skin. It does not see cultures that originate in the Tropics or cultures that originate in the Arctic. It sees different expressions of beauty, just as it looks upon an alpine meadow filled with flowers of great beauty and diversity and does not say, "The purple ones are my people" and "Those that are not purple are less or are threats or are limiting to me." A Universal Human does not look at the red flowers and think or say the same, or the white flowers. A Universal Human does not look at trees and think, "They are my culture, not flowers." A Universal Human is flower. A Universal Human is tree. A Universal Human is all else.

Universal Humans are Universal.

# 62

# Beyond Religion

U niversal Humans are beyond religion.

Religious institutions profess Universal truths such as love and oneness. Yet they are among the most divisive organizations in the Earth school. They are purely pursuits of external power. How did this happen?

Oysters encrust irritants to protect themselves, to isolate themselves from them. Their defense systems are analogous to autoimmune systems in human bodies that encrust, so to speak, bacteria and viruses with antibodies. Five-sensory collectives also encrust irritants. Kernels of Universal truth are irritants to them. Religious institutions are the encrustations they form around them. From the perspective of a five-sensory collective, a Universal truth is a pathogen, like an irritating grain of sand, metaphorically speaking.

The Universal truths at the heart of all our religions are the ultimate irritants to five-sensory collectives. They challenge the very reason that five-sensory collectives exist—fear. They replace fear with radically new understandings, such as the understanding of power as alignment of the personality with the soul.

In the case of Christianity, the irritant was the Universal truth of Love, the oyster was the five-sensory collective into which the Christ placed it, and the encrustation is the institution of Christianity.

Every religious institution is an encrustation around a kernel of Universal truth. In other words, the energy of a religious institution is never the same as the energy of the Universal truth at its core, such as, in this case, Love. Religious institutions pursue external power. They look after themselves. They manipulate and control practitioners and compete with one another for them. They promise the inside track. They build barriers between *us* and *them*. *They* will go to hell. *We* will not. Divinity is on *our* side. *They* are infidels.

Religious institutions consume cultures, demonize differences, and attack adversaries, including nations and other religious institutions. A religious institution insulates individuals within it from the transformative power of the Universal truth at its core, and confines them to shallow experiences instead of guiding them to experiences that move mountains. For example, most Christians speak of love. Many Christians believe love is a principle to live by, but few Christians *live* love as the Christ modeled it. Billions of Christians remain insulated (by the encrustation of Christianity) from the transformative power of love. They tolerate others, but they do not accept them. They smile at others and judge them silently or loudly. They kill in the name of love. How many Christians live love like Martin Luther King Jr.? "I have a DREAM" he roared, and the world transformed as he touched it with his courage, integrity, and Love—as he showed and shared the kernel, not the encrustation.

At the memorial service for the American singer, Whitney Houston, the Baptist preacher shared a story that has never left me. "The Muslim said," said the Preacher, "'I wish I had met the Christ before I met the Christian.'" What would the Earth school be like if every Christian lived by the Universal truth of love instead of the religious institution of Christianity? What would the Earth school be like if every Christian loved *you* enough to *die* for you?

Maya Angelou often told us, "When someone says to me, 'I am a Christian,' I say, 'Really? I am in my eighties, and I am still trying.'" The Christ, we are told, declared that you will do all the miraculous things that He did *and more*. When will you begin? What will be your first step?

In the case of Buddhism, the irritant was the Universal truth of enlightenment—perception beyond the Earth school, freedom from all attachment, consciousness clear as a diamond and brilliant as ten thousand suns—awareness of worlds numerous as "motes of dust," each with Buddhas and paths to enlightenment. The oyster was the five-sensory collective into which the Buddha placed it, and the encrustation is the institution of Buddhism.

Buddhists seek their "original face" without the "marks" (characteristics) of mind and desire. Yet their original face remains invisible to them. They desire, suffer, and die as the Buddha described without using the tools that the Buddha gave them. They jostle one another to light incense before statues of the Buddha. They believe in reincarnation, yet relatively few live as though consciousness and responsibility continue after death, as though every experience is a Karmic necessity. How would the world be different if every Buddhist created constructive consequences in every moment with every choice and *never* blamed anyone for his or her experiences?

Every religious institution is an encrustation around a kernel of Universal truth. Each stands *against* the truth, power, and beauty of the Universal truth at its core. Each proclaims its Universal truth, and each models otherwise.

This is deeply confusing to millions of adherents and sometimes to religious professionals, yet they see no way to challenge their religious institution and treasure the Universal truth at its core at the same time. The Universal truth is their proverbial baby, and their religious institution is their proverbial bathwater. So they strive to keep both—the Universal truth that they cherish and the ruthless religious regimen that claims it.

Universal truths come from beyond the Earth school. They calm the personality with the impersonal perceptions of the soul. Now that we are evolving beyond the limitations of five-sensory perception, the Universal truths at the core of our religions are becoming *our* Universal truths. They cease to be properties of institutions.

Multisensory perception makes visible the difference between religious institutions and the Universal truths at their cores. Religious institutions compete. Universal truths do not. Religious institutions restrict creativity. Universal truths release it. Religious institutions have no future. Universal truths are timeless.

If you feel superior or above others, RIGHT instead of WRONG, because of your religion, you are not experiencing the Universal truth of your religion. You are experiencing the fear of the five-sensory institution that claims to own it. Five-sensory religious institutions *prevent* our evolution. Their hideous behaviors are products of fear. They have no future. Multisensory humans strive for harmony, cooperation, sharing, and reverence for Life. They strive for humbleness, clarity, forgiveness, and love. Universal Humans embody these things.

When you ask yourself "What would my life be like if I lived the Universal truth at the core of my religion or any religion?" you ask the Universe for an experience of the Universal Human.

# 63

# Beyond Nation

U niversal Humans are beyond nation.

"Nation" is a word for the enormity of the brutality and the cruelty in the human experience. It is a linguistic symbol for what we are leaving behind as we transition from five-sensory perception to multisensory perception and from the understanding of power as the ability to manipulate and control to the understanding of power as the alignment of the personality with the soul. It is deeply and unconsciously entrenched. Understanding "nation" presents us simultaneously and unambiguously with the two sides of the choice that must be made between love and fear, and how vital and insightful is the awareness that is required to make it.

Nations share the same genetic code, metaphorically speaking, as frightened parts of personalities. Absolute monarchies, empires, religious institutions, and cancer cells also share this code. Affection for a nation is a sentimental delusion. It obscures the nature of nations. Once you understand the nature of "nation," you will understand why.

A nation is a collective, but it is not a collective of individuals as it appears. It is more a collection than a collective. It is a collection of diverse pursuits of external power.

The nation itself, the entity that we call a "nation," is a pursuit of external power that comes frequently into conflict with other nations that are the same. The nation with the most external power imposes its will upon those with less. This is the only dynamic among nations.

Within nations the dynamic is identical. Some pursuits of external power are more effective than others, and they impose their wills upon the other pursuits. In political arenas those pursuits are called "parties." Yet within the nation are also myriad other concerns, for example, social concerns. The status of females in relationship to males is one of them. Here the collection of males has more external power. That is shifting and creating great resistance. The relationship of white people to black people is another example. An analogous circumstance prevails in the United States—white people have more external power.

The relationship of religious populations to one another is another example. In the United States one religion is dominant and has more external power than the others combined. In other nations the situation is the same, but the dominant religion is different. In yet other nations the balance is different. This is also the relationship, as we have seen, between individuals. Individuals, through the frightened parts of their personalities, pursue external power and come into conflict with one another.

In other words, from top to bottom and from bottom to top a nation is a pursuit of external power and simultaneously a hollow shell that contains countless pursuits of external power within it at every level of interaction, from social to personal, from political to religious. Each nation is a miniature reflection of the pursuit of external power that characterizes five-sensory humanity. External power is everywhere and inescapable.

The most aggressive nations distend, like cancer-infested organs, into bloated entities incapable of self-perpetuation. The Roman empire distended from Britain to Babylonia and from North Africa to the Middle East. The British empire distended to a quarter of the earth's land area and four hundred twelve million people. It became so distended that the sun could not set on all of it at the same time, thus did the British boast "the sun never sets on the British empire." Eventually, it did.

Five-sensory humans glorify all this. They call Alexander from Macedon, whose relatively small empire distended from Greece to India, Alexander the Great—undefeated in battle and unquenchable in his appetite for it. Multisensory humans call him Alexander the Terrified. He feared no adversary, army, or collective, but the pain of powerlessness terrified him. He conquered country after country and put his name on twenty cities trying to avoid it. He pursued external power until his death, and the pursuit of external power ripped his empire apart after he died. Today Alexander's empire, the Roman empire, and the British empire are no more.

There is no sense of relationship between nations except in the continual search for advantage over one another. In this they perfectly reflect the relationship of frightened parts of one personality to frightened parts of others. From the five-sensory perspective interactions among personalities (such as connecting with neighbors) are at the lowest level of a hierarchy, and interactions among nations (such as empire-building) are at the highest level. Multisensory perception and the understanding of power as the alignment of the personality to the soul invert this hierarchy. The highest and most meaningful level is that of interactions among individuals (because human evolution requires creating authentic power). The lowest and most meaningless level is that of interactions among nations (because there is no spiritual dimension to them). Nations have no ability to move forward. They are empty.

A nation is something similar to a hall of mirrors. Entering it and viewing experience from its perspective, there is nothing but itself, and it projects itself upon all other collections called "nation." In other words, nations are collections of pursuits of external power that are themselves reflections of other pursuits of external power.

Where do nations come from?

64

# Far Beyond Nation

The origin of nations is important not only in the history of our nation and the history of other nations, but also in the history of the human species. It illuminates all that needs to be changed in the human species and the awareness of what is required to change it. These exist simultaneously in both collectives and in individuals. What exist simultaneously are the two sides of the choice that must be made between love and fear. We have explored this choice throughout this book. It is the heart of creating authentic power. The origin of nations reveals the significance of making it consciously and constructively.

While humankind was five-sensory and power was understood as external, "nation" began to emerge as the ossification of this understanding. The continual pursuit of it among individuals was reflected in social institutions, including, ultimately, empires and dynasties. As the understanding of power as external and pursuits of it began to coalesce into entities—and the participants in each entity became cohesively dependent—the "nation" itself reflected them as it came into being, a monstrous collection of all that is destructive in the human psyche.

A cohesive dependence of participants within an entity that is pursuing external power is the dependence of all the participants in the entity upon the structures and experiences of pursuing external power. Five-sensory humanity evolved by pursuing power. Therefore, it can be said that all of five-sensory humanity had a cohesive dependence upon the pursuit of external power. Whether the activity was an interaction between individuals, groups of individuals, or larger collectives of individuals, the interaction was the pursuit of external power. This was understood by all and was not questioned.

In other words, all interactions among five-sensory individuals and five-sensory collectives, including larger collectives, were based upon this common understanding and experience of power as the ability to manipulate and control. It is that which brought them together and kept them together, put them into continual competition, generated hoarding, created discord, and required exploitation of one another and Life. All of this—destructive as it was—was the cohesive energy of five-sensory participants in all their interactions large and small. Said another way, it was the commonality of not feeling emotional pain and instead attempting to mask it through the pursuit of external power. As this commonality grew in scope, it gave birth to the hollow, empty, destructive entities called nations.

As these pursuits of external power over quite long periods of time began to come into structured form, so to speak, these structures grew in size and encompassed more individuals. That was the coalescence of these experiences into entities, each of which had the cohesion of participants in pursuit of external power. As these structures grew in size and efficacy, they eventually emerged as the entities that we now call "nations."

Every interaction among nations illuminates the structure of experience that we have been calling the pursuit of external power—focus of attention on the world with the intention of changing it. It is the opposite of the structure of experience that we have been calling the creation of authentic power—focus of attention on interior dynamics with the intention of changing oneself. Nations have no content but external power. They have no purpose but the pursuit of external power. They have no usefulness but the pursuit of external power as it served the survival of five-sensory humanity. They embody all that the pursuit of external power without reverence represents and has accomplished.

Individuals often say or feel that they have an allegiance to their nation, and they call that patriotism. The word "patriotism" itself is an expression of fear. It expresses dominance in terms of external power of males over females. As it is commonly understood, "patriotism" is allegiance to the pursuit of external power. There is no consideration of the other. There is no compassion. There is zero wisdom. Matriotism used in the same way would be as destructive. The pursuit of external power is not restricted by gender.

Individuals often feel attractions to one another, but those attractions are self-serving when they are unconscious. They serve the unconscious pursuit of external power. This is visible in the unconscious interactions that we refer to as romantic attractions, for example, when individuals say to each other, "You make me feel complete" or "You make my world." When that is gone, the attraction changes. This dynamic infuses friendships, communities, and all collectives. Therefore we could say that the pursuit of external power is the essence of "nation," except that "nation" has no essence. It is the empty pursuit of external power populated by myriad pursuits of external power, all reflected, expressed, and acted upon by this thing called "nation."

Nations have no further use in human evolution, just as the pursuit of external power has no further use in human evolution. They prevent human evolution.

Universal Humans do not judge this. Universal Humans are beyond the pursuit of external power, and therefore they are beyond the mindless destruction, suffering, and inhumanity that it creates. Universal Humans see this. They see also what can be done to assist fellow students in the Earth school in expanding their awareness, using their volition consciously, and creating a constructive world. In this world nations will have no place, for there will be no need for them.

Nation is the only social structure that will not have a replacement.

# 65

# Beyond Ethnic Group I

Universal Humans are beyond ethnic group.

"Race" is a relatively new word. It is only a few centuries old, but the energy behind it is very old. It applies only to humans. We do not speak of a race of elephants, or a race of mammals, or races of fish. "Race" carries covert meaning. It implies that one human collective can be more valuable, worthy, intelligent, beautiful, or creative than another. Words carry consciousness. "Race" carries the consciousness of fear. "Race" is a declaration of superiority and inferiority. Collectives that see themselves as superior wield this word as a weapon.

Nazis defined their biological inheritance as the "Aryan race" and declared themselves *übermenschen*, which means "superhumans." The "Aryan race" was white and German. It claimed supremacy over millions of humans who were also white and German, such as Jews, Gays, Lesbians, and Gypsies. It claimed supremacy over millions of humans who were merely white, such as French, Spanish, Swedish, and many others. It also claimed supremacy over every black, yellow, and brown human. Claiming supremacy meant entitlement to enslave, torture, and kill.

The goal of the Aryan "superhumans" was a "Thousand Year Reich," an empire that would last a millennium. It survived twelve years. During this short time the viciousness, mercilessness, and brutality unleashed in the name of "race" engulfed the world in the most destructive conflict endured by humans, World War II. It enveloped the earth. Historians needed to create a new category to describe it, "Total War"— unconstrained use of weapons and targets (think atomic bombs), mass death of civilians (think labor camps and death camps), collective punishment (think London and Tokyo burning), death to all involved (think unrestricted submarine warfare).

Six million Jews and five million individuals from "inferior races" in Europe were methodically murdered in thousands of facilities specifically built to exterminate them (not only the huge and infamous ones, such as Auschwitz and Buchenwald). An estimated *eighty million* people died in World War II. The word "race" did not cause the carnage. The energy that utilized it did—fear. When you think in terms of "race," you participate in this energy.

The German physiologist and anthropologist Johann Blumenbach (1752–1840) was one of the first to use the word "race" to categorize humans by appearance. He did not assign values to the five races he identified (white, black, brown, yellow, red), but he admired the beauty of the white race (his race). This opened a door through which countless thoughts shaped by fear were to pass.

The Atlantic slave trade was huge by Blumenbach's time—it brought *millions* of West Africans as slaves to Europe, the American colonies, and Brazil. Its degrading and murderous treatment of these individuals could not be ignored. Europeans began to use Blumenbach's ideas to justify the unjustifiable. The malignant reasoning that developed in Europe and then in the American colonies was this: Races are unequal. The white race is superior to the black race. Slave traders and slaveowners are not immoral when they brutalize an inferior race. This behavior is the natural order of things. I am not immoral when I acquiesce to this brutality.

Blumenbach himself opposed slavery and strongly objected to this kind of reasoning (he was twenty-four when the American Revolution began). "There is no so-called savage nation known under the sun," he pointedly wrote, "which has so much distinguished itself by such examples of perfectibility and original capacity for scientific culture, and thereby attached itself so closely to the most civilized nations of the earth, as the Negro," but this kind of reasoning happened anyway and continues to happen today.

The unjustifiable was huge in the American colonies. On July 4, 1776, the Second Continental Congress declared the thirteen American colonies to be "Free and Independent States" and all political connection between them and Great Britain "totally dissolved." Even more thrilling was their pronouncement that "all men are created equal" with "unalienable Rights" including "Life, Liberty and the pursuit of Happiness." How could *that* be reconciled with slavery?

The always explosive flash point in America appears to be "race." It is not. It is the unresolved conflict between the radiant potential of the United States that shines at its essence—equality for all—and what it is and offers. This conflict is as virulent today as it was in 1776, and it continues to create dissonance in the symphony of American experience that will not disappear, that becomes more frequent and louder with each century, each year, each month, and now with each day.

Slavery is as old as human history. It existed in Babylonia, and it exists today. Slaves probably cast some of the nets that caught the shrimp on your table. Countless women are slaves in cultural prisons as much as women who are slaves in brothels. They cannot leave, drive, vote, or educate themselves. Itinerant farmworkers in the United States and garment workers in Bangladesh live in functional slavery. They are exploited continually and they cannot escape. Slavery exists everywhere people are bound by the shackles of poverty.

Some ancient forms of slavery allowed slaves freedom after certain requirements were met. Some allowed children of slaves to be born free. Some allowed owners to educate slaves, as did the Roman master who educated Terence and also freed him. However, the form of slavery in the American colonies was among the most savage, brutal, and degrading. Slaves were "chattel" (personal, movable property). They were enslaved their entire lives. Their children and grandchildren were chattel (personal, movable property of the same owner). Education was violently prohibited to them. Their ability to travel, even into a town, was severely limited. Many lived in bestial conditions provided by owners who brutalized them at will.

All slaves in the American colonies were black. All slaveowners were white. White people bought and sold black people as animals. White people exploited, discarded, and killed black people. White men raped black women with no fear of disapproval or punishment. What circumstance could be more receptive to a hierarchical theory of race based on appearance? Blumenbach's 1775 dissertation provided one.

Slavery in the American colonies distorted the perceptions of white Americans of Africans and the perceptions of Africans of themselves. These distorted perceptions exist in the United States today. Contemporary white Americans and black Americans are filled with emotions, thoughts, and rationalizations that would be familiar to Colonial slave owners and slaves. Slavery excluded Africans from humanity, denied their rich histories and cultures, and defined them as animals. These exclusions, denials, and definitions are part of the collective consciousness of the United States, but they are not confined to the collective consciousness of the United States.

Many white Americans, including those who profess otherwise, fear African-Americans, see them as inferior, and hold them at a distance. Some use relationships with African-Americans, including the most superficial, to demonstrate open-mindedness. Almost all are ignorant of African histories and cultures. They do not know that Adam and Eve came from Africa. They do not know that a thousand years before the Pre-Roman Iron Age (400 BC), Africans were smelting and working with iron (1500 BC). In other words, they do not know that while Europeans were still using crude stone tools, Africans were exploring the technology that enabled the Industrial Revolution. They are unaware of African-American poets, artists, and scholars.

African-Americans struggle everywhere with the legacy of slavery—customs, laws, police, policies, and economics. Even the most successful of them face inner demons that declare them inadequate, hopeless, and unworthy. Every human encounters these demons, but African-Americans feel the weight of slavery upon them as they do. Millions of African-Americans are enslaved in the permanent under-caste of America, struggling daily to survive economically, psychologically, or physically. When you think in terms of race, you participate in all of this. But all of this was not the end point of "race" in the United States as justification for pursuing external power.

It was the beginning.

# 66

# Beyond Ethnic Group II

White settlers used Blumenbach's ideas to justify their genocide of red people.

Their justification for murdering red people was virtually identical to their justification for enslaving black people: Races are unequal. The white race is superior to the red race. White people are not immoral when they brutalize an inferior race. This behavior is the natural order of things. I am not immoral when I acquiesce to this brutality.

However, there were big differences between the red people that white settlers murdered and the black people that they enslaved. The black people did not want to be in the American colonies or in the United States (to say the very, very least), and the red people were determined to remain on their homelands. White settlers wanted those lands, and they took them with lethal force. The more heroically red people defended themselves, the more white settlers considered them savages and treated them savagely. The origin of this ugly chapter in American history is older than Blumenbach's dissertation and the United States.

In 1493, a pope (Alexander VI) published a Papal Bull (decree) that gave Spain (think Ferdinand and Isabella) ownership of the land that Christopher Columbus discovered the previous year. It also gave them ownership of all the land in a very large part of the world that Spanish explorers might discover in the future. In other words, the Pope gave Spain virtually all of the "New World" even while it was being discovered! (He had self-serving reasons for doing this.)

The Pope also decreed in the same Bull that the first white Christian to step onto land previously undiscovered by a white Christian (except in the part of the world reserved for Spanish white Christians to discover) (think North America and South America) automatically made that land (by right of first toe-touch) property of his white Christian sovereign (think Isabella and Ferdinand again, and also England, Portugal, France, Holland, Germany, and Belgium)! Further, everything and *everyone* on the land (according to the Pope, and, therefore, according to the Pope's God) henceforth belonged to that white Christian sovereign. (Really.) Even if that white Christian sovereign or a representative never visited the land, the land and everything and everyone on it belonged to him or her *forever*! (This *actually happened*.)

The Pope also instructed the white Christian sovereigns who benefited from his Bull to "lead" their newly acquired peoples "to embrace the Christian profession." Other than that, they were free to do as they pleased with their newly acquired peoples.

The external power (think warships and cannons) of the European nations that profited from the Pope's self-serving proclamation quickly made it into a reality that shapes international relations today. (The first American on the moon did not kneel in gratitude, pray for peace, or even rejoice. He planted a flag.) The Pope's proclamation became known as the "Doctrine of Discovery." It could also be known as the "First-White-Christian-Takes-All" doctrine.

American settlers used this doctrine to justify being in the "New World" (their name) in the first place (actually, the second place, since it was occupied before they arrived), and to justify their "Manifest Destiny." "Manifest Destiny" translates roughly as "Everything on this continent is ours." When the red people who lived on the land objected, the white people killed as many of them as they could. American history calls this savagery the "Indian Wars" and blames it on the Indians.

In short, white people took land that red people held sacred and enslaved black people to work it. The white people prospered. The red people and the black people did not. This is the situation today. Genocide and slavery are open lesions on the collective consciousness of the United States, and they continue to create ugly consequences.

From the Virginia Colony to the Massachusetts Colony, from Wounded Knee to Standing Rock, from 1776 to now, "race" continues to distort American experience. White settlers saw Native Americans as savages. Today Americans confine Native Americans to the least desirable parts of the United States. White settlers saw Africans as animals. Today Americans incarcerate (cage) more African-Americans than any other Americans.

Five-sensory humans think the Pope's Bull, Blumenbach's dissertation, and white settlers are the causes of these cruelties. Multisensory humans know that the pursuit of external power without reverence is the cause. Five-sensory perception and the pursuit of external power are parts of a package. That package is the dying consciousness. Now another package has arrived. It contains multisensory perception and the creation of authentic power. In order to evolve, we need to throw the old package away, unwrap the new package, and begin using what is in it.

Half a century ago geneticists discredited the theory that "races" originate in geographically distinct gene pools. UNESCO declared "race" a myth in 1952, and social scientists call it a "social construct." From the multisensory perspective, "race" does not exist. Souls do not have genes, DNA, IQ, geographical origins, or physical characteristics.

However, *racism* exists. *Racism* is fear—the opposite of love. It is the lethal liaison between ignorance and fear wherever it appears, even where differences in "race" do not exist! The Nazi genocide of Jews (same race), Rwandan Hutu genocide of Rwandan Tutsis (same race); Pakistani genocide of Bangladeshis (same race); Soviet genocide of Ukrainians (same race); Ottoman genocides of Armenians, Christian Greeks, and Assyrians (same race) are some examples.

Racism is a cork thrown up from a sea of fear, bobbing on the surface, violent and ugly, but not the source of the suffering it produces. The sea itself is the source. There is no more genetic significance between black skin and white skin than there is between brown eyes and blue eyes or big athletes and small carpenters. If we were to assert "races" of brown-eyed and blue-eyed people, or big people with athletic ability, small people who build things, and medium-size people who write books (like me), would these "races" be absurd? Totally.

Race is a fantasy of fear, a progeny of the pain of powerlessness, and a desperate, unconscious, self-tormenting attempt by five-sensory humans to avoid the pain of powerlessness. These dynamics are invisible to five-sensory individuals, but multisensory individuals see them.

Defining a fellow student in the Earth school as different from yourself in any essential way is racism by whatever name called. It is equally absurd. All Earth suits are unique. All souls are immortal. All souls incarnate voluntarily. All souls evolve through choices of their personalities. All personalities have loving and frightened parts. The pain of powerlessness torments all personalities. Five-sensory personalities pursue external power to mask it. Multisensory personalities create authentic power to move beyond the control of it.

Maya Angelou also told us, "We are more alike than we are different." Now we can say with multisensory certainty, "We are *much* more alike than we are different." We are all souls. We are all Life.

Universal Humans celebrate this.

# 67

# Beyond Gender I

Universal Humans are beyond gender.

The most inclusive social structure in the human experience governs relationships between five-sensory females and five-sensory males. It predates all other social structures. It is more pervasive and influential than any others even though it has no organizing body, no communications networks, not even a website. It establishes the roles and responsibilities for every five-sensory female and every five-sensory male.

This social structure has no compliance arm, but its demands are ruthlessly enforced. Penalties for ignoring them are severe. Penalties for resisting them can be savagely brutal. The penalty for challenging them in many places is death. This social structure is built on external power like all other five-sensory social structures, and therefore, like all other five-sensory social structures, it is obsolete and disintegrating.

New archetypes of female and male have appeared. They are different from the old archetypes of female and male. An archetype is a pattern of energy that shapes the experiences of individuals in its gravitational field, so to speak, as the sun shapes the orbits of planets revolving around it. Father, Mother, Warrior, and Priest are examples of archetypes.

The old archetype of female is the Old Female. Old Females are five-sensory. The old archetype of male is the Old Male. Old Males are also five-sensory. Old Females are fulfilled by bearing and raising children. Old Males are fulfilled by providing and protecting. The Old Female and the Old Male together created a natural division of labor that enhanced the probability of their survival.

The new archetype of female is the New Female. New Females are multisensory. The new archetype of male is the New Male. New Males are also multisensory. Therefore, the archetypes of New Female and New Male are as different from the archetypes of Old Female and Old Male as multisensory perception is from five-sensory perception—and more so.

New Females are not bound by the roles of the Old Female. They can be heads of state, CEOs of corporations, surgeons, architects, financiers, nannies, carpenters, poets, plumbers, and stay-at-home mothers. They can build bridges as well as bear children. They can fight for freedom as well as raise families. They accomplish whatever they intend. Their lives illuminate the powerful words of Johann Wolfgang von Goethe: "Whatever you can do, or dream you can, begin it. Boldness has genius, power, and magic in it."

New Females say what needs to be said, do what needs to be done, and build what needs to be built. They are unstoppable.

New Males are not bound by the roles of the Old Male. They cradle infants in airports, push baby carriages through grocery stores, and drive children to playdates, as well as pilot airplanes (with New Females), build businesses (with New Females), and contribute to multisensory social structures (with New Females). They are sensitive, intuitive, and loving. They laugh, cry, care for others, nurture the sick, guide the young, help the poor, and support the elderly. They redefine masculinity.

New Females and New Males cocreate in the new archetype of Spiritual Partnership. They choose their roles in their spiritual partnerships. They are parts of the consciousness that is being born. Old Females and Old Males are parts of the consciousness that is dying.

The purpose of the five-sensory social structure that governs relationships between five-sensory females and five-sensory males is to impose the roles of the Old Female onto all females and the roles of the Old Male onto all males. New Females and New Males are not confined to these archaic roles.

The Garden of Eden story portrays Eve as the second-class citizen in the Garden of Eden and the Mother of All Problems as well as the Mother of Humanity. *She* listened to the only nonhuman in the Garden (the snake). *She* yearned to learn. *She* is responsible for the catastrophic collapse of our perfect lives in paradise. *She* is a derivative! *She* is made from a male to be his companion (not cocreator, co-explorer, or even colleague). The male is the first-class citizen.

The Garden of Eden story did not create this perception of females. This perception created the Garden of Eden story. Five-sensory humans called themselves "huMANity." They chronicled their "HIStory" (not "HERstory"). Their choices of fear created female genital mutilation, "honor" killings, rape of females as a weapon of war, females as property (think chattel), sex slaves (think harems), without rights (think education), without freedom (think passport), without choice (think arranged marriage), and without voice (think vote).

Multisensory humans chronicle "OURstory." The disintegrating five-sensory social structure that imposes the values of Old Females and Old Males upon all females and males cannot control New Females or New Males any more than streams can run uphill or rivers can flow from the ocean.

New Females and New Males create authentic power in spiritual partnerships and support one another in spiritual partnerships. They plumb the depths of emotional awareness and develop the discipline of responsible choice. Nonphysical Teachers become their friends, and they are delighted to learn that they have always been their friends. They become captains of their own vessels, following the great ships that are their souls. They deepen their commitment to spiritual growth through practice, strengthen their courage through creating authentic power, and grow spiritually in cocreation with the Universe. They become receptors of love and conveyors of love, livers of love and givers of love. Fear comes but it cannot stay because it does not frighten them.

A new experience of gender is emerging. The archetypes of the New Female and the New Male are not related to genitals, sexual desires, or sexual identities. They are patterns of energy that shape the experiences of New Males and New Females regardless of whether their genitals are male or female, they desire to be with males or females, or they experience themselves as male or female.

They are even freer of gender than this.

# 68

# Beyond Gender II

Gender is an aspect of the human experience that has immovable functions, so to speak. The bearing of children is a function of the female gender. Males cannot bear children. Therefore, this aspect of gender cannot change, yet because of that there is an understanding from the five-sensory perspective that the relationship between males and females cannot change. This is incorrect.

From a multisensory perspective male and female are aspects of Earth suits. Every aspect of an Earth suit provides opportunities for experiences that the soul agreed to prior to incarnation. Gender is one of them. The relationship between males and females transcends even gender, for that relationship from a multisensory perspective is soul-to-soul. From a five-sensory perspective the relationship is personality-to-personality, and that is where male-and-female seems to be forever a divide that cannot be crossed.

In fact, that divide disappears when the relationship between students in the Earth school becomes soul-to-soul. Then gender becomes part of the Earth suit that was chosen by the soul. In other words, an Earth suit that is male provides opportunities for experiences that are necessary for the spiritual growth of that student, and the same is true for an Earth suit that is female. For example, one personality may have frightened parts that are angry or strive to be dominant, and the frightened parts of another personality may be submissive or feel inferior.

From a five-sensory perspective these are often thought of as male and female aspects, yet they are not. They are Earth suit aspects, for there are male personalities that must struggle with speaking what they know is important, with not being submissive, with contributing with integrity, and there are female personalities that must challenge frightened parts that would dominate conversations, would manipulate and control in ways that are more overtly the pursuit of external power.

As we have seen, both males and females have frightened parts of their personalities, and those frightened parts, no matter what personality they belong to, pursue external power. This is an inherent aspect of the Earth school, an aspect of souls incarnating into the realm of time, space, matter, and duality as personalities. Each of those personalities has parts of itself that its soul has given to it that are already aligned with its soul. These are the loving parts. Each of those personalities also has parts that are not aligned with its soul. These are the frightened parts.

The frightened parts of a personality require unearthing, experiencing, and challenging to move beyond the control of them. The loving parts of a personality require unearthing, experiencing, and cultivating to bring them more frequently into the awareness of the personality. It is in this context that the difference between male and female becomes simply another difference between personalities, a difference that is tailor-made, so to speak, for the spiritual development of a particular personality.

The physical characteristics of a male and the physical characteristics of a female are defined in terms of bearing children, but the frightened and loving parts of a personality emerge as it develops emotional awareness so that it can move beyond the control of fear. Personalities that are creating authentic power support one another in this process, in other words, they become spiritual partners. Male-or-female is not the defining characteristic of this relationship. It is experiencing and challenging fear and experiencing and cultivating love. That is why the dynamic of New Male and New Female is not determined by genitals. These are different ways of saying the same thing.

Universal Humans are beyond gender because gender does not define their relationships. The relationship of individuals as they become multisensory is the relationship of spiritual partners assisting one another in the creation of authentic power. Just as one individual may have experiences in the military that other individuals have not had, another individual may have experiences as a mother that other individuals have not had. However, from a multisensory perspective bearing a child is more than becoming a mother. It is the fulfilling of an agreement that a soul made prior to incarnation to work closely with another soul as it enters the Earth school, which means, as it incarnates as a student, as a personality.

As New Females emerge, they are able to have experiences that were previously reserved for Old Males, for example, military experiences such as fighting in the infantry, flying jet aircraft, and becoming senior officers—and with that come the same challenges of transforming the social structures in which they become involved. These are the five-sensory social structures that are now disintegrating and will be replaced by multisensory social structures. The five-sensory social structures are based upon the personality and the understanding of power as external. The multisensory social structures that are replacing them are built upon the soul and the understanding of power as the alignment of the personality with the soul.

All of this occurs independently of personality characteristics, and from the multisensory perspective, gender is a personality characteristic, an Earth suit aspect. Gender no longer defines the relationship of New Males to New Females as it defined the relationship of Old Males to Old Females and the reverse.

New Males and New Females choose one another as spiritual partners, as individuals with whom they choose to undertake the difficult and demanding journey of spiritual growth. In other words, the emergence of a New Male and a New Female is simply a reflection in terms of internal dynamics of a new multisensory species leaving behind the limitations that it associated with gender as a physical function and perceiving gender instead as a personality aspect.

The Universal Human is beyond all that is five-sensory. The Universal Human is multisensory. The Universal Human is authentically empowered. The Universal Human does not see its experiences in terms of spiritual development as defined by the five-sensory experiences of Old Males and Old Females, but instead by multisensory experiences of its world and multisensory experiences of itself and its fellow students as souls with a common function, a common purpose, a common destination—a journey into Life and the experience of Life without fear, a journey into Love and the cultivation of Love. For Universal Humans there are no other experiences.

As you look at the sky on a starry night that is clear, there is no alternative to it. That is Life presenting itself to you in that spectacular way. As you look at a soul, there is no alternative. That soul is Life presenting itself to you in that spectacular way. Universal Humans experience this. They experience all of it. They are beyond every five-sensory experience. They are beyond every five-sensory limitation, and in their movement beyond those limitations and experiences they expand into gratitude, into appreciation of Life itself.

There is nothing more important to them. There is nothing more significant to them because as they grow in their awareness, they realize that there is nothing but Life. They honor Life. They revere Life. They appreciate Life. They enjoy Life. They support Life. They are Life. They are Universal Humans.

Five-sensory humankind is transforming into multisensory humankind. This is the phase that is emerging now. It is the transformation that is reshaping all experience—the transition from five-sensory limitations into the more expanded perceptions of the soul. Beyond that comes another transformation as magnificent, as indescribable, as the transition from five-sensory perception and interactions of personalities in the Earth school into multisensory perception and interactions of souls in the Earth school.

Just as multisensory perception cannot be meaningfully described to a five-sensory species, the species of multisensory humans cannot meaningfully understand a species of Universal Humans. Yet multisensory humans can begin to feel the call of it, the magnitude of it, the beauty of it, the expansiveness of it, for it is the Universe. It is Love. It is Consciousness. It is Life, and that is the source, that is the destination, that is the journey, that is the joy, that is the completion, and that is the ever-present fulfillment of the Universal Human.

# 69

# Universal Humans

The most intimate sharings are the most universal. I see this again and again in our events. General statements, nonspecific references, and vague wording do not change the one who shares or those who listen. Eventually, participants in our events recognize this. Then they must choose to remain silent, share thoughtlessly, or speak honestly. Fear-based parts of their personalities strive for invisibility, bluster, or inundate us with torrents of words. Love-based parts of their personalities long for the truth of the heart, the communion of sharing the truth of the heart, and the freedom the truth of the heart offers. They reach outward to connect, and the reach is always worth the courage. Years later, I remember what these participants shared, how permanently it changed me, and how deeply it affected all in the room.

One woman spoke of her mother with Alzheimer's. Her mother would mistake her for her sister. Then she would mistake her for her mother. At other times she would mistake her for her brother. At last in frustration she said, "No, Mother. I am not your sister! I am not your mother! I am not your brother! I am your daughter!" Then her mother, in tears of frustration, cried, "I don't know who you are. I only know my soul wants to be with you."

Other participants shared fears of abandonment, ridicule, betrayal, failing their expectations, shame, or self-loathing—all in the context of describing (not speaking from) a fear-based part of his or her personality. They shared their most guarded and dark places, and they discovered that others already knew them. They displayed their humanness, and

they became human. That is the power of the heart. The heart always
recognizes the heart.

Universal Humans and the heart are inseparable. Universal Humans
cannot *be* without the heart. Universal Humans are the goal of the heart,
the fulfillment of the heart, and the completion of the heart. They are the
heart unleashed, unbound, and without limit. Where Universal Humans
are, the heart shines. The heart is the center and the periphery, the above
and the below, the in and the out of Universal Humans. It is the sun that
never sets, the bloom that never fades, and the ceaseless source of Love
that animates Universal Humans. It cuts through all barriers of language
and belief.

Mother Teresa told us, "We cannot do great things, but we can do
small things with great love." She tended to wounds, sickness, and thirst
one wounded, ill, and thirsty person at a time. She did small things with
great love. From the perspective of the old consciousness, the greatest
things affect the most people. From the perspective of the new consciousness, the smallest thing is the greatest thing: the choice of love
instead of fear that one person makes in the intimacy of her or his experience. Universal Humans pay attention to the details of love.

Mother Teresa was a Universal Human.

Mohandas Gandhi marched two hundred forty miles to the sea
from his ashram to gather salt and publicly violate the British salt mo-
nopoly in India. Seventy-eight colleagues who had trained for fifteen
years in *satyagraha*, the power of love, began with him. Millions more
joined with their feet or hearts as they marched to the ocean. Gandhi
walked consciously toward his possible (probable) death, his possible
(probable) crippling, his possible (probable) imprisonment, and India
walked consciously with him. His intention was to provoke a British
reaction that would reveal the brutality of British rule in India to the
world. He had no doubt it would come. When it did, its cruelty shocked
the world, and the massive civil disobedience that followed was the beginning of the end of British rule in India, although difficult struggles
remained.

Two weeks before the march Gandhi published an article, "When I
Am Arrested." He wrote in it, "Not a single believer in nonviolence as an

article of faith for the purpose of achieving India's goal should find himself free or alive at the end of the effort."

He wrote with love, acted in love, went to prison with love, endured beatings with love, guided India to independence with love, and died in love. He practiced "noncooperation" with love (not the same as "nonviolent protest"). "Love" is the operative word. "Love" is the operative energy. "Love" is the transformative force. Love was Gandhi's tactic and Gandhi's strategy.

Gandhi was a Universal Human.

We are told that zealots offered Jesus from Nazareth command of an army and that He declined. We know little about Jesus, especially his early life, except from words that were written centuries after He walked the Earth, words that were frequently and sometimes intentionally changed. Gaining knowledge this way is analogous to children playing a game of "telephone," where whispered messages are immediately distorted. These hearsay accounts tell us that love was important to Jesus—He fed people, healed people, and cared for prostitutes and tax collectors. All of them tell us that Jesus usually sought to teach love, even for the soldiers who tortured Him and killed Him.

Jesus was a Universal Human.

These Universal Humans emerged in our past. They call us still to higher visions, healthier lives, more sensitive societies, and the fulfillment of our highest potential.

The Universal Humans that are emerging now call us to the same.

# 70

# Emerging Universal Humans

E merging Universal Humans are appearing around us like grass in the spring. Here are some examples.

≈

Jayesh guided Linda and me patiently through a large slum—one hundred twenty thousand people—near Gandhi's ashram in Ahmedabad, India. Jayesh was born in that ashram, and now he is a trustee of it. People rushed from their "houses"—some without walls, some with dirt floors, and all filled with people and animals—to greet him joyfully. Laughing children danced beside him. He playfully cleaned the nose of a boy, then washed his own hands to model the rest of the lesson. People everywhere met him with unrestrained joy.

An old woman gestured to us. "She is inviting you to have tea with her," Jayesh told us with a smile. An old man who had become a sadhu—a holy man—after Jayesh's last visit showed us his small, bare, clean room that he had made into a temple. "Did you not have even two minutes to be with me these seven years?" he reproached Jayesh lovingly, with tears of joy flowing from his eyes.

Seven years earlier Jayesh and his colleagues taught these same people, some of them children then, how to build and use toilets, clip children's fingernails, clean noses, and wash hands to reduce the cause of eighty percent of preventable illnesses in India—poor sanitation.

As we walked and talked, Jayesh lifted his left hand palm down, as though dropping something from it, like a gift. "This is no good," he said. Then he extended his right hand palm up below it, as though receiving something from above, as a beggar holds her hand. "This is no good," he said again. Then he extended his right hand as though to shake the outstretched hand of another. "This is good," he explained. "We cooperate, cocreate, and step back."

On our walk we discovered that Jayesh had not visited this slum for seven years! He had "stepped back," to use his words, eighty-four months to let new knowledge integrate, creativity emerge, and strength grow! Without knowing this, I had asked him to show to us this slum before we left India. I wanted to see if the generosity, kindness, and joy that flowed to us from the people we had met in the Old Town of Ahmedabad—a place much, much, much poorer than a "slum" in the West—would also flow to us from the people in this slum. They did.

Jayesh Patel is an emerging Universal Human.

I met Masami on a video call. "I want *you* to create with me," she announced laughing as her daughter translated from Japanese. Playfully she poked her finger at me as she spoke, and, amazingly, I felt her poke. The joy in her laugh and enthusiasm filled me. How could her body be so small and her energy be so great? Linda and I met Masami and her family in Tokyo the following spring, and she blessed us again with her joy, vitality, and clear, unwavering focus. Her focus was peace. Peace for all. Peace everywhere. The energy of peace. The intentions of peace. The spiritual growth that alone produces peace, and supporting that spiritual growth around the world. Her entire family joined her in this focus, even grandchildren too young to speak.

We gathered at the base of Mount Fuji for an annual Symphony of Peace Prayers. The celebration was gorgeous: Snow-covered Mt. Fuji in the background and twelve thousand people sitting on the grass. A representative from every religion blessed us; a small group of participants from around the world shared its discoveries at a preceding conference on Peace, which Linda and I had attended. Then the flag of every country was paraded to music, one by one, as people on the grass held high plastic replicas of the flag of their country when it appeared or the flag of a country they wanted to pray for when it appeared. I was surprised at how deeply I enjoyed praying for every flag. Our prayers were not for a nation, but for the well-being of a country and its people—prayers for each country to attain its highest and most healthy potential.

Then Masami took us to a huge room in one of the buildings. I was profoundly moved by what I saw there. It was filled with mandalas that had been cocreated by thousands of visitors. Each mandala was a piece of paper with concentric circles drawn on it. The space between the lines of the concentric circles was quite small. On each of these lines—around each of these circles—were carefully hand-printed the words "May Peace Prevail on Earth," over and over, by a visitor or visitors to this room. The smaller mandalas were about twelve inches in diameter. Each took hours to finish. Others were much larger. One was twelve FEET in diameter! It covered a wall. On each was the focused intention, the focused prayer, the focused gift, "May Peace Prevail on Earth," offered again and again and again.

As I knelt on my hands and knees, pen in hand, carefully writing the words, "May Peace Prevail on Earth," onto an unfinished mandala, I felt the company of thousands of brothers and sisters, or tens of thousands, who had knelt on their hands and knees in this same room, or in rooms around the world, carefully writing "May Peace Prevail on Earth." This huge room was a Heart of Peace emanating its beneficence to an awakening world.

The Peace Pole that Linda and I planted by our home in a small mountain community in the United States decades before we met Masami—a square pole with the words, "May Peace Prevail on Earth" painted on each side in a different language—now reminds us daily of how far the love of a great soul reaches.

Masami Siaonji is an emerging Universal Human.

Nipun, then a college student, asked his parents if they would open their house each week for friends to sit together in silence for an hour, share insights for an hour, and then eat in silence together for an hour. His parents happily agreed. Those gatherings in Santa Clara, California, were the first of many. Today individuals around the world open their houses or apartments weekly for gatherings like them, now called Awaken Circles. Volunteers cook meals, and volunteers clean up. "No teachers. No donation box. Nothing to belong to," as Nipun describes them.

Nipun took Linda and me to a restaurant with a wonderful caring atmosphere and delicious healthy food and, I quickly learned, much more. When a diner asks for a bill, the server replies, "There is no bill. Your meals are free." If the diner asks "How does this restaurant pay you?" the server says "I am a volunteer." If the diner insists on paying for something, the server suggests, "You can pay for that family over there," nodding to a table nearby. This was a Karma Kitchen. A Karma Kitchen is a pop-up "gift economy" restaurant. "We rent a restaurant for a night," explained Nipun, "like you would rent one for a birthday party, except we turn it into a Karma Kitchen." Karma Kitchens have popped up in twenty-three countries and given a "gift-economy" dining experience to hundreds of thousands of people.

Smiling, Nipun gave Linda and me some small cards with "Smile" printed on the front. On the back was an invitation to pass it on. Mine made me smile. Then I learned that volunteers around the world have given away millions of Smile Cards—paying kindness forward millions of times and providing millions of opportunities for others to do the same.

The small group of volunteers that began with Nipun and three college friends has now grown into a worldwide ecosystem called ServiceSpace with over six hundred thousand members. Awaken Circles, Karma Kitchens, and Smile Cards are some of their cocreations, and all of them have been accomplished without fund-raising, advertising, or soliciting media attention.

ServiceSpace was conceived by volunteers, built by volunteers, and is run by volunteers, all for the benefit of all. "We believe in the inherent generosity of others and we aim to ignite that spirit of service," explained Nipun, "creating both inner and outer transformation." Nipun calls ServiceSpace an example of "giftivism," which he defines as the practice of radically generous acts that change the world. Because ServiceSpace is volunteer-run, its overhead is so low that it can do things without a business plan; because it is built on the gift economy, it can do everything for free, and word spreads rapidly. Five thousand people join ServiceSpace every month.

Combining the intention of inner transformation (instead of external power) with volunteers, small acts of kindness, and many-to-many interactions on the internet provides deeply meaningful experiences—such as receiving kindness and generosity and paying them forward—to the most people.

These experiences can be life-changing. Karma Kitchen diners, for example, generally leave *more* for meals that they buy for people they do not know than they would have paid for their own meals. ServiceSpace is a new prototype, among many others, of an emerging commerce of compassion that reflects the new and fulfilling potential of business (pure service) just as the obsolete and unfulfilling commerce of pure profit has become irreversibly destructive.

Nipun Mehta is an emerging Universal Human.

≈

These are some of the emerging Universal Humans that I know. There are many, many more.

Where are they?

# 71

# Recognizing Emerging
# Universal Humans

U niversal Humans are beginning to appear even as our species first glimpses the dawn of a new multisensory humanity. The light of the new dawn makes them visible. They may or may not think in terms of authentic power and spiritual partnerships, but they all realize that the road is clearer, more rewarding, and more fulfilling from the perspective of love, and the road is steeper, more challenging, and more difficult from the perspective of fear, and they all practice, each in his or her own way, choosing the perspective of love.

Like multisensory humans who are creating authentic power, emerging Universal Humans are transforming their lives into vehicles of love from vehicles of fear. Like multisensory humans who are creating authentic power, emerging Universal Humans are becoming aware of their choices and the consequences of them. Like multisensory humans who are creating authentic power, emerging Universal Humans are using their free will to align themselves with their highest impulses, their most loving impulses, their most accepting, compassionate, giving, satisfying, fulfilling impulses.

To recognize emerging Universal Humans, look for them consciously. Begin by creating authentic power. If you are not creating authentic power, you will not be able to see those who are. Distinguish love from fear in yourself. Whenever the two conflict (they always conflict), choose love instead of fear until fear ceases to control you and love fills your awareness.

Make your choices:

To love instead of fear.

To love instead of hate.

To love instead of envy.

To give instead of take.

To cooperate instead of compete.

To harmonize instead of fight.

To share instead of hoard.

To revere Life instead of exploit.

Then add to this a continual, constant, commitment to contribute to Life an ever-present love of Life. Ask yourself if Life is more important to you than being male or female, and if Life is more important to you than being American or Brazilian or Japanese. Ask yourself if Life is more important to you than anything you are or have. If contributing to Life is not the most important and fulfilling experience for you, you will not be able to recognize those for whom it is.

These things are the essence of emerging Universal Humans—humans who are beginning to see Life wherever they look, feel Life wherever they go, hear Life wherever they listen, and touch Life wherever they reach. Emerging Universal Humans also experience themselves in ways that are very different from the ways that most multisensory humans experience themselves, such as, for example, sensing sometimes that the Universe sees through their eyes, feels through their hands, and speaks with their words.

Last, don't forget to look inside yourself. You can do this by saying each time you act (and after you act), "I do this and everything I do at each moment in my life so the Universal Human can come into being fully." If this feels good or satisfying or natural to you, and you are creating authentic power, you are an emerging Universal Human.

—

I learned to express myself unambiguously, or to try, long before I met the person who would become my life partner, spiritual partner, and cocreator for decades to come. She would often speak about a "he" or a "she" or an "it" but without explaining *which* "he," "she," or "it." She spoke in generalities. I had explained quantum physics to nonscientists.[7]

My frustrations with her opaque (to me) ways of expressing herself grew until one day she smiled at me and said simply, "Beloved, language is my second language." In that moment I began to see in new ways. While I shared concepts, she shared her heart. While I communicated, she connected. I have learned much from her, and I continue to learn.

When I try to explain a multisensory perception, or a higher order logic or understanding of the heart, I reach for the most loving parts of my personality I can access to help me. I search my memory, my experiences, and my imagination for ways to make it as personal and intimate as I can. I remember why I am writing—to give voice, image, and action to love; to share about emotional awareness, responsible choice, authentic power, spiritual partnerships, and Universal Humans. Sometimes when I am seeking the best way to express myself, and I think there is only one best way, Rumi's beautiful words return to remind me, "There are a thousand ways to kneel and kiss the Earth."

Whenever you find someone who is multisensory, who strives to distinguish love from fear within him- or herself and choose love, who is moving beyond the bounds of culture, religion, nation, ethnic group, and gender, and who is becoming attracted to Life first and all else second, you have found an emerging Universal Human.

It may be you.

---

7  *The Dancing Wu Li Masters: An Overview of the New Physics* (New York: HarperOne, 1979).

# 72

# Our New Creation Story Part 2

Five-sensory creation stories are about nonhuman creators that shape or manipulate five-sensory humans as they choose. Most of them tell five-sensory humans what they are, how they were created, and sometimes how they ought to behave. All of them are all hearsay accounts of ancient circumstances—some historical, some mythical—handed down by five-sensory personalities long dead to five-sensory personalities also long dead—with the perversions that this process produces—all in the context of five-sensory cultures. Only the most fervent believers of a five-sensory creation story proclaim the contrary and only for their own creation story.

Our new creation story is completely the opposite. Our new creation story is *our* new creation story. It is not given to us from above or anywhere else. We are writing it now. We are bringing it into being choice by choice. We are deciding what will be in it and what will not. Multisensory perception is transforming human consciousness *now*. We are recognizing our significant creative capacity for the first time *now*. Our responsibility for what we create is becoming undeniable to us *now*. The horror, destruction, and suffering that five-sensory humanity created and our new potential of unbound compassion, health, and wonder now present themselves to us everywhere, always asking us, "Which do you choose?" and we must always answer.

There are no excuses in our new creation story. There are causes and effects. There are no villains or victims, no right or wrong, no should, ought, or must. There is potential. The power of creating our experiences in the Earth school is ours alone. It always has been. Now we know it.

The consequences of our choices extend far beyond the imagination of five-sensory humans. Now we are glimpsing how far. A new and startling, completely unexpected experience of ourselves is upon us—*we are powerful and creative, compassionate and loving spirits.*

The potential of the Universal Human is at the heart of our new creation story. This potential stands before us like a great mountain on the horizon. It is the ocean calling to us as the moon calls tides. We move toward the Universal Human each time we create authentic power. Waiting for a "critical mass" to transform us into Universal Humans prevents us from becoming Universal Humans. Waiting for a "hundredth monkey" to become a Universal Human prevents us from becoming Universal Humans. The Universal Human must manifest in the micro before it can manifest in the macro. You are the micro.

Until you become an authentically powerful adult citizen of the Universe (not child of the Universe), beyond culture, religion, nation, ethnic group, and gender—an authentically powerful human whose allegiance is to Life first and all else second—you will remain a member of this culture or that, this religion or no religion, this nation or that, this ethnic group or mixture of ethnic groups, and this gender or that. They will shape your identity, form your thoughts, and determine your perceptions of yourself and others. The demands of these collectives come from fear. That is why satisfying them cannot bring fulfillment, peace, and joy.

Becoming a Universal Human requires creating authentic power. As you challenge fear and cultivate love in yourself—distinguish intentions of love from intentions of fear and act with intentions of love—you move toward the Universal Human. As you create harmony, cooperation, sharing, and reverence for Life, you move toward the Universal Human. The intentions of your soul become doable, then desirable, and then enticing. You look for opportunities to create with them. You search for ways to support others in creating authentic power, and you are open to their support. You cocreate spiritual partnerships. The Universal Law of Attraction brings you to those who are creating authentic power and them to you.

You cannot climb a mountain in an hour. You must condition your body—train with the intention of climbing the mountain. You must learn about weather, snow, ice, and avalanches. You must learn to use crampons, ice axe, and ropes. Most important, you must climb with your heart, because of your heart, at the direction of your heart, if you are to gain anything at all from the climb.

You cannot leap from ignorance into Universal Humanity in a single bound. You must create authentic power. You must develop emotional awareness, practice responsible choice, and consult intuition. Most important, you must create the ability to speak and act with love, even while frightened parts of your personality demand to speak and act from fear.

As you challenge your fears, they control you less. As you cultivate love, more experiences of love fill your awareness. As you welcome your emotions, experiences, and all that the Earth school gives you, your life transforms from resistance to relief to acceptance and then to joy. You marvel at the beauty of all personalities and the radiance of the souls they serve, whether or not others see what you see, whether or not the personalities that you encounter see these things in themselves.

Your perception goes deeper, your appreciation goes deeper, your gratitude goes deeper. Your identity moves from your personality to your soul to Life, and you become a Universal Human.

This is our new creation story. It is happening *now*, and it is happening in *us*. *We are creating it!* Our new creation story is not an amalgam of ancient memories and primordial miracles bequeathed in archaic five-sensory prose. It is the ongoing and always-current creation of *our* ongoing and always-current experiences, insights, and choices of intention.

We are not created by, in, or because of our new creation story. *We are creating our new creation story.* It requires *our* commitment, courage, compassion, and conscious communications and actions. *We* choose to journey consciously to and through our greatest fears. *We* choose to cultivate love—of ourselves, our fellow students in the Earth school, our world, and the Universe. *We* choose to make Life more important to us than anything we thought we were or desired.

Our new creation story is the story of *us*, multisensory humans, changing ourselves with our choices. It is the story of *us* becoming authentically powerful adult citizens of the Universe, bringing *our* responsibility, intelligence, and love into the service of Life first and all else second. It is the story of spiritual partnerships that *we* create enveloping the Earth. It is *our* ongoing experience of the infinite, eternal Universe of compassion and wisdom and *our* choices to honor that above all else.

Now.

# 73

# From Journey to Expansion

All books about Universal Humans end with the heart. They begin with the heart. The heart fills all the spaces in between. Without the heart, all is idea. Without the heart, all is fear. Without the heart, nothing human can evolve. This is our new path. The heart is the treasure. The treasure is around us and within us, however, finding it requires intention and focus. That is creating authentic power.

If you intend to understand something, it is necessary to study it. The intention to understand it is not sufficient. If you intend to climb a mountain, as we discussed, you must learn the skills of climbing. If you intend to live a life of love, you must do more than learn about love. You must develop the ability to recognize it in yourself and express it.

This is a journey. Humankind has been on this journey since its origin, and it has been a long journey. Now something dramatically, previously unimaginably new has appeared in ourstory. Our evolution is no longer determined by circumstances external. Our experiences are no longer forced upon us. We are no longer twigs in a stream swept forward as it flows toward the ocean. We now determine how the stream will flow and our experiences in it. We are no longer twigs. We are the stream, and we know that we are headed for the ocean. We ARE our evolution. We are aware, in intimate terms, of the role we play in our evolution. We determine our contributions to our evolution. We determine our experiences in our evolution. HUMAN EVOLUTION HAS BECOME CONSCIOUS!

Every experience in the Earth school now supports conscious human evolution. It is now the sole course in the Earth school. Creating authentic power is its discipline. We are its students. Emotional awareness, responsible choice, intuition, authentic power, and spiritual partnership are its subjects, and multisensory perception has immersed us in them.

There are phases to every evolution. Five-sensory perception was one of ours. Now we are in the phase of multisensory perception—awareness of the soul and creating authentic power. As we move forward into and through this phase, yet another phase appears. So accelerated is our evolution that even as we are in the second phase, the third phase is becoming visible, like a premonition of light in the early hours of the morning. This is the Universal Human.

Every evolution requires learning and developing. Learning and developing never cease. What is learned and developed changes. As a student moves through an educational process, he or she learns many things in many ways—for example, she becomes literate, and then literacy allows her to continue learning in new ways, and that level of learning allows the student to develop further in yet new ways. Now, as the potential of the Universal Human appears, our evolution continues, and we are continuing to learn and develop.

The goal of evolution for five-sensory humans was survival. The goal of evolution for multisensory humans is authentic power, alignment of the personality with the soul. The goal of evolution for Universal Humans is Love—Love, Life, Consciousness, and Universe seen, experienced, and expressed as one. Just as multisensory humans existed within five-sensory humanity, Universal Humans exist within multisensory humanity. They are beacons of light, or indicators of direction, like signposts. Beacons, indicators, and signposts have no value to an individual who does not recognize them or recognizes them and does not follow them.

There is always more to evolution. Think of your evolution not as a journey, but as an expansion. A journey that has no end leads you ever onward. An expansion that has no limit keeps you always at its center. The center does not move. The expansion does not cease. Yet they are the same. This is how a sun radiates endlessly, contributes light and warmth endlessly, nurtures endlessly.

We are all becoming suns. Each of us is the center. Universal Humans are part of this process. We are part of this process.

We are this process.

# THE NEXT STEP

THE NEXT STEP

# 74

# Beyond Universal Humans

T he Universal Human is the last step in the evolution of human. Beyond the Universal Human are domains of experience that are as different and beyond multisensory humanity as multisensory humanity is different and beyond five-sensory humanity. The evolution of five-sensory humanity and multisensory humanity and Universal Humanity begins in physical form. It is anchored in physical reality, which means the reality of the Earth school.

The evolution of the Universal Human takes the consciousness of humanity beyond the limitations of physical form. Multisensory humanity is a stepping stone, a bridge, between five-sensory humanity, or consciousness, and the consciousness of the Universal Human. The sole source of information for five-sensory humans is the five senses, and the five senses are designed to detect the physical reality that we have been calling the Earth school. The bridging consciousness, or multisensory humanity, frees multisensory humans from the necessity of providing data for comprehension that are obtained from physical circumstances. That is the shift from the limited logic of the intellect into intuition. Intuition, the voice of the nonphysical world, as it replaces five-sensory and intellectual considerations, opens multisensory humans not only to new experiences but also to new sources of insight and inspiration and information about themselves. Universal Humanity is the last step in this three-part process. Universal Humans walk on the Earth. They have five senses which inform them. They have intuition which informs them. They communicate regularly with nonphysical Teachers. They are not bound by identification with aspects of the personality. They are free to interact soul-to-soul in the Earth school.

Yet their focus is already beyond the Earth school. Their focus is on Life. This is yet a new domain of exploration, a new arena of spiritual development. As humankind moves beyond the Universal Human, it moves into entirely new experiences that are beyond human. Just as Universal Humans recognize the Universe, Consciousness, Life, Love as that which they are, beyond the Universal Human lies awareness as Life.

The transformation from five-sensory humankind, or consciousness, to multisensory humankind, or consciousness, is occurring very rapidly after a prolonged period of the evolution of five-sensory humanity. The evolution of multisensory humanity into Universal Humanity is already taking place. The movement of human consciousness beyond Universal Humanity and into realms of awareness and experience that are nonhuman cannot be expressed so simply in terms of years. That framework is one that is disappearing or that will disappear as Universal Humanity moves beyond that which is human.

Within the Earth school there is the termination of the personality called death. As humanity becomes multisensory, that termination is seen to be not the termination of human consciousness but the termination of a vehicle that the soul adapts for its own learning and evolution in the domain of physicalness. Multisensory humans understand that consciousness and responsibility for how they use their consciousness continues after the death, or the termination, of a personality.

As Universal Humans begin to emerge as a species-wide phenomenon, the lines become blurred, so to speak, between that which was once all that humans knew, and we call physical, and the larger domain of experience that is beyond human and which does not include time or space or matter or duality. Beyond human lie infinite domains and modes of evolution that cannot be grasped by five-sensory or multisensory humans but that can be, to a certain extent, intuited by Universal Humans. These are experiences and domains of experience that are not limited to a single focal point, so to speak.

Beyond Universal Humans is the direct experience of these new dimensions. Five-sensory humans have in their collective wisdom, which is often thought of as mythology, direct communication with intelligence that is nonhuman, such as Angels and deities. Multisensory humans have direct communication with nonphysical Teachers. Communication with nonphysical Teachers is becoming a species-wide characteristic of multisensory humanity. Multisensory humans, within a relatively brief period of time, will communicate with nonphysical Teachers as easily as they communicate with one another.

This can be imagined as the interaction between two physical human bodies can be imagined, but in terms of the expansive relationship—the facile, fluid relationship—between multisensory humans and nonphysical Teachers, it cannot be imagined, although it is beginning to be experienced. Universal Humans move more into that experience. Their thoughts are thoughts of Life. Their perceptions are perceptions of Life. Their care is for Life. Their sole allegiance is to Life. As you can see, they are already taking on the characteristics of a nonphysical Teacher from the perception of multisensory humanity.

Moving beyond the human does not mean that each Universal Human as it moves beyond human becomes a nonphysical Teacher. It moves into new neighborhoods, so to speak. Part of the experience of those new neighborhoods is the support of Life as it is not detectable by five-sensory, multisensory, or Universal Humans. In other words, we are involved in an evolution that has not suddenly grown larger and will at some point become immeasurably larger, incomprehensibly larger. That evolution has been in place since the appearance of the first five-sensory human and its predecessor. Awareness of this process is now becoming much fuller, complete, and inclusive. Yet as that happens, human consciousness moves into a realm in which the word "inclusive" has no meaning. What more can be included in the concept of "everything"? What more can be included in the concept of "Life" when Life is the direct experience beyond comprehension of all that can be and cannot be comprehended?

Now is a good time to begin to experience this evolution, as it appears with more fullness, with more richness, with the knowledge that where you are is the appropriate place for you to be. This is what multisensory humans see as they look at the world that was the limitation of five-sensory humans. It is what Universal Humans live without effort, and it is what consciousness in the domain beyond human is.

To say that there are more realms or domains of experience beyond the Universal Human is an attempt to describe that which cannot be described, even to a Universal Human. It is analogous to attempting to describe colors in domains that are beyond human in which color as we think of it in terms of the five senses, or in terms of what multisensory humans experience at times when they interact with nonphysical Teachers, is not detectable or describable. It simply is. In other words, experience beyond human cannot be described. It cannot be imagined. Yet it is real.

The process of expanding perception—five-sensory to multisensory, personality to soul, soul to Life, multisensory humans to Universal Humans—is all an indication, the emerging appearance of a pathway toward that which cannot be described. Yet the pathway is becoming part of human experience. Multisensory humans understand that they are on a path, and they call it evolution, as do five-sensory humans.

Universal Humans are on the path. Beyond the consciousness of human lies not the path, but the path and all else. Path in terms of a line, path in terms of a bounded road, path in terms of a linear progression toward a destination, no longer exists, ceases to exist, and instead is Life itself, Consciousness itself, the Universe itself, Love itself, and the countless ways that it can be experienced, enjoyed, and shared.

Evolution does not stop when Universal Humans step beyond the boundary of human.

Infinite new phases of it begin.

# 75

# Hope

Hope is essential. It is necessary for spiritual development. It is necessary for a grounded, aware, creative, and healthy life. Hope and air are the most necessary ingredients for a healthy life—a physical life in the Earth school and a spiritual life in the Earth school—that reflects health in different dimensions of experience. When humankind was five-sensory, awareness was limited to the first dimension, physical health. Now that we are becoming multisensory, awareness of health in a larger dimension is becoming a major part of human consciousness, that is, health in a spiritual dimension, the dimension of conscious relationship with the soul.

Hope is necessary because without hope, there is no intention to grow. Without hope there is no intention to reach for that which might be or could be or promises to be better. Better not in a material sense, but in a sense of more fulfilling, of more gratifying.

Hope has generated every religious organization. As we have seen, religious organizations are formed as encrustations around a Universal truth that lies at the heart of each, a different Universal truth. Without the sun to rise each morning, the world would be cold and barren. Without hope, that is the nature of internal experience. Hope is the bringer of warmth, of growth, of fulfillment, like blossoming or blooming.

What is hope? Hope is connection with the soul, and beyond that, a connection with Divine Intelligence. The soul is beyond the dualities of the Earth school. It is a reflection of the larger reality that we have been calling Divine Intelligence—the Universe, Consciousness, Love, and Life. It is the glimpse of all of those. It is the first appearance of light in the sky after a night of darkness. Without hope of that, there can only be surrender or resistance to the darkness. In either case, the darkness is the determining overall factor in experience. With hope, all of that changes.

Hope is insight into the essential human nature. Your personality was created from compassion. All of your experiences are created with compassion. The opportunities that the Earth School presents you at each moment are gifts of compassion, compassionate gifts of the Universe. Suspicion of that, premonition of that, is hope. Glimpsing that is hope revealing its power, flooding awareness with new perspectives. Awareness of these things is hope—hope not embodied but expressed as a fulfillment in action.

Love has no need of hope. Only fear has need of hope. Therefore, a personality that is hopeful is a personality with a frightened part of itself active. The hope does not come from fear. The hope is an aspect of the Universe, and the Universe is a Universe of love. It is only a frightened part of the personality that is not aware of this and that does not participate in it consciously.

Fear brings five-sensory humans together, and hope gives value to their togetherness. Love brings multisensory humans who are authentically powerful together. It binds Universal Humans, for Universal Humans realize that they are the Universe. It belongs to them and they belong to it. They are not separate from it or from anything in it.

Wonder at the Universe, wonder at the starry sky, wonder at mountains aglow with evening sunlight, wonder at green fields, wonder at the depth and incomprehensibility of the ocean, wonder at Life itself with its endless diversity—all of those are experiences of hope. Hope is an experience of one who is not yet part of all of that. It is the realization of the potential of all of that. Stepping into all of that without fear is the fulfillment of hope. It is the manifestation of the potential. In other words, hope lies at the heart of all that calls us to health, to goodness, to relationship, to connection, to Life.

The experience of hope has many levels. It can be a lifeline, a life preserver thrown into an angry ocean in which an individual experiences him- or herself as hopeless and lost and powerless. It can be experienced as an insight, an insight that awakens a desire to share it, not from fear, but with joy.

Hope is an experience of connection soul-to-soul, a glimpse into the eyes of others or another that reveals depth, fullness, presence, and reminds you that that depth, fullness, and presence exist within you or they could not be recognized by you.

Hope initiates all endeavors. Five-sensory humans see that there is a possibility of survival that comes with the pursuit of external power, and it gives them hope. As they accept that hope as real, as a possibility that they intend to bring into being, they move forward with more ability, more clarity or confidence, you might say, more courage.

Hope inspires courage—hope in the goodness of others, hope in the goodness of yourself. The experience of these things removes the need for hope and brings your life into new realms of experience, insight, and understanding. Hope initiates the inquiry into authentic power for multisensory humans. The development of authentic power is continually inspired by hope. Then as multisensory humans begin to experience authentic power, that experience itself draws them to it.

You can think of hope as a small ball of snow beginning to roll downward over the surface of a snow-covered mountain. As it rolls, it skims along the surface of the snow, bouncing, gaining speed, until it impacts the snow enough to begin to accumulate more snow to it. When that happens, it grows, and with each impact on the surface of the snow it grows in size, and its downward movement accelerates.

This metaphor has its limits, but the products of hope have no limits. Hope is an experiential connector to the limitlessness of the Universe. Hope is insight into the compassionate nature and wisdom of the Universe. As you become that, compassion and wisdom replace hope for compassion and wisdom. Joy, meaning, and purpose replace hope for those things. That is the path that humankind is on. That is the path of evolution. Evolution could not and would not occur without hope.

Hope is more than a thought. It is more than a feeling. It is an energy. It is the energy that initiates evolution. Evolution itself is the growing body of hope. Cells do not think or feel, yet they are not without consciousness. Multicelled organisms in their primitive states do not think or feel, yet they express the energy of hope as they connect with other cells and form more complex cellular organisms. That movement continues without end for five-sensory humans. Multisensory humans are able to begin to glimpse an end of this process, and Universal Humans step into that process which has no end.

Hope is the energy that permeates all of this. Yet hope now becomes an inadequate word, for it is not a psychological dynamic. It is not an emotional dynamic. It is an energy, and that energy is the energy of the Universe itself, of Life itself, of Consciousness itself, of Love itself. All that you see around you is the manifestation of this energy. It is the manifestation reaching toward ever more fulfillment, reaching toward Divine Intelligence, yet Divine Intelligence cannot be reached toward, except in the limited perception of five-sensory and multisensory humans. Universal Humans begin to move past those limitations.

Hope is an initiator of conscious evolution. Hope is the initiator of star systems and galaxies, not that star systems and galaxies are hopeful. They themselves express the energy, the expansive, ever-including, ever-expanding, ever-fulfilling energy that is at the heart of Life and Consciousness and Love and the Universe itself.

That is what humans—five-sensory, multisensory, and Universal—call hope.

# An Invitation

To learn more about authentic power, spiritual partnership, and Universal Humans, please visit www.seatofthesoul.com.

Also, will you please send me your experiences as an emerging Universal Human to gary@seatofthesoul.com? I am looking forward to hearing from you.

—GARY ZUKAV

# Index

291

CPSIA information can be obtained
at www.ICGtesting.com
Printed in the USA
BVHW071332280422
635538BV00006B/6

9 781982 169886